ARBITRARY POWER

LITERATURE IN HISTORY

———————— SERIES EDITORS ————————

David Bromwich, James Chandler, and Lionel Gossman

The books in this series study literary works
in the context of the intellectual conditions,
social movements, and patterns of action
in which they took shape.

OTHER BOOKS IN THE SERIES

Lawrence Rothfield, *Vital Signs: Medical Realism in
Nineteenth-Century Fiction*

David Quint, *Epic and Empire: Politics and Generic
Form from Virgil to Milton*

Alexander Welsh, *The Hero of the Waverly Novels*

Susan Dunn, *The Deaths of Louis XVI: Regicide and the
French Political Imagination*

Sharon Achinstein, *Milton and the Revolutionary Reader*

Esther Schor, *Bearing the Dead: The British Culture of
Mourning from the Enlightenment to Victoria*

Elizabeth K. Helsinger, *Rural Scenes and National
Representation: Britain, 1815–1850*

Katie Trumpener, *Bardic Nationalism: The Romantic Novel
and the British Empire*

Karen Chase and Michael Levenson, *The Spectacle of Intimacy:
A Public Life for the Victorian Family*

Joshua Scodel, *Excess and the Mean in Early Modern English Literature*

ARBITRARY POWER

ROMANTICISM, LANGUAGE, POLITICS

William Keach

PRINCETON UNIVERSITY PRESS

PRINCETON AND OXFORD

COPYRIGHT © 2004 BY PRINCETON UNIVERSITY PRESS
PUBLISHED BY PRINCETON UNIVERSITY PRESS, 41 WILLIAM STREET,
PRINCETON, NEW JERSEY 08540
IN THE UNITED KINGDOM: PRINCETON UNIVERSITY PRESS,
3 MARKET PLACE, WOODSTOCK, OXFORDSHIRE OX20 1SY
ALL RIGHTS RESERVED

LIBRARY OF CONGRESS CATALOGING-IN-PUBLICATION DATA

KEACH, WILLIAM, 1942–
ARBITRARY POWER : ROMANTICISM, LANGUAGE, POLITICS / WILLIAM KEACH.
P. CM. — (LITERATURE IN HISTORY)
INCLUDES BIBLIOGRAPHICAL REFERENCES AND INDEX.
ISBN 0-691-11766-7 (CL : ALK. PAPER)
1. ENGLISH LITERATURE—19TH CENTURY—HISTORY AND CRITICISM. 2. POLITICS AND LITERATURE—GREAT BRITAIN—HISTORY—19TH CENTURY. 3. ENGLISH LANGUAGE—POLITICAL ASPECTS—GREAT BRITAIN. 4. ENGLISH LANGUAGE—19TH CENTURY—RHETORIC. 5. POWER (SOCIAL SCIENCES) IN LITERATURE. 6. ROMANTICISM—GREAT BRITAIN. I. TITLE.
II. LITERATURE IN HISTORY (PRINCETON, N.J.)
PR468.P57K43 2004
820.9'358—DC22
2003057953
ISBN 978-0-691-16800-5
BRITISH LIBRARY CATALOGING-IN-PUBLICATION DATA IS AVAILABLE

THIS BOOK HAS BEEN COMPOSED IN SABON

PRINTED ON ACID-FREE PAPER. ∞

PUP.PRINCETON.EDU

PRINTED IN THE UNITED STATES OF AMERICA

10 9 8 7 6 5 4 3 2 1

To Sheila Emerson

CONTENTS

Preface ix

Acknowledgments xiii

Abbreviations xv

1
Arbitrary Power 1

2
Words Are Things 23

3
The Politics of Rhyme 46

4
Vulgar Idioms 68

5
"'A Subtler Language within Language'" 95

6
The Language of Revolutionary Violence 122

Notes 159

Index 185

PREFACE

I BEGAN THINKING about this book in the mid 1980s, when what had been called the "linguistic turn" in literary studies generally, and in Romantic studies more particularly, was yielding priority to a "return to history."[1] The shift coincided with and accentuated a turn in my own work. Having written a book about Shelley and language that says relatively little about the political contexts, motivations, and force of his writing, I wanted to undertake a project that would foreground these very realities. But I also knew that important questions about Romantic linguistic theories and practices remained unanswered, even (in some cases) inadequately posed. So I started where *Shelley's Style* left off—with a problem that has to do, inescapably, with both linguistic and political power or agency. Working through the ramifications of this problem has taken me a long time, in part because it traverses a very broad and diverse spectrum of what we call "Romantic" literature and culture.

The most generalized level of argument advanced here shares some central concerns with James Chandler's *England in 1819* (1998). Like Chandler I emphasize "the vexed issue of determination" and see as foundational "the question of agency in relation to the concept of the 'historical situation.'"[2] Whereas Chandler's purpose is to rethink, through a process of historical reflexivity, what the construction and analysis of a "historical situation" involves—in Shelley's moment and in our own—my aim is to return to and extend unfinished work on Romantic theories of linguistic agency, practice, and institution and to show how deeply implicated they are in defining social changes and conflicts. These changes and conflicts are, I believe, significantly continuous with the world we now inhabit. This is a book written in opposition to notions of the "posthistorical," the "postrevolutionary," the "posthuman," and various related kinds of "post"-ness. I especially value the aspect of Chandler's agenda that responds with such amplitude to Fredric Jameson's call to study a literary text by attending to "the historicity of its form and of its content, the historical moment of emergence of its linguistic possibilities, the situation-specific function of its aesthetic."[3] As my way of responding to this exhortation from *The Political Unconscious* (1981), I want also to return to Jameson's much earlier reflections on "the doctrine of the arbitrary sign," to his argument in *The Prison-House of Language* (1972) that "to isolate the signified as such for purposes of description, would seem to imply that it had already found *some determinate type of organization*" (my emphasis).[4] What Jameson located and articulated in the early 1970s is a problem not just of linguistic, but also of historical and political, conceptualization. This problem has distinctive antecedents in Romantic writing; it also has incompletely explored consequences for how we read such writing now.

The "return to history" has produced a good deal of criticism that casts itself, sometimes unreflectingly, in "political" terms that are overt and yet vague in their orientation, unclear in their commitment. Richard Cronin is right to complain, reflectingly, that "the view that all poetry is political" can function as a banal truism, and to note that "the practice of designating as political any relationship that can be described as an exercise of power by one individual or group over another" has led to a suspect proliferation of academic books and articles with titles that take the form "The Politics of _____."[5] But as he goes on to say what it means that his own title takes this form (*The Politics of Romantic Poetry* [2000]), Cronin demonstrates that its status as current academic fashion need not obviate its usefulness in critical work that makes a priority of recognizing the manifold, often contradictory, ways in which literary representation depends on "an exercise of power by one individual or group over another." This book is about representing language itself as just such an exercise of determinative "power over"—and at the same time as the apparent opposite of this, as a constitutive dimension of social and cultural practice unavoidably linked to chance and random association.

In each of the six chapters that follow I look for the convergence of pronouncements about language with representations of the political, and of both of these with salient stylistic conventions, gestures, experiments. Sometimes, though, textual instances strike me as telling because, in the absence of any explicit thematizing of language, stylistic practices themselves register, bear the pressure of, political forces. Nowhere in British Romanticism does this happen more powerfully, or more disarmingly, than in *Don Juan*. In the middle of the War Cantos Byron takes the opportunity afforded by his narrative of relentless, ridiculous mutual slaughter between the Turks and the Russians to glance sarcastically at Wellington and Waterloo. Then he returns to the Siege of Ismail by way of these stanzas:

> But never mind;—"God save the king!" and kings!
>   For if *he* don't, I doubt if *men* will longer—
> I think I hear a little bird, who sings
>   The people by and by will be the stronger:
> The veriest jade will wince whose harness wrings
>   So much into the raw as quite to wrong her
> Beyond the rules of posting,—and the Mob
> At last fall sick of imitating Job:

> At first it grumbles, then it swears, and then,
>   Like David, flings smooth pebbles 'gainst a giant;
> At last it takes to weapons such as men
>   Snatch when despair makes human hearts less pliant.
> Then comes "the tug of war";—'twill come again,
>   I rather doubt; and I would fain say "fie on't,"
> If I had not perceived that Revolution
> Alone can save the Earth from Hell's pollution.
>   (8. 393–408)

This is the only passage in Byron's poetry in which the word "Revolution" appears, and it would be easy to dismiss it as opportunistic posturing—as rhyme-enforced positioning. But it is significant that on this one occasion Byron's narrator, without entirely forgoing the lofty disdain for the "Mob" he evinces elsewhere, finds himself compelled to proclaim "Revolution" from below as the only alternative to the "Hell" of imperialist war and the national systems of class rule that promote and benefit from it.

Byron's lines call attention to the linguistic and rhetorical forces that drive and enable his making this political and stylistic passage from the mock-patriotic "'God save the king'" to the reluctant perception that only getting rid of kings altogether "can save the Earth." The passage enacts not an identification with, but rather an understanding of, the limits of endurable oppression, limits that determine where and when "the people" will rise up and draw the line. The phonetic and semantic associative sequencing of rhyme—that most rule-governed and yet chance-dependent dimension of verse—takes on here as elsewhere in *Don Juan* an organizing life of its own. Could Byron have known that if he began with "kings" he would eventually come to "Revolution"/ "pollution"? Maybe not—and yet there is an undeniable political logic in the sequence. The characteristic pseudoapology for having digressed into Wellington and Waterloo—"But never mind"—makes the reader expect, but also suspect, a revival of ostensible authorial control. As part of the narrator's performative self-representation, each stanza contains a quoted phrase, neither of which is traceable to a particular speech act. "God save the king" is something mouthed by everyone who admires the Duke of Wellington; Byron's narrator mouths and extends it into an ironic example of imagining the King's death.[6] "[F]ie on't" is a phrase the narrator both says and unsays: that is, he says it in saying he "would fain say" it "if" he were not aware of a social and political reality that makes saying it historically pointless. The voice of the narrator contains and is partly defined by voices that are his own and not his own, ironically alienated voicings of a social identity and class position by which he is entitled but also marginalized. Byron told John Murray in February 1821 that he eventually planned to move his hero on from the world of the English Cantos and "make him finish as *Anacharsis Cloots*—in the French revolution" (*BLJ* 8: 78). Jean Baptiste Clootz (he named himself "Anacharsis") was the Prussian aristocrat who passionately supported the Revolution but was executed in 1794 during the Terror.[7]

Such are the kinds of intersections between political and linguistic "possibilities," between historical reference and stylistic performance, that this book attempts to bring into focus. The first chapter analyzes a multiply doubled and divided discourse of the arbitrary as it evolved out of the Enlightenment into the Romantic era, and as it continues to evolve and function in current literary, linguistic, and cultural theory. Chapter 2 explores one of the consequences of understanding language as an arbitrary system of representation: an intense problematizing of relations between the materiality of the word and the material world that carries critical implications both for incipient discourses of the aesthetic and for explicitly political uses of speech and writing. The theoretical and practical issues foregrounded in the first two chapters bear sharply on the politicizing of poetic styles during the Regency. The third chapter examines two antithetical cases to show how practices so apparently "literary" as following and thwarting the conventions of rhyme came to be motivated and marked by the politics of class antagonism. New kinds of class antagonism in the early decades of the nineteenth century—defensive anxieties about an emergent working class, and about an increasingly bourgeois and commercial literary culture—shape the language of "vulgarity" examined in chapter 4. This language reveals shifts in gender as well as class relations: chapter 5 traces the complications in Romantic efforts to represent women's access to new sources of verbal and political power during the 1790s and again in the tense years immediately after Waterloo. The intertwined linguistic and political account of "arbitrary power" in the first five chapters culminates in a detailed textual analysis of the language of revolutionary violence in the final chapter.

Writing this book coincided at various stages with political work that matters to me—organizing opposition to U.S. military intervention in Latin America, the Balkans, the Middle East; joining picket lines that won at UPS and Verizon, and picket lines that lost at GE and American Airlines; campaigning against the death penalty in Massachusetts and Illinois; protesting police brutality in Providence and Boston. This work taught me much about arbitrary power and was interconnected with, even as it interrupted, my reading and writing about arbitrary power in the Romantic era. I continue to draw inspiration from the fact that the writers most important to this study believed that politics could neither be excluded from nor confined to literary and intellectual work, and that making a political difference always means more than casting a vote in support of a dominant party responsible for things as they are.

ACKNOWLEDGMENTS

MY FIRST AND deepest thanks are to Sheila Emerson, for her generosity, intelligence, vision, courage—and for her love. She is my best reader. She is my best hope.

James Chandler and James McKusick read the book in its entirety and wrote responses that were very helpful in their detail and in their critical grasp of the larger argument. James Chandler supported the project in its later stages in many additional ways; I am very grateful to him for his professional advice and friendship. Susan Wolfson followed the genesis of the book with enlivening attention and offered many valuable suggestions. Anne Janowitz has been a specially supportive friend and literary comrade.

Among colleagues and students at Brown University who have contributed to my thinking about the issues in this book, I particularly wish to thank Ashley Cross, Jim Egan, Diane Elam, Phil Gould, Cole Heinowitz, Neil Lazarus, Kevin McLaughlin, Laura Morrissey, Steve Murray, Robert Scholes, Zachary Sitter, Zachary Sng, and Stefan Wheelock. Many other colleagues shared with me their insights and information: I thank Derek Attridge, Alan Bewell, John Brenkman, David Bromwich, Marilyn Butler, Jerome Christensen, Stuart Curran, Kelvin Everest, Neil Fraistat, Bruce Graver, Spencer Hall, Paul Hamilton, Kurt Heinzelman, Sonia Hofkosh, Jerrold Hogle, Theresa Kelley, Jon Klancher, George Levine, Peter Manning, Alan Richardson, Christopher Ricks, Jeffrey Robinson, and Charles Rzepka. Earlier versions of chapter 1 and chapter 4 formed the basis of presentations to the seminar on Romantic Literature and Culture at the Humanities Center, Harvard University. I am grateful to the participants in the seminar for their attentive responses.

Thanks to Mary Murrell, Ellen Foos, and other members of the Princeton University Press editorial staff; to my copyeditor Jonathan Munk; to my indexer James Curtis. Their work was accurate, resourceful, and comprehending. Sam Keach has given me the kind of support that only a brother and a fellow writer can give. Jeanne and Henry Spiller have been wonderful in their steadfast interest and encouragement. Susan Spruce has helped me in many ways through her honesty and determination. I thank Linda Khalastchi for her witty, imaginative hospitality and for giving me access to her distinctive collection of eighteenth- and nineteenth-century books. Paola Cabibbo's personal and intellectual friendship, extended between Boston and Rome, means a great deal to me.

To my comrades in the International Socialist Organization and in the

Campaign to End the Death Penalty, thanks and "solidarity"! Among these comrades I am especially grateful to Helen Scott, Ashley Smith, Annie Zirin, and Jason Yanowitz. And I pay tribute to my comrade and friend Paul Foot, whose passion for Shelley and belief that the world can be made a freer, more democratic place are always with me.

A Guggenheim Fellowship supported most of a year's leave from teaching and enabled me to get started on this book.

Parts of chapter 2 appeared in somewhat different form in "'Words Are Things': Romantic Ideology and the Matter of Poetic Language," *Aesthetics and Ideology*, ed. George Levine (New Brunswick: Rutgers University Press, 1994). Earlier versions of parts of chapter 3 appeared in "Cockney Couplets: Keats and the Politics of Style," *Studies in Romanticism* 25 (1986) and "Political Inflection in Byron's *Ottava Rima*," *Studies in Romanticism* 27 (1988). One section of chapter 5 includes material from "Cythna's Subtler Language," *Studies in Romanticism* 37 (1998). An earlier version of the section on Blake in chapter 6 appeared in *Representing the French Revolution: Literature, Historiography, and Art* (Hanover: University Press of New England, 1992). All are reprinted by permission of the publishers.

ABBREVIATIONS

BLJ	*Byron's Letters and Journals*. Edited by Leslie A. Marchand, 12 vols. Cambridge, MA: Harvard University Press, 1973–1982.
CC	*The Collected Works of Samuel Taylor Coleridge*. General Editor Kathleen Coburn. Princeton: Princeton University Press and London: Routledge, 1969–. CC citations refer to the individual titles and vols. in this edition.
CLSTC	*The Collected Letters of Samuel Taylor Coleridge*. Edited by Earl Leslie Griggs, 6 vols. Oxford and New York: Oxford University Press, 1956–1971.
CPPWB	*The Complete Poetry and Prose of William Blake*, rev. ed. Edited by David V. Erdman, commentary by Harold Bloom. Garden City, NY: Anchor Press/Doubleday, 1982.
CPWB	Lord Byron [George Gordon], *The Complete Poetical Works*. Edited by Jerome J. McGann, 7 vols. Oxford: Clarendon Press, 1980–1993.
CWTP	*The Complete Writings of Thomas Paine*. Edited by Philip S. Foner, 2 vols. New York: Citadel Press, 1945.
LPBS	Percy Bysshe Shelley, *Letters*. Edited by Frederick L. Jones, 2 vols. Cambridge, MA: Harvard University Press, 1958.
Notebooks	*The Notebooks of Samuel Taylor Coleridge*. Edited by Kathleen Coburn, 4 vols. Princeton: Princeton University Press and London: Routledge, 1957–.
PS	*The Poems of Shelley*. Edited by Kelvin Everest and Geoffrey Matthews, 2 vols. to date. Harlow: Longman-Pearson Education, 1989–.
PWWW	*The Prose Works of William Wordsworth*. Edited by W.J.B. Owen and Jane Worthington Smyser, 3 vols. Oxford: Clarendon Press, 1974.
SPP	*Shelley's Poetry and Prose*, 2d ed. Edited by Donald H. Reiman and Neil Fraistat. New York: W.W. Norton, 2002.
SPW	*Shelley: Poetical Works*. Edited by Thomas Hutchinson, corrected by G. M. Matthews. London, Oxford, New York: Oxford University Press, 1970.
WMW	*The Works of Mary Wollstonecraft*. Edited by Janet Todd and Marilyn Butler, 7 vols. Washington Square, NY: New York University Press, 1989.

WPBS   *The Complete Works of Percy Bysshe Shelley.* Edited by Roger Ingpen and Walter E. Peck, 10 vols. London: Ernest Benn, 1926–1930.

WPW   *The Poetical Works of William Wordsworth.* Edited by Jonathan Wordsworth and Helen Darbishire, 5 vols. Oxford: Clarendon Press, 1940–1949.

1

ARBITRARY POWER

1.

THE CRITICAL issues in this book are framed by the eighteenth- and nineteenth-century discourse of the arbitrary—or rather, and more precisely, by what appear to be two discourses of the arbitrary that do not, at least at the level of explicit theorization and articulation, converge. On the one hand, "arbitrary power" establishes itself in the course of the eighteenth century as the concept through which republican or liberal or even Whig political discourse names monarchical, and in some cases patriarchal, tyranny and despotism. Here are two instances that cross the conventional historical span of British Romanticism:

> He saw talents bent by power to sinister purposes, and never thought of tracing the gigantic mischief up to arbitrary power, up to the hereditary distinctions that clash with the mental superiority that naturally raises a man above his fellows. (Mary Wollstonecraft on Rousseau in *A Vindication of the Rights of Woman*, 1792)[1]

> [The Tories] will yield nothing of the patronage of the Crown; and, until forced, they will lessen none of the people's burdens. They are friendly to large military establishments; patrons of arbitrary power [at home and] abroad ... (*The Edinburgh Review*, 1818)[2]

This is the overtly political discourse of "arbitrary power," and it marks virtually all writing during the late Enlightenment and Romantic eras in which the tyrannical authority of monarchy and aristocracy is contested. It is there in the Declaration of Independence of the United States, where George III is charged with "abolishing the free system of English laws in a neighboring province, establishing therein an arbitrary government, and enlarging its boundaries so as to render it at once an example and fit instrument for introducing the same absolute rules into these Colonies."

On the other hand, "arbitrary" gets established at the end of the seventeenth century and variously repeated and worried over through the eighteenth and into the nineteenth century as the prevailing term for characterizing the distinctive features of the linguistic sign. My own preoccupation with this discursive strain began as I was trying to understand what Percy Shelley means when he says in *A Defence of Poetry* that "language is arbitrarily produced by the Imagination and has relation to thoughts alone" (*SPP*, 513). My first impulse was to read forward and see Shelley anticipating a central tenet of Saussurian and post-Saussurian linguistic theory. Then I read Hans Aarsleff and realized that I also had to read backwards, against the grain of Blake- and Coleridge-induced accounts of the enemies of Romanticism, into Locke's *An Essay Concerning Human Understanding*.³ And there it was, of course, in the second chapter of Book 3:

> Words . . . come to be made use of by Men, as *the Signs of* their *Ideas*; not by any natural connexion, that there is between particular articulate sounds and certain *Ideas*, for then there would be but one Language amongst all Men; but by a voluntary Imposition, whereby such a Word is made arbitrarily the Mark of such an *Idea*. (3.2.1)⁴

Part of getting our historical bearings on Shelley's notion of language "arbitrarily produced by the Imagination and ha[ving] relation to thoughts alone" involves our seeing in his prose and letters that he had not thought of Locke as the enemy or an enemy at all—that he had read him with great interest early in his career and kept reading and re-reading him at important junctures later on.⁵

But even with these fresh historical bearings on Shelley's notion of language as an arbitrary production, the discourse of the arbitrary remains deeply contradictory. It is not just that Shelley's affirmative commitment to the arbitrariness of language in the *Defence* stands so directly against the ways in which Wordsworth and Coleridge try to resist the arbitrariness of words. It is that, as Coleridge says in an often-quoted letter to Godwin, there is something arbitrary about the word *arbitrary* itself, something inherently and inescapably contradictory about it in Shelley and Locke, and in modern and postmodern theoretical discourse, too. "Arbitrary power" is the name of a problem—not just about the relation between the two aspects of the sign, but about the relation between political power and agency on the one hand and linguistic institution and performativity on the other.⁶ This problem is a constitutive feature of much that we are still trying to understand about Romantic literary ideology, practices, and institutions.

One way of moving further inside this problem, through a predictable and conservative route, is to look at the *OED* and Johnson's *Dictionary*. Locke's meaning of *arbitrary*—"not by any natural connexion," "by a voluntary Imposition"—does not fully appear in either of them, although Johnson's fourth and last definition comes closest: "Voluntary, or left to our own choice." We are left to infer that the rather specialized linguistic meaning that Locke and his contemporaries give the word is somewhat askew to, though constantly colored by, its more common uses. What we learn from the *OED* is that the word originates in Latin as part of a specifically legal or juridical set of terms: a noun *arbiter* (from *ad + be/itere*), literally "one who goes to see" [an eye-witness], "one who looks into or examines," subsequently "a judge in equity," and from there "a supreme ruler"; and a verb *arbitrari* deriving from the legal/ juridical nouns. These legal terms come into English early on, through Old French, and the legal senses remain prominent in most variants into our own day: think of *arbitrate, arbitration, arbitrator,* or *arbitrage* (the latter names a financial practice which is, as it turns out, quite often illegal). But alongside this tradition of legal meaning another tradition evolves, a tradition at times antithetical to the original ideal of looking into, examining, judging. Even in Latin of the second century A.D. (Aulus Gellius) *arbitrario* could mean "depending on the will, inclination, pleasure"; and in English by the sixteenth century *arbitrary* comes to mean "to be decided by one's liking; dependent upon will or pleasure," and a little later "derived from mere opinion or preference; not based on the nature of things . . . capricious, uncertain, varying," and also "unrestrained in the exercise of will . . . despotic, tyrannical."

This divergence in the meanings of *arbitrary* and its variants appears to arise out of the dissolution of an originally constituted social or legal authority, out of the degradation of such authority into despotism or whimsy. The divergence is strong in Johnson's *Dictionary*. Johnson defines the adverb *arbitrarily* only as "with no other rule than the will; despotically; absolutely," and the adjective *arbitrary* as: "1. Despotick; absolute; bound by no law; following the will without restraint . . . 2. Depending on no rule; capricious." But when you move down the page to the verb *arbitrate*, you find Johnson returning to the cool Latin legalisms that contrast so sharply with the despotic and capricious: "1. To decide; to determine . . . 2. To judge of."

Strikingly undeveloped and only intermittently implicit in these traditional lexicological sources is the identification of the *arbitrary* with randomness, chance. We are made indirectly aware of this difficulty in Hugh Roberts's recent effort to "reconcile" the "skeptical" and "idealist" impulses in Shelley by rethinking the influence on him of Lucretius from a perspective informed by late twentieth-century "chaos science" and by the work of Michel Serres. In "nonlinear dynamic systems," Roberts writes, "arbitrarily small effects have a tendency to take on a life of their own under feedback amplification," producing "negentropic subsystems" within "a system that is globally entropic."[7] Though Roberts never reflects on his own use of *arbitrary* ("arbitrarily small" could have several different meanings) or on Shelley's distinctive relation to Enlightenment discourses of the arbitrary, he brings the conceptual strategies of "chaos science" to bear on Shelley's texts and on the complex natural and political processes they often represent (storms, revolutions) in ways that provoke fresh questions about the place of randomness in his writing, and that bring into sharp focus the distinction between modes of the arbitrary that depend on human agency (whether tyrannical or capricious) and modes that do not. I will have more to say later about the arbitrary as mere contingency. What I want to insist on here is that in both political and linguistic frames of reference it is not only the doubleness of the *arbitrary*—its signifying at once absolute determination and utter indeterminacy—that characterizes the problematic I am attempting to define. It is also the interaction between the terms of the doubleness—the historical and social processes through which what is initially random and contingent becomes absolute, or conversely through which absolute will and authority give way to the random and contingent.

When we go back to Locke and Shelley with the contradictory or at least divergent semantic history of arbitrariness in mind and look at how they use *arbitrary* and its variants in contexts that are not explicitly linguistic, we may be struck by how oddly the nonlinguistic uses sit next to the neutral or celebratory sense of phrases such as "a Word made arbitrarily the Mark of such an *Idea*" and "language is arbitrarily produced by the Imagination." Here is Locke in *The Second Treatise of Government* (1689), in a passage I am sure Wollstonecraft was remembering in her sentence on Rousseau, speaking "of Paternal, Political, and Despotical Power, considered together":

> *Paternal* or *Parental Power* is nothing but that, which Parents have over their Children, to govern them for the Childrens good, till they come to the use of Reason. . . . The Affection and Tenderness, which God hath planted in the Breasts of Parents, towards their Children, makes it evident, that this is not intended to be a severe Arbitrary Government, but only for the Help, Instruction, and Preservation of their Off-spring. (Ch. 15, sec. 170)

And here again is Locke, in the next section, on "Political Power":

> *Political Power* is that Power which every Man, having in the state of Nature, has given up into the hands of the Society. . . . with their express or tacit Trust, that it shall be employed for their good. . . . it can have no other *end or measure* . . . but to preserve the Members of that Society in their Lives, Liberties, and Possessions; and so cannot be an Absolute, Arbitrary Power over their Lives and Fortunes. (Ch. 15, sec. 171)

Locke's political uses of *arbitrary* are consistently negative in this way and coincide exactly with Johnson's definition—"Despotick . . . following the will without restraint . . . capricious." In Shelley's political writing the word has a wider and more subtly graded range of meanings: in the *Essay on Christianity*, for instance, he can say that "some benefit has not failed to flow from the imperfect attempts which have been made to erect a system of equal rights to property and power upon the basis of arbitrary institutions" (*WPBS* 6: 252). But for Shelley, too, the predominant ethical and political meanings of *arbitrary* are negative: "The savage brutality of the populace is proportioned to the arbitrary character of their government" (*A Philosophical View of Reform, WPBS* 7: 51).

Beyond making evident this divergence between the overtly political and the linguistic uses of *arbitrary* in Locke and Shelley, what the instances I have cited help us see is that *arbitrary* is a word deeply and inextricably embedded in material and political life, and that Locke's effort to give it a neutral philosophical meaning in his crucial attempt to confine linguistic signification to the interaction of "articulate sounds" and "ideas"—bracketing the entire process of referring to the world of "things"—and Shelley's related conviction that language is "produced by the Imagination and has relation to thoughts alone"—are both shadowed by the material and political frames of reference and value they momentarily set aside. Listen again to Locke's formulation: in speaking of "voluntary Imposition," he claims a remarkable kind and degree of power for the mind in its verbal invention and operations, a power that functions independently—at least in the context of Book 3 of the *Essay*—of "things" and nature. And while he goes on in this part of Book 3 to speak of the "Advantage of Society" and its dependence on "Communication of Thoughts," he says almost nothing about how this collective social impulse manifests itself through "voluntary Imposition," through the "arbitrary" appropriation of certain sounds for certain ideas. Locke never looks analytically at arbitrary linguistic institution, at "voluntary Imposition," as a collective historical process. "Voluntary" carries with it the ancient notion of words being instituted *ad placitum*—"according to what is pleasing, agreeable, acceptable"—and reproduces the ambiguity of the Latin phrase. As expounded in the *Essay* Locke's idea of the arbitrary has little explicitly to do with notions of "convention," "compact," or "custom," though it has often been assumed that these are the notions he intends by "arbitrary," and though later in the eighteenth century some of Locke's followers slide loosely back and forth between *arbitrary* and terms for referring to socially instituted signs.[8] As a result, Locke's linguistic discourse of the arbitrary is left confusingly vulnerable to those senses of the "despotic," "willful," and "capricious" that are dominant in his political discourse of the arbitrary.

With Shelley's passage on language in the *Defence*, the case is even more striking. "Poetry," he says, "expresses those arrangements of language ... which are created by that imperial faculty, whose throne is curtained within the invisible nature of man." Shelley the radical democrat and revolutionary is suddenly associating "language arbitrarily produced by the Imagination" with an "imperial faculty" whose seat of power, a "throne," is usually a figure for the despotic patriarchal authority he detests. And he goes on to celebrate language for being "more plastic and obedient to the controul of that faculty of which it is the creation." Not only is this language about the power that produces language politicized, but it is politicized in a direction that runs directly counter to Shelley's explicit political convictions and ideals.[9] His sense of the imagination's verbal power is verbally at odds with his sense of political power, and this being at odds has to do with his using the term *arbitrary*, as Locke does, to deny that linguistic signs are constituted through a "natural connexion" rooted in things, to restrict the signifying representational function of language "to thoughts alone."

In the political language of the eighteenth and early-nineteenth centuries, *arbitrary* is the epithet of power that is unnatural, irrational, and unrepresentative, in that it does not derive or arise from the represented will of citizens who make up the polity. As such, it names a condition of political tyranny or despotism that may be either absolute or capricious, or both. In linguistic discourse, however, *arbitrary* is the epithet of a power that is socially, but not naturally or rationally, constitutive: words originate through collective acts of "Imposition" (Locke) or "institution" that are not founded in nature or reason. In the historical course of communicative use, they evolve in ways that may be or should be—but rarely are—both natural and rational.

2.

Far from having been resolved in post-Saussurian semiotic theory, the Enlightenment and Romantic problems that inhere in the discourse of the arbitrary sign have persisted and confounded efforts to relate language as a formal system to its social origins, functions, and meanings. Derrida takes note of the difficulty in *Of Grammatology* by calling *arbitrary* a "gross" misnomer, but he never pauses to elaborate a sustained critique of the term itself; his musings on Warburton and hieroglyphics in the 1979 essay "Scribble" are tantalizing and provocative but finally elusive on this point.[10] 1979 was a productive year for pronouncements about "arbitrary power." There is de Man in "Shelley Disfigured," saying that in *The Triumph of Life* "the positing power of language is both entirely arbitrary in having a strength that cannot be reduced to necessity, and entirely inexorable in that there is no alternative to it. It stands beyond the polarities of chance and determination and can therefore not be part of a temporal sequence of events."[11] De Man's distinction between "entirely arbitrary" and "entirely inexorable" creates the significant opening for further intervention here. And there is Umberto Eco in *A Theory of Semi-*

otics, putting valuable critical pressure on such received semiotic binarisms as "conventional vs. natural" and "arbitrary vs. motivated" (the latter binarism may be taken to epitomize one version of the problem I am posing) and arguing that even so-called iconic signs are arbitrarily coded.[12] In general, however, semiotic and poststructuralist theory has tended to move on by taking the principle of arbitrariness as established and no longer interestingly problematic.[13] This tendency is itself, I am arguing, a problem.

Within some sectors of theoretical linguistics, though not within currently dominant academic styles of the philosophy of language, the debate about arbitrary signs has been kept alive.[14] In *Reading Saussure* (1987), Roy Harris situates his discussion of the principle of arbitrariness within what he calls a "prolonged controversy, which still continues," though the books and articles in this part of his bibliography are not widely known to most of us working in literary and cultural studies. Harris emphasizes both the uncompromising priority of the principle of arbitrariness for Saussure and its apparent contradictoriness and obscurity.[15] One difficulty, noted but dealt with only briefly by Harris, is famously thrown into relief by Emile Benveniste in his 1939 paper on "The Nature of the Linguistic Sign." Saussure's account of arbitrariness, Benveniste claims, "is falsified by an unconscious and surreptitious recourse to a third term which was not included in the initial definition [of the sign as an arbitrary relation of "sound-image" and "concept"]. This third term is the thing itself, [material] reality." Benveniste's example is Saussure's own: Saussure can only claim that the two French "sound-images" *böf* and *oks* arbitrarily signify the same concept by referring covertly to the actual animal in the world from which that concept is derived.[16] Harris deals with this objection by insisting that Saussure's principle of arbitrariness applies only to the level of *la langue* and "has nothing to do with *la parole*," with historically and socially situated acts of language use. But as Harris later acknowledges, questions of reference do bear importantly on linguistic change and continuity at the level of *langue*; the bracketing of the world of things in Saussure, as in Shelley and Locke, may defer but can never resolve key questions about linguistic agency and institution. Harris usefully articulates the fundamental tension in Saussure: "although *la langue* is a social institution—and in certain respects the very archetype of a social institution—its arbitrariness gives it a structural autonomy vis à vis society" (69). So language is archetypally social, but neither the individual nor the social collective "has any power to alter either *signifiant* or *signifié*." "[T]he *Cours* is committed both to the proposition that the linguistic sign is arbitrary and also to the proposition that *la langue* is a social institution," Harris continues. "The latter proposition, however, is left in considerably deeper obscurity than the former" (81). It is in fact the interdependence of these two sources of Saussurian obscurity that I want to insist upon. When Harris draws out the obscurity of Saussure's insistence on language as a social institution by saying that "language is imposed on its speakers, not agreed to by them" (8), he is in fact rearticulating the problem of arbitrariness—the problem lurking in Locke's appeal to "voluntary Imposition," in Shelley's figure of the linguistic imagination as an "imperial faculty."

The status of these questions within the tradition of Chomskyan generative grammar—a tradition usually taken to be antithetical to that of Lockean-Saussurian semiotics—is a complicated matter, particularly when pursued historically with reference to Chomsky's own effort to link his work to Cartesian rationalism and to the seventeenth- and eighteenth-century tradition of universal or general grammar.[17] Shifting the terrain of the discussion from that of the constitution and operation of the sign to the production of the grammatical and syntactic sequence immediately situates the problem of the arbitrary very differently. Oswald Ducrot helpfully summarizes the position of the seventeenth-century *Port-Royal* grammarians, whom Chomsky especially looks to as his predecessors: "To the extent that the logical aspect of grammar is regarded as its deepest level and that the idiomatic specificities only graft themselves onto it secondarily, language, from the perspective of the general grammars, may be regarded as fundamentally motivated and only accidentally arbitrary."[18] What this formulation catches is how theoretically loose the discourse of universal grammar gets when it comes to addressing that aspect of linguistic experience that it regards as secondary. Saying that language production is "accidentally arbitrary" exposes, among other things, the limitations in the opposition of "motivated" to "arbitrary" as it operates here. For Chomsky and the tradition with which he identifies his work, language is arbitrary, but only at the level of historical particularity and contingency that he often relegates to a secondary realm of "external stimulus." Steven Pinker can toss off the claim that "words have stable meanings, linked to them by arbitrary convention," without breaking his stride in *The Language Instinct* (1994)—and without pausing to consider what this claim means for his account of "How the Mind Creates Language."[19] At the level of those "linguistic universals" that make possible the generation of infinite meaningful possibilities from finite cognitive structures—and that are understood with increasing conviction to be "hard-wired" in the human brain—at this level, language is said by the Chomskyans to be anything but arbitrary.

The Chomskyan vantage point is important to my argument because of the degree to which it converges with the anti-arbitrarian strain in Romantic thinking about language. Chomsky's *Cartesian Linguistics* warmly embraces not just Descartes, Arnauld, and Lancelot, but Herder,

Coleridge, the Schlegels, and Wilhelm von Humboldt. The second item in Chomsky's bibliography is *The Mirror and the Lamp*. This is of interest not simply because of the Romantic campaign to sustain a belief in the "natural" as against the "arbitrary" sign, but because that campaign was intermittently invested in a grammatical rather than a semiotic approach to the sources of linguistic authority and agency. In Coleridge's unfinished manuscript "treatises" that have come to be known as the *Logic*, the focus is on what he calls a "grammatical discourse" that "reflects the forms of the human mind" (*CC*, 18). Drawing on Berkeley's speculations about a divinely authorized grammar encoded in the natural world and imperfectly reflected in human language (*Treatise Concerning the Principles of Human Knowledge*, 1710) and on James Harris's *Hermes, or a Philosophical Inquiry concerning Universal Grammar* (1751), Coleridge works his way toward a transcendentalist grammar that absorbs the problem of the arbitrary sign into a constitutive "unity of apperception . . . presupposed in . . . all consciousness" and active in fully potentiated human discourse.[20] I will return momentarily to an earlier stage in Coleridge's contention with arbitrariness. The point of emphasis here is not its identity but its companionability with the Chomskyan position.

The problem of the arbitrary has also had a vexed place within the tradition of historical and cultural materialism. In his chapter on "Language" in *Marxism and Literature*, Raymond Williams draws extensively on Vološinov's *Marxism and the Philosophy of Language* and argues that the latter was able to preserve many of the strengths of Saussure's insistence on thinking about language as an autonomous system of signs while at the same time overcoming the two debilitating restrictions that Saussure—and Locke before him—had depended upon: the strategic severing of the connection between words and material things on the one hand, and the bracketing of social reality into a deferred formal abstraction on the other. In seeing "The process of [linguistic] articulation" as "necessarily . . . a *material* process," Williams writes of Vološinov, "the sign itself becomes part of a (socially created) physical and material world":[21] "consciousness takes shape and being in the material of signs created by an organized group in the process of its social intercourse" (13). In making this case, Williams demonstrates how troublesome the term *arbitrary* can be:

> The relation within the sign between the formal element and the meaning which this element carries is . . . inevitably conventional (thus far agreeing with orthodox semiotic theory), but it is *not* arbitrary and, crucially, it is not fixed. On the contrary the fusion of formal element and meaning . . . is the result of a real process of social development, in the actual activities of speech and in the continuing development of a language. . . . signs can exist only when this active social relationship is posited (37).

In a note on this passage, Williams explains that it is the sense of *arbitrary* as "random" or "casual" that he opposes, and this at least has the virtue of facing up to, if not resolving, some of the unstable implications of the word in Locke, Shelley, and Saussure. But Williams says nothing about that other pattern of implication, the "despotic" or "tyrannical," even in his later discussion of "domination" and "hegemony." It is never made clear why what he calls the "real process of social development" and "the actual activities of speech" rule out acts of linguistic power— "Imposition," to use Locke's word—that are *arbitrary* in senses other than "conventional," that are either "random" or "tyrannical." A fully realized Marxist account of language as socially produced and subject to change needs to be clearer on this fundamental issue.

Williams is important to Tony Bennett's *Formalism and Marxism* (1979), a book that takes us back into an aspect of Saussure's thinking that, as Harris makes evident, is easy to lose touch with—back into Saussure's own remarks about the connection between "The Arbitrary Nature of the Sign" and the historical and social dimension of language. At the level of theoretical principle, the arbitrary relationship between signifier and signified, Bennett says, "does not constitute a flight away from historical considerations so much as a mode of entry into them." Bennett quotes Jonathan Culler on this point: "Because it is arbitrary, the sign is totally subject to history, and the combination at a particular moment of a given signifier and signified is a contingent result of the historical process."[22] This is consistent with Harris's reading of Saussure. More emphatically than Harris, however, Bennett demonstrates the degree to which Saussure's formal position becomes obscure and contradictory once you try to work with it in the realm of material historicity and temporality. As Saussure puts his principle of arbitrariness into play, "Chance and necessity . . . play a gleeful game of tag with one another," Bennett writes, "as first one and then the other is allowed a central role" (73). In the end Saussure's principle of arbitrariness is "crucially debilitating," Bennett argues, because although it allows for the essential principle of historical variation, it never explains the historical determination it also implies. Like Williams, Bennett looks back to Vološinov and Bakhtin and calls for "a theory of language which will explain the particular unity of form and meaning established by the system of signs which constitute language with reference to the socially based and historically changing linguistic practices on which the system rests" (77–78). This call for a critical ideological semiotics that can incorporate the Chomskyans' findings about the common human capacity for syntactic production is appealing. But we are still left wondering whether the contradictory forces swirling around and through the word *arbitrary* in Saussure's "gleeful game of tag" are to be so optimistically subdued or subsumed, particularly in texts where a writer willingly submits to or willfully resists constraints and possibilities understood as arbitrary. Bennett's 1979 appeal signaled, in any case, unfinished work for Marxist theories of language.

Some of the most important resources for carrying this work forward are to be found, I believe, in the writing of the late Pierre Bourdieu. Bourdieu's relation to Marxism is nowhere more complex than in his analysis of language. Even those intent on differentiating Bourdieu's from a "traditional type of Marxist analysis" have had to acknowledge that "his work is deeply influenced by Marx's approach."[23] Yet in important respects Bourdieu positions himself at a critical distance from existing Marxist paradigms; his 1984 essay "Social Space and the Genesis of 'Classes'" sees itself as making a "break with the Marxist tradition" in terms that have come to sound all too familiar in post-1968 French theory (*Language and Symbolic Power*, 233). Bourdieu's self-positioning is different, however, from that of the poststructuralists: his "break" with Marxism often has the effect of returning us to the fundamental principles and commitments of this tradition and is crucial to what enables him to contribute so productively to the unfinished Marxist project of grasping language as a social and historical system and process.

In the essays comprising *Language and Symbolic Power*, Bourdieu begins by emphasizing the theoretical and descriptive limitations "constituted, in the work of Saussure, by the exclusion of all inherent social variation, or, as with Chomsky, by the privilege granted to the formal properties of grammar to the detriment of functional constraints" (32). Bourdieu resumes this orienting critique at the beginning of "The Production and Reproduction of Legitimate Language," where it clears the theoretical space for an alternative paradigm, that of "the linguistic market," in which different social groups with different, often conflicting interests exercise their competency in deploying the resources of the formal language system (understood both as Saussurian *langue* and as Chomskyan generative grammar). Though the model of a "linguistic market" may appear to be anti- or non-Marxist, it is in fact deeply convergent with Marx's own approach to human social behavior in capitalist society—and in all forms of society hierarchically structured primarily by class and secondarily by other "distinctions." For Bourdieu, language must be understood in terms of "an economy of symbolic exchanges" in which there exists, on the one hand, "the socially constructed dispositions of the linguistic habitus . . . which involves both the linguistic capacity to generate [in Chomsky's sense] an infinite number of grammatically correct discourses, and the social capacity to use this competence adequately in a determinate situation" and, on the other hand, "the structures of the linguistic market, which impose themselves as a system of specific sanctions and censorships" (37). "What circulates on the linguistic market," he argues, "is not 'language' as such, but rather discourses that are stylistically marked both in their production . . . and in their reception" (39).

Within this framework Bourdieu addresses the problem of the arbitrary in ways that are diversely enabling for an exploration of Romantic language theories, practices, and institutions. His sense of the interactive doubleness of the arbitrary—of the processes through which the unmotivated and the random acquire the force of absolute power and authority—pervades his account of the social construction of "legitimate language":

> [I]f one fails to perceive both the special value objectively accorded to the legitimate use of language and the social foundations of this privilege, one inevitably falls into one or other of two opposing errors. Either one unconsciously absolutizes that which is objectively relative and in that sense arbitrary, namely the dominant usage, failing to look beyond the properties of language itself, such as the complexity of its syntactic structure, in order to identify the basis of the value that is accorded to it, particularly in the educational market; or one escapes this form of fetishism only to fall into the naïvety *par excellence* of the scholarly relativism which forgets that the naïve gaze is not relativist, and ignores the fact of legitimacy, through an arbitrary relativization of the dominant usage, which is socially recognized as legitimate, and not only by those who are dominant. (52–53)

Bourdieu writes with an awareness of the dialectical historicity of the arbitrary that is very close at times to what we find in Williams, though unfortunately Williams and those shaped by his kind of cultural materialism form no part of what Bourdieu in the early 1980s understands as "the Marxist tradition."[24] What particularly concerns Bourdieu is the process through which "political unification and the accompanying imposition of an official language establish relations between *the different uses of the same language* which differ fundamentally from the theoretical relations (such as that between *mouton* and 'sheep' which Saussure cites as the basis for the arbitrariness of the sign) between different languages, spoken by politically and economically independent groups" (53). What "political unification and the accompanying imposition [remember Locke's 'voluntary Imposition'] of an official language" mean historically for Bourdieu comes to carry powerful implications for Romanticism as a cultural formation produced by the conflict between the older monarchies and the new actually existing or emergent bourgeois republics. "Until the French Revolution," Bourdieu writes, "the process of linguistic unification went hand in hand with the process of constructing the monarchical state." "[T]he Revolutionary policy of linguistic unification" involved a very different regime of language "imposition":

> [The] imposition of the legitimate language in opposition to the dialects and *patois* was an integral part of the political strategies aimed at perpetuating the gains of the Revolution through the production and the reproduction of the 'new man'.... To reform language, to purge it of the usages linked to the old society and impose it in its purified form, was to impose a thought that would itself be purged and purified.... The conflict between the French of the revolutionary intelligentsia and the dialects or *patois* was a struggle for symbolic power in which what was at stake was the *formation* and *reformation* of mental structures. In short, it was not only a question of communicating but of gaining recognition for a new language of authority. (46–48)

Bourdieu opens up critical new dimensions of the problem of the arbitrary. Not only does "arbitrary" name a place of conflicted convergence between language (as formal system) and political power, between the imagined acts of "imposition" through which signs are initially constituted and the social process through which the semiotic vestiges of "voluntary Imposition" are themselves "imposed." "Arbitrary" also names the linguistic aspect of nation-formation under the conditions of class rule that obtain within a representative republic. In terms closer to home, "arbitrary power" in this sense applies not only to King George III but to those of his former subjects prepared to revolt against his power and form a republic independent of his authority.

3.

The theoretical and historical problematic I have been setting out implies a range of specific questions about the interrelationships among political determination and contingency, linguistic representation, and literary form in Romantic writing. On my way to exploring some of these questions in depth in the chapters that follow, I want to suggest more broadly their centrality to ongoing debates about language, social and political conflict, and the writing that we have come to think of as characteristically or distinctively "Romantic."

The Preface to the second edition of *Lyrical Ballads* is a contradictory effort to counter or minimize the arbitrary power of language. The fundamental point of linguistic reference in the Preface is what Wordsworth calls "language really used by men." And in the familiar passage where Wordsworth contracts his ideal of "language really used by men" to the language of "Humble and rustic life," he makes explicit his antagonistic sense of the arbitrary:

> The language . . . of these men has been adopted (purified indeed from what appear to be its real defects, from all lasting and rational causes of dislike or disgust) because such men hourly communicate with the best objects from which the best part of language is originally derived; and because, from their rank in society and the sameness and narrow circle of their intercourse, being less under the influence of social vanity, they convey their feelings and notions in simple and unelaborated expressions. Accordingly, such a language . . . is a more permanent, and a far more philosophical language, than that which is frequently substituted for it by Poets, who think that they are conferring honour upon themselves and their art, in proportion as they separate themselves from the sympathies of men, and indulge in arbitrary and capricious habits of expression, in order to furnish food for fickle tastes, and fickle appetites, of their own creation. (*PWWW* 1: 124)

Wordsworth is responding directly here to Locke's doctrine that words are signs of ideas, not of "objects," and that they exist as signs not by virtue of any "natural connexion" but "arbitrarily," "by a voluntary Imposition." The term "arbitrary" in the Preface takes on a significance, political as well as poetic, that cannot simply be limited to Wordsworth's polemic against the artifice of eighteenth-century poetic diction.

In articulating his idea of "language really used by men" who "hourly communicate with the best objects from which the best part of language is originally derived," Wordsworth appears to address exactly those two spheres of experience that semiotic ways of thinking about language, whether Locke's or Saussure's, bracket or ignore: actual social life and the material world. Wordsworth's appeal sounds in many ways like Raymond Williams's appeal to "a real process of social development," to "the actual activities of speech." Of course Williams would say that Wordsworth's delimitation of "language really used by men" to "Humble and rustic life" does not constitute "a real process of social development" at all, but rather a primitivist ideal abstracted from actual social and historical conditions and invoked on behalf of other ideological considerations. And he would be right: what is most striking about Wordsworth's linguistic and social range of reference is how coercively he has to manipulate it to accommodate his own poetic practice. Even as Wordsworth appeals (in a sentence I omitted from the quotation above) to "the *necessary* character of rural occupations" in his campaign against "arbitrary and capricious habits of expression," he has to "purify" the language of those occupations from "its real defects." (One wonders whether these "defects" are themselves "necessary" or "arbitrary.") Certainly Wordsworth's acts of purification or "selection" (as he says elsewhere) involve an arbitrary compositional power both in their being "voluntary Impositions" and, at times, in their being "despotic." It is partly because he knows he has to perform these acts that Wordsworth says so little in the Preface about "these men" talking to each other—it leaves him freer to do their poetic talking for them. They talk instead with nature; they "hourly communicate with the best objects."

This reading of Wordsworth's Preface differs somewhat from Olivia Smith's account in *The Politics of Language, 1791–1819* (1984). "The thesis which the Preface argues," she says, is "that language is a democratic vehicle of expression."[25] Smith convincingly maintains that "'Arbitrary' refers . . . throughout the Preface . . . to what is socially imposed and socially divisive," and that "at its simplest" the Preface claims "that the rustic does not suffer the risk of 'arbitrary' connections between words and ideas."[26] But she overestimates Wordsworth's success in evading "'arbitrary' connections between words and ideas" on behalf of a "democratic" view of language. The difficulty is partly a matter of political tone of voice: it is hardly "democratic" of Wordsworth to claim that "these men," "from their rank in society, and the sameness and narrow circle of their intercourse . . . convey their feelings and notions in simple and unelaborated expressions." No wonder the *Anti-Jacobin* was not disturbed by the politics of *Lyrical Ballads*. More importantly, Wordsworth himself knows that he cannot use the language of peasants to escape from the arbitrariness of language and says so near the end of the Preface: "[M]y language may frequently have suffered from those arbitrary connexions of feelings and ideas with particular words and phrases, from which no man can altogether protect himself." This is the attitude that finally prevails in Wordsworth, the recognition, as he says in the *Essay, Supplementary to the Preface* to *Poems* (1815), "that the medium through which, in poetry, the heart is to be affected, is language; a thing subject to endless fluctuations and arbitrary associations" (*PWWW* 3: 82).

Granting to or finding in language a distinctive power to affect the heart has a long tradition in eighteenth-century discourses of sentiment and sensibility, and of what would come to be called aesthetic theory. Not all such discourses regard Lockean semiotics as antithetical to their affective emphasis. It is a strength of Tom Furniss's chapter titled "The labour and profit of language" in *Edmund Burke's Aesthetic Ideology* (1993) that he sees how readily and with what contradictory results "Burke invokes the authority of Locke" in the *Enquiry into the Origin of Our Ideas of the Sublime and the Beautiful*. Burke's unstable relation to Locke's philosophy of words is significant in ways that include a powerful and still-debated influence on Wordsworth. The *Enquiry* depends, Furniss argues, on a belief that the mind has "an unmediated engagement with reality"—with words-as-sounds and, through them, with things ("it is not only of those ideas which are commonly called abstract . . . but of particular real beings, that we converse without having any idea of them excited in the imagination"; *Enquiry*, 170)—a belief that Burke grounds in Locke's alleged assertion that "the senses are the great original of all our ideas."[27] At the same time Burke not only accepts Locke's premise that words are arbitrary, not natural, signs of ideas and therefore of things but links this to his argument for the immediate affective power of language: "[S]o far is a clearness of imagery from being absolutely necessary to an influence upon the passions, that they may be considerably operated upon without presenting any image at all, by certain sounds adapted to that purpose" (*Enquiry*, 60). It is this stress on the immediate emotive effects of words as mere "sounds" that allows Furniss to argue that "Burke begins from what ostensibly looks like a Lockean view of language in order to celebrate precisely what Locke would remedy"—the tendency of language to generate irrational, passionate states of mind (*Edmund Burke's Aesthetic Ideology*, 99). Language for Burke in the *Enquiry* functions "independently of referents or concepts" (101) and according to an "arbitrary" dynamic that is shifted away from the Lockean notion of "voluntary Imposition" toward what will later become the characteristic Burkean ideas of "habit," "custom," and "prejudice."

The political implications of Burke's emotive and affective account of the arbitrariness of language play themselves out in even more deeply contradictory ways in his writing of the 1790s. Already in the *Enquiry* the affirmed immediacy of connection between "sound" and "emotion" that is central to Burke's analysis of the literary sublime is also a source of anxiety about the disposition of the "common sort of people" to respond to what they hear or read solely through "their passions" (61). As Furniss argues, in the *Reflections on the Revolution in France* this anxiety returns and is extended to "the people's susceptibility to the sublime," to "the condition which enables their repression within the traditional order and, at the same time, . . . makes them responsive to . . . the 're-publican' or 'radical' sublime": "It is necessary for Burke that the people should be motivated and manipulated by power rather than knowledge, yet this is precisely what makes them dangerous" (*Edmund Burke's Aesthetic Ideology*, 103). In the subsequent discussion of how the Burkean sublime becomes "a 'revolutionary' aesthetic which depends for its very power on a particular *relation* to custom," and of how "discourses of tradition and revolution become mirror images of one another," there is an element of rhetorical formalism in Furniss's argument that tends to minimize the specific historical content of "revolutionary" and turn it into little more than a rhetorical category. Yet his account very usefully shows, along lines that need to be reinforced by Bourdieu's analysis in "The Production and Reproduction of Legitimate Language," that the problem of the arbitrary does not disappear but is profoundly transformed in the movement from monarchy to republic.

The question of which class in society is imagined as either agent of or subject to the arbitrary power of language is recurrently determinative in Romantic discourse. When Coleridge takes issue in chapter 17 of the *Biographia Literaria* with Wordsworth's claim that "the best part of language is originally derived" from the kind of "communicat[ion]" with the "best objects" of nature characteristic of peasants, he does so in terms that momentarily draw him surprisingly close to Locke and to Shelley: "The best part of human language, properly so called, is derived from reflection on the acts of the mind itself. It is formed by a voluntary appropriation of fixed symbols to internal acts, to processes and results of imagination, the greater part of which have no place in the consciousness of uneducated man" (*CC* 2: 54). The phrase "by a voluntary appropriation" sounds like an effort to turn Locke's "by a voluntary Imposition" in a more comfortable direction. Like Shelley, and in keeping with one of the deepest impulses in Romantic language theory, Coleridge appropriates for the poet working *within* an already existing language a power that Locke ascribes to the origination of language. Thus the arbitrary institution of linguistic signs comes to be exuberantly transferred by Shelley, through what we might call the trope of perpetual origination, to a celebration of poetic agency and production. Coleridge is far more cautious, and more critical of the Lockean principle (the tension between "fixed symbols" and "internal acts," "processes and results of imagination," is the clearest indication of this). The most striking moment in his early thinking about these matters comes in the letter to Godwin of 22 September 1800, where he responds to the first volume of John Horne Tooke's *EPEA PTEROENTA, or The Diversions of Purley.*

> I wish you to write a book on the power of words, and the processes by which human feelings form affinities with them—in short, I wish you to *philosophize* Horn Tooke's System, and to solve the great Questions—whether there be reason to hold, that an action bearing all the *semblance* of predesigning Consciousness may yet be simply organic, & whether a *series* of such actions are possible—and close on the heels of this question would follow the old 'Is Logic the *Essence* of Thinking?' in other words—Is *Thinking* impossible without arbitrary signs? &—how far is the word 'arbitrary' a misnomer? Are not words &c parts & germinations of the Plant? (*CLSTC* 1: 625)[28]

Like Derrida, Coleridge sees the discourse of the "arbitrary" as a negative instance of itself, as a misnaming of the fundamental semiotic relationship. His organicist reaction to this misnaming is of course deeply un-Derridian. His questions to Godwin simultaneously collapse the bracketed and deferred sphere of reference into signification, and push both in the direction of a constitutive transcendental symbolization. In a double sense Coleridge wants words to be instances of what he will later call *natura naturans*: he wants them to be "part" of the organic processes they refer to and signify, and the best evidence the mind offers of its own deep unity with natural process.[29] Coleridge is by implication already anticipating generative grammarians like Chomsky and Pinker, with their methodological preferences for transformational "roots" and "trees," with their elaborate diagrams of "right-branching" and "left-branching" syntactic structures. Coleridge does all this in hopeful opposition to his radical friend Horne Tooke, whose revision of the Lockean principle of arbitrariness assumes that language develops primarily through a social imperative of quicker, more efficient communication.[30]

The range of practical stylistic consequences of the conditions and conceptualizations of language I have been investigating becomes evident when we move from Wordsworth, Burke, and Coleridge to Byron, whose writing enacts by opportunistically revelling in the linguistic arbitrary in its contradictorily domineering and capricious, absolute and random, modes of operation, in contexts where both "arbitrary power" in the explicit political sense, and the liberal discourse of "convention," "compact," and "contract," are recurrently at stake. The most prominent stylistic marker of the Byronic arbitrary is rhyme, an aspect of his writing with contradictory political attachments that I will look at in detail in chapter 3. Byron comes to see rhyme as an occasion for performative rhetoric that produces willfulness from whimsy, strength from chance:

> If I sneer sometimes,
> It is because I cannot well do less,
> And now and then it also suits my rhymes.
> (*Don Juan* 13. 58–60)

Jerome Christensen reads these lines as generalizing the gesture by which Byron disposes of the dead Cockney highwayman Tom two cantos earlier: "But Tom's no more—and so no more of Tom. / Heroes must die . . ." (11. 153–54). "That Tom can die to suit the poet's rhyme is the condition of possibility for the condition that Lyotard calls Auschwitz," Christensen writes, deliberately pushing the performative implications of Byron's aristocratic strength over the top.[31] This is also the "condition of possibility" for that act of linguistic and narrative coercion and opportunism in which the poem originates, or at least with which it begins: wanting a hero, Byron finds "Barnave, Brissot," and a whole list of "many of the military set, / Exceedingly remarkable at times, / But not at all adapted to my rhymes" (1. 17–24). The anglicizing imposition that compels "Ju-an" into rhyming convergence with "new one" and "true one" signifies Byron's larger imposition on the legendary narrative of aristocratic seduction and damnation. That such imposition depends upon and is constrained by patterns of semiotic chance at once peculiar to English and shaped by a formal stanzaic convention borrowed from Italian poetry determines—establishes the terms for, sets the limits of— Lord Byron's arbitrary performance.

One more brief excursion into the unfinished debates within semiotic theory will suggest what is at issue in Byron's representing himself as "The grand Napoleon of the realms of rhyme" (11. 440). Contending with Saussure's claim that "the arbitrary character of *la langue* fundamentally distinguishes it 'from all other [social] institutions,'" Harris argues that "other social institutions (political, religious, legal, economic, etc.) deal with things which are already interconnected, directly or indirectly, in a variety of non-arbitrary ways." In contrast to the "superficial arbitrariness of the price" in market capitalism, for example, "the profound arbitrariness of the linguistic sign" means that "it would make no difference to" any specific "linguistic transaction" whether the signfier-component of a given word were what it is or something else. "It would make no difference to the linguistic transaction (the act of *parole*)," Harris says, "if the word for 'sister' were not *soeur* but *zoeur*, or *soeuf*, or *pataplu*" (*Reading Saussure*, 67–68). Harris's generally insightful analysis is wrong here in ways that can disable us from understanding the possibilities of rhyme and of puns. It does make a difference that the word in French for "sister" is *soeur*, because (putting the case negatively) a French poet cannot do what Byron does with this sign. In Canto 14 Lord Henry Amundeville departs from Lady Adeline "and, as [he] went out, calmly kiss'd her, / Less like a young wife than an aged sister" (14. 551–52). You cannot do this exact thing in any language but English, any more than you can work Shakespearean changes on semantically antithetical rhymes like "womb" and "tomb," or "breath" and "death." The fundamental arbitrariness of linguistic signs generates possibilities distinctive to particular languages; the chance convergence that Byron rather predictably seizes upon here is as English as Lord Henry ("He was a cold, good, honourable man, / Proud of his birth," 14. 553) and Lady Adeline ("Cool, and quite English, imperturbable," 13. 108) themselves.

Byron understands that the arbitrary constraints of rhyme are its arbitrary possibilities, and he exploits this peculiar resource again and again not just to assert a lordly or imperious strength against, but to situate such strength within, what he sees as a national culture in decline. But since Byron also has the strongest claim to an internationalist position of any English Romantic writer, his translingual or interlingual rhyming and punning are worth thinking about from just this perspective. So is his ironic assimilation of Regency political and social idiom. Dudù's confusion about her dream in the harem episode of *Don Juan* provokes the narrator to comment on the arbitrariness of his own dreams:

> I've known some odd ones which seemed really planned
>   Prophetically, or that which one deems
> "A strange coincidence," to use a phrase
>   By which such things are settled now-a-days.
>
>   (6. 621–24)

The quoted phrase, identified in the 1832–1833 *Works* as having been used by one of Queen Caroline's parliamentary defenders in dismissing her alleged sexual transgressions, captures something strange about dreams—and about the couplet rhyme that comments on and instances "'A strange coincidence'": "phrase" / "now-a-days." British national identity and party politics—specifically the Whig discourse that had a lasting claim on Byron and in which "arbitrary power" names the abuses of aristocracy, monarchy, and empire—become the reference points for sarcastically condemning the post-Napoleonic version of the new world order.

4.

In political theory and in the philosophy of language, the problem of the arbitrary is intrinsic to the problem of representation. Chandler's extended meditation on the "tension between the 'representative' and the 'representational'" and on the "representative state" in *England in 1819* demonstrates how complexly entangled the apparently distinct discourses of the arbitrary become in the late eighteenth and early nineteenth centuries. From Marx's distinction between *Vertretung* and *Darstellung* in *The Eighteenth Brumaire of Louis Bonaparte* and from Gayatri Spivak's elaboration of this distinction in "Can the Subaltern Speak?," Chandler draws out the double problematic as it applies to the development of historical and historicizing discourse during the Romantic period: "discussion of literary representation or representativeness in this period often intersects with the dominant political topic of the day: the issue of reform in political representation" (187).[32] I want to situate this intersection even more intensively at the theoretical and practical level of verbal representation itself. The problem of the arbitrary occupies multiple levels of representation simultaneously, as Chandler indicates in observing that "Hazlitt's couching of his comments [in *The Spirit of the Age*] about literary popularity in the terms of political suffrage is ... by no means an arbitrary metaphor" (187).

Moving Chandler's analysis further onto the plane of linguistic theory and stylistic practice will enable us to deepen our sense of why and how his account of Romantic literary culture in general, and of Romantic historicism in particular, matters to our reading of individual texts. Chandler's own reading of the poem from which he takes his title, Shelley's "England in 1819," stands as a kind of proleptic response to the imagined challenge that he has appropriated Shelley's title for "an arbitrarily framed subject matter" (23) and begins to suggests ways in which the language of Shelley's sonnet is itself "arbitrarily framed." The rhetorical and grammatical structure of the poem, Chandler implies, enacts an arbitrary compositional power that may seem willful and coercive in its framing of a historical situation in which despotism produces hope: "The grammatical device by which this transformation is accomplished could scarcely be more overt: the sheer predication ('Are graves') that at once turns the catalogue into a compound subject and reduces its items to a common fate" (24). In the closing couplet "Shelley makes a historical turning point appear to coincide with the formal turning point of the poem" (27). Yet at the same time, Chandler says, this "formal turning point occurs in a scrambled sequence of rhymes"—in a stylistic trajectory that would appear, on his reading, to move us in the opposite direction of the arbitrary understood as the capricious, the random. But is the rhyme sequence scrambled? *a b a b a b c d c d c c d d* is a willfully unscrambled though decidedly unconventional formal order, one that depends, as all rhyme sequences do, on the accidents or contingencies that generate "King" / "spring" / "cling," "flow" / "know" / "blow," "field" / "wield" / "sealed" / "unrepealed," and "prey" / "slay" / "may" / "day." It is the shaping of such contingencies through and across the conventions of sonnet form into a single sentence whose copulative grammar completes itself in "Are graves" at the beginning of the penultimate line, only to open out into the liberatory but indeterminate future possibility stretched across the line-ending of the couplet—"may / Burst, to illumine"—it is this stylistic action, I think, that makes "England in 1819" what Chandler calls "a project of making history by making it legible" (78). Shelley's stylistic making engages all senses of arbitrary linguistic power, and it does so in ways that represent the contradictions of arbitrary social and political power as well.

We are now in a better position to take the measure of de Man's dark pronouncement in "Shelley Disfigured": "The positing power of language is both entirely arbitrary in having a strength that cannot be reduced to necessity, and entirely inexorable in that there is no alternative to it. It stands beyond the polarities of chance and determination and can therefore not be part of a temporal sequence of events." The "positing power of language" can be grasped dialectically only *within* "the polarities of chance and determination," and as part of a sequence that is at once "temporal" and a matter of grammatical necessity. Being subject to chance and to temporality, the force of language cannot indeed be entirely "reduced to necessity," but neither can it be produced or received except in relation to binding rules of meaningful, communicable thought. What de Man provokes us negatively to see about Shelley's figuring of the power and the limits of language in *The Triumph of Life* is a registering of cultural and political history. Language is one of the forms that cultural and political history takes; it is one of the forms of thought through which human beings make history.

"Human beings make their own history, but they make it not 'out of free pieces' [voluntarily, of their own accord] — not under self-chosen, but under immediately found, given, and transmitted, circumstances."[33] Marx's famous sentence from *The Eighteenth Brumaire* generates interpretive resources that have too often gone unrealized in literary and cultural criticism that quotes it. In Shelley's "England in 1819," the "circumstances" of sonnet form, no less than the "circumstances" of Regency state corruption and oppression, are "found, given and transmitted" from the past, and it is from both that Shelley makes history poetically, in Chandler's terms, "by making it legible." Chandler gets to the nub of what it means to "make history" when he says that "to see how [Marx's] formulation sets the terms for the debate about the historian's code is to see how the question at issue relates to the vexed issue of determination" (36). Whether as a question of the "general will" of the polis or of the individual will of a political agent or writer, "determination" structures nineteenth-century efforts to understand the constitution of society and culture. The problem of the arbitrary is, as I suggested earlier, one form of the problem of determination (and, from an Althusserian perspective, of overdetermination)[34] — the setting of ends or limits, the bringing about of results, the exerting of specific pressures, the willing of particular ends, limits, or results. Understanding the problem of determination, in all of these senses, by attending critically to the discourse of the arbitrary enables us to see more precisely how this problem inheres in language itself as semiotic and grammatical system and as social and historical institution. Romantic writing finds, in the circumstances given to it and transmitted by it during the great revolutionary crises of modern Europe before the twentieth century, its historically distinctive relation to forces that were and still are contradictorily called "arbitrary." Often it denies or ironically submits to these forces. Occasionally it imagines not an organicist or theological escape from the arbitrary but a transformation of privileged will and privileged caprice, necessity and chance, the causal and the casual, into new, less destructive, more commonly productive forms of discourse and social life.

2

WORDS ARE THINGS

WITHIN THE Enlightenment paradigm that, variously developed and inflected, remains central to the philosophy of language into the nineteenth century, the claim that language is "arbitrary" depends on understanding words as signs—primarily of ideas, secondarily of things. This paradigm performs contradictory functions not only in the ideologies of Romanticism but also in the discourse of the aesthetic that emerged from Alexander Baumgarten's *Reflections on Poetry* (1735) through Kant's *Critique of Judgment* (1790) and on into the major nineteenth-century contributions of Hegel, Coleridge, and their contemporaries.[1] The aesthetic, even when placed most conspicuously at the service of transcendent "spirit" or "idea," was above all invented to provide new philosophical grounds for valuing the sensuous, and therefore raised new questions about the materiality of form in artistic representation.[2] In literary representation, how was the material and sensuous dimension of language to be regarded and valued in an intellectual culture that understood this dimension as "arbitrarily" related to the conceptual or emotive content of words-as-signs?

This chapter explores questions of material form and aesthetic ideology as they appear in British Romantic understandings of poetic language, and as they give the complications I have traced within the discourse of the arbitrariness of language a defining role in literary practice.[3] The signature of these questions in most of the texts I will be looking at is the claim that "words are things"—a claim that in shifting and conflicting ways will take us from affirmations and interrogations of the material efficacy of the Romantic symbol to confrontations with the marketing and consumption of literary texts: the transformation of poems into commodities.[4]

1.

Again, the critical passage from Coleridge's letter to Godwin of 22 September 1800:

> Is *Thinking* impossible without arbitrary signs? &—how far is the word 'arbitrary' a misnomer? Are not words &c parts & germinations of the Plant? And what is the Law of their Growth?—In something of this order I would

endeavor to destroy the old antithesis of *Words* & *Things*, elevating, as it were, words into Things, & living Things too. (*CLSTC* 1: 625–26)[5]

Byron also, at various moments in his life as a writer, denies "the old antithesis," but his ways of doing so are, if not antithetical to, mainly at odds with the emphasis of Coleridge's "elevating" endeavor. Most famously in Canto 3 of *Don Juan*, the narrator observes that poets "in these times" are all said to be "such liars," reflecting on the performance of a court poet whose situation is remarkably made to connect Robert Southey's career with Byron's own:

> But words are things, and a small drop of ink,
> Falling like dew, upon a thought, produces
> That which makes thousands, perhaps millions, think;
> (3. 793–95)[6]

For Byron, the power of words as things comes not from any transcendent coalescing of verbal signs with natural objects perceived through the impassioned imagination, but rather—as Kurt Heinzelman so impressively shows—from a complexly practical grasp, at once ambitious and anxious, of printing and publishing. *Don Juan* is "overtly—even self-consciously—conscious of its own status as a commodity," Heinzelman observes; "The Byron of the *Don Juan* period not only accepts income from his work but is acutely aware that 'Byron' is both a political and a saleable 'thing.'"[7] The socioeconomic and political perspectives on words-as-things opened up initially by Heinzelman need to be extended—and they need to be linked to questions about linguistic representation such as those posed in Coleridge's letter to Godwin. In the lines from Canto 3 of *Don Juan*, the way in which "ink" gets formally taken up into its rhyming partner "think" is, as Sheila Emerson suggests, emblematic of the productive material force Byron attributes to the recognition that "words are things."[8] Such argumentative rhyming calls attention to its own phonetic and graphic materiality as one of the means by which the passage "produces" the responses Byron imagines.

The issues raised divergently by these passages from Coleridge and Byron engage a wide range of theoretical work. Foucault never explicitly addresses the claim that "words are things" in *Les mots et les choses* (1966), but his version of the old belief in a radical "break" between classical and Romantic attitudes to language offers one possible model for understanding why Coleridge in his way, and Byron in his, want to "destroy the old antithesis of *Words* & *Things*." If the Enlightenment really held, as Foucault says, that words provide a spontaneous and transparent representational "table" or "grid for the knowledge of things," and if "at the beginning of the nineteenth century, [words] rediscovered their ancient, enigmatic density" and withdrew from representation into their own immanent order, then Coleridge and Byron might be read as articulating their awareness of such an epistemic crisis.⁹

I trust it is clear from my summary of the Foucauldian position on this matter that I do not find it historically or conceptually convincing. It must be addressed here, though, because it offers an influential and relevant account of historically shifting relations between words and things, and because it contains local insights that may prove helpful in thinking about the questions I am pursuing. Foucault points out, for instance, that already in the *Port-Royal Logic* and in Condillac we find a recognition that the verbal sign, "in order to function, must be simultaneously an insertion in that which it signifies and also distinct from it."¹⁰ Foucault offers an important insight into the problem of the arbitrary, one that I will later pursue in some detail. As for his general position, he is most persuasive when he says, in *The Archaeology of Knowledge*, that " 'Words and things' is the entirely serious title of a problem," of the ironically revealed "task" of "no longer treating discourses as groups of signs . . . but as practices that systematically form the objects of which they speak."¹¹

Further poststructuralist help in thinking about words-as-things might be sought, and sporadically found, in Lacan's doctrine of what he variously calls the "autonomy," "supremacy," or "materiality of the signifier," and especially in such Marxist efforts to enlist Lacan in the quest for a materialist theory of language as Rosalind Coward's and John Ellis's *Language and Materialism* (1977) and Michel Pêcheux's *Language, Semantics, and Ideology* (1982). But the trouble with the Lacanian doctrine and its neo-Marxist appropriations is that isolating the physical (phonetic or graphic) aspect of the verbal sign from the larger social matrix and changing semiotic entity of which it is by definition a part often yields a conceptually weak and ultimately trivializing kind of materialist stance. Jameson objects to efforts to ground a "genuinely materialistic view" of language in "the Lacanian notion of a 'material signifier'" by arguing that "Marxism is . . . not a mechanical but a historical materialism: it does not assert the primacy of matter so much as it insists on an ultimate determination by the mode of production."¹² Derek Attridge cites this passage from *The Political Unconscious* in support of his own more focused and pertinent argument that an "account of 'poetic' language as involving a heightened awareness of the production of meaning by language is . . . more amenable to a materialist philosophical (and political) position than an emphasis on the material signifier alone."¹³ The curious phonetic and graphic connection of "ink" to "think" in Byron's rhyme is powerfully provoking not because of any "supremacy" or "autonomy" established by the physical properties of the signifiers themselves, but because the arbitrary rhyming connection is part of a generative relationship between two signs that are themselves part of the passage's production of social, economic, and political meanings.

To see what is theoretically at stake in Romantic assertions that words are things, it is helpful to look back past Coleridge and remind ourselves of just how insistent Enlightenment philosophy had been in driving words and things apart. We may remember Thomas Sprat's ideal of a "close, naked, natural" scientific prose that would deliver "so many *things*, almost in an equal number of *words*";[14] we certainly remember Swift's wonderful parodic satire of this ideal in the Academy of Lagado's "Scheme for entirely abolishing all Words whatsoever" by refusing any representation of things at all.[15] But behind both Sprat's ideal and Swift's parody is the philosophical recognition, misleadingly downplayed by Foucault, that words are related to things not directly and transparently, but indirectly and arbitrarily. "*Words in their primary or immediate Signification*," writes Locke in Book 3 of the *Essay*, "*stand for nothing but the* Ideas *in the Mind of him that uses them*, how imperfectly soever, or carelessly, those *Ideas* are collected from the Things, which they are supposed to represent" (3.2.2).[16] Locke's clear implication is that even if our ideas were perfectly and carefully derived from things, the primary signifying relation between word-form and idea could carry no guarantee of transparency and stability. Swift's satire hardly touches this aspect of Locke's position, which may best be summarized in his skeptical formulation of the concept of "double Conformity" in Book 2 of the *Essay*: "Men are so forward to suppose, that the abstract *Ideas* they have in their Minds, are such, as agree to the Things existing without them, to which they are referr'd; and are the same also, to which the Names they give them, do by the Use and Propriety of that Language belong. For without this *double Conformity* of the *Ideas*, they find, they should both think amiss of Things in themselves, and talk of them unintelligibly to others" (2.32.8).

It is commonplace to read Romantic endeavors such as Coleridge's "to destroy the old antithesis of *Words* & *Things*" as projects (once regarded as triumphs, now more often as mystifications and evasions) to overcome the gaps and slippages acknowledged in Locke's analysis of "double Conformity." Less common are recognitions of the degree to which deconstructions of the Romantic symbol (like de Man's) are anticipated in Enlightenment thinking itself. From this angle, the assertion that "words are things" may be read as a truculent, truncated defiance of Lockean semiotics. But such a reading fails to take in the force of Byron's version of the claim, with its concern for words as material text and as commodity. For this, we need to go back and connect what Locke says about the "Propriety" of language with what he says about "property," and work forward through Smith and Ricardo until we can reimagine historically what kind of status as an economic "thing" early nineteenth-century writers could attribute to a text, to a literary "thing" made out of language. Heinzelman and subsequent critics have begun this process; I want to suggest extensions in the direction of Romantic thinking about language. We can begin to pose the problem in Lockean terms by setting the commitment to "Natural Law" on which his analysis of property is grounded against the unstably conventionalist and institutionalist assumptions of his analysis of language, and to ask: if the "right" or "title" to property derives from the appropriation and transformation of nature by human labor for human use, what "right" or "title" to property can derive from work on and in language, which for Locke originates not in any "natural connexion" but in "arbitrary Imposition"? Is language inherently enough like money to place any property made from it outside the range of Locke's labor theory of value? In Locke's theory, we recall, it is "the *invention of Money*, and the tacit agreement of Men to put a value on it, introduced (by Consent)," that disrupts the natural constraints on the accumulation of property, and thus its allegedly self-governing social function.[17]

2.

I will come back to these questions in a direct way when I come back to Byron. For the moment, it is important for my argument that we pursue more indirect and still inadequately explored linguistic matters by working our way further inside Coleridge's view of words-as-things, and now alsoWordsworth's. Perhaps the best known of all Romantic claims that "words are things" is the one Wordsworth makes in his 1800 note to "The Thorn." The specific occasion for the claim is his defense of "repetition and apparent tautology" in the language of "The Thorn" and of other poems in *Lyrical Ballads*, on the ground that in attempting "to communicate impassioned feelings" a "speaker will cling to the same words, or words of the same character."[18] "There are also various other reasons why repetition and apparent tautology are frequent beauties of the highest kind," Wordsworth continues: "Among the chief of these reasons is the interest which the mind attaches to words, not only as symbols of the passion, but as *things*, active and efficient, which are of themselves part of the passion" (*WPW* 2: 513). Frances Ferguson says in commenting on Wordsworth's note that it "puts into question the primacy of the symbol in literary language."[19] But in fact Wordsworth's setting not words-as-signs but words-as-"symbols" in opposition to words-as-"things" disguises his offering, under the latter category, a compressed version of "symbol" as Coleridge famously defines it in *The Statesman's*

Manual: "a Symbol . . . always partakes of the Reality which it renders intelligible; and while it enunciates the whole, abides itself as a living part in that Unity, of which it is the representative" (*CC* 6: 30). In this sense "symbols" are "things" for Coleridge, and his definition shares with Wordsworth's note a Romantic rewriting of that recognition that Foucault locates in Enlightenment theory: the verbal sign "must be simultaneously an insertion in that which it signifies and also distinct from it."[20] The "symbol," it might be said, seeks to redeem words from their arbitrariness by a short-circuited aestheticized materialism in which both signification and reference are collapsed into an identity that is haunted by its own covert act of arbitrary imposition.

For Wordsworth more emphatically than for Coleridge, what makes words take on the force of things is "passion." Behind the theoretical claim of Wordsworth's note we can hear and feel the force of all those astonishing moments in his writing when "things," under the pressure of passion, come movingly, hauntingly to life—and when other people are loved, valued, and mourned as "things":

> A motion and a spirit, that impels
> All thinking things, all objects of all thought,
> And rolls through all things.[21]
>   (*Tintern Abbey*, 100–102)

>   . . . ye who pore
> On the dead letter, miss the spirit of things;
>   (1850 *Prelude*, 8. 296–97)

> As a huge stone is sometimes seen to lie
> Couched on the bald top of an eminence;
> Wonder to all who do the same espy,
> By what means it could thither come, and whence;
> So that it seems a thing endued with sense:
>   (*Resolution and Independence*, 57–61)

> No mate, no comrade Lucy knew;
> She dwelt on a wide moor,
> —The sweetest thing that ever grew
> Beside a human door!
>   ("Lucy Gray," 5–8)

> She seemed a thing that could not feel
> The touch of earthly years.
>   ("A Slumber Did My Spirit Seal," 3–4)

Contextualized in this manner, Wordsworth's sense of words-as-things seems to recede from any obvious emphasis on the materiality of language. And "things" do recurrently lose their materiality in Wordsworth. The childhood moment recollected in the Fenwick note to the *Intimations* ode is paradigmatic in this regard: "I was often unable to think of external things as having external existence, and I communed with all that I saw as something not apart from, but inherent in, my own immaterial nature" (*WPW* 4: 463). This relation to things is predominant throughout Wordsworth's writing—so that when, in the first stanza of "The Thorn," the thorn itself is seen as "A wretched thing forlorn" (9), we connect it retrospectively with "our mortal Nature" and its capacity to "tremble like a guilty thing surprised" (*Intimations* ode, 146–47). Words are things for Wordsworth when things are spirits, or ghosts.

Nowhere are the complications in Wordsworth's attitude toward words-as-things more apparent than in what he says about books-as-things in Book 5 of *The Prelude*. At the beginning of this Book, thoughts about the materialization of spirit in printed words produce generalized elegiac lamentations:

> Thou also, man! hast wrought,
> For commerce of thy nature with herself,
> Things that aspire to unconquerable life;
> And yet we feel—we cannot choose but feel—
> That they must perish.
>   (5. 18–22)

Books for Wordsworth are preeminently "Things that aspire," objects that breathe forth, and the contradictoriness of this perception compels him to ask

> why hath not the Mind
> Some element to stamp her image on
> In nature somewhat nearer to her own?
>   (5. 45–47)

The word "stamp" here is one of many indications in Book 5 of the material concreteness of Wordsworth's anxiety about printed books as material objects. Even a volume of Shakespeare or Milton, when "held . . . in my hand," seems but a "Poor earthly casket of immortal verse" (5. 163–64). This figure of the book as tomb or sepulcher haunts even such moments of recollected pleasure as the memory of the "little yellow, canvas-covered book" of Arabian tales, since Wordsworth's regarding it as "but a block hewn from a mighty quarry" links it to tombstones, his favorite image for writing that is at once more permanently materialized than a book and more at home with matters of the spirit, with "A promise scarcely earthly" (5. 460–68). The ostensible resolution of these broodings on the material word as a matter of life and death resides in appeals to "Nature," in such moments of affirmation as "this verse is dedicate to Nature's self, / And things that teach as Nature teaches" (5. 230–31). Yet at the end of Book 5, the realm of things that words come to inhabit is again undeniably sepulchral:

> Visionary power
> Attends the motions of the viewless winds,
> Embodied in the mystery of words:
> There, darkness makes abode, and all the host
> Of shadowy things work endless changes there,
> (5. 595–98)

As embodiments of thought or spirit, in becoming "things" words for Wordsworth enter a realm of perishable materiality and frail mortality that is the precondition of their passing over into "Visionary power."

Wordsworth agrees with Coleridge that words may become "living things"—"active and efficient," as he says in the note to "The Thorn"—but for him this means that they also become mortal, perishable things. The difference from Coleridge is accentuated, and another pertinent aspect of this issue opened up, in a passage from one of Coleridge's notebooks: "The focal word has acquired a *feeling* of *reality*—it heats and burns, makes itself be felt. If we do not grasp it, it seems to grasp us, as with a hand of flesh and blood, and completely counterfeits an immediate presence, an intuitive knowledge."[22] Here words are not so much reified as corporealized in a gesture that makes them both less and more arbitrary, less and more matters arising from natural connections. Despite Coleridge's self-consciousness about the rhetorical figure ("seems to grasp us, as with a hand . . . counterfeits"), the emphasis is on words themselves, not on writer or reader, as active agents. In the note to "The Thorn," Wordsworth characteristically balances such an awareness of words-as-living-things against his recognition of "the interest which the mind attaches to words." That "the mind" here may refer to the poet, to the dramatized fictive speaker, or to the reader is consistent with Heinzelman's argument that Wordsworth ideally sees writer and reader engaged in an act of "reciprocal labor," though I would want to argue that the reciprocity is less a matter of stable cooperation than of power struggle—of "mutual domination" and "interchangeable supremacy," to adopt Wordsworth's language for the interaction between mind and nature in the final book of *The Prelude* (14. 78–86).[23] Most conspicuous in Wordsworth and Coleridge are the curious textual transformations through which words-as-things come to testify not to language as a material process or product, but to the mind's privileged work in giving all things, including words, life.

In Coleridge we can see a concerted effort to repudiate materialist accounts that identify words as things as well as Lockean accounts that insist on their discrepancy. (It has to be acknowledged that by the end of the eighteenth century Locke's position had been interpreted along increasingly sensationalist—and, in that limited sense, materialist—lines.) Coleridge was fascinated, as James McKusick has shown, with Horne Tooke's etymological derivation of *think* from *thing*, on the model of the Latin noun *res* and its dubious derivative, the verb *reor*, "I think, I imagine."[24] According to Horne Tooke, "*Res*, a thing, gives us *Reor*, i.e. I am *thing-ed* . . . where we now say, *I think*, the antient expression was—*Me thinketh*, i.e. *me thingeth*, It *Thingeth me*."[25] In an 1806 notebook entry Coleridge cribs Horne Tooke's speculative etymology and, with an almost malicious self-delight, inverts it, as McKusick says, "to support the idealist position that things are generated by thought and have no logical priority to consciousness."[26]

> Reo = reor probably an obsolete Latin word, and res the second person singular of the Present Indicative—If so, it is the Iliad of Spinozo-Kantian, Kanto-Fichtian, Fichto-Schellingian Revival of Plato-Plotino-Proclian Idealism in a Nutshell *from* a Lilliput Hazel. Res = thou art thinking.—Even so our 'Thing': id est, thinking or think'd. Think, Thank, Tank = Reservoir of what has been *thinged*. (*Notebooks* II, #2784; Jan. 1806)

That Coleridge and Tooke are equally in the dark as to the most likely etymological origins of *things* (it comes from Old English and Old Norse sociopolitical words meaning "meeting," "public assembly") is less interesting than the divergent efforts they both make to coerce *things* to their respective ideological and philosophical perspectives. Both are engaged in what at times appear to be arbitrary efforts to ground signification in something beyond Locke's notion of arbitrary imposition. Coleridge deploys his *think-thing* etymology recurrently in later notebook entries. In 1809, for instance: "Words as distinguished from mere pulses of Air in the auditory nerve must correspond to Thoughts, and Thoughts is but the verb-substantive Participle Preterite of *Thing* . . . a thing acts on me but not on me as purely passive, which is the case in all *affection*, affectus, but res agit in co-agentum—in the first, I am *thinged*, in the latter I thing or think" (*Notebooks* III, #3587; July–Sept. 1809). Coleridge understandably bypasses that aspect of words that might identify their thing-ness as pure phonetic signifier ("mere pulses of Air in the auditory nerve"), but instead of going on to inquire into the production of linguistic meaning as a material social process, he identifies words-as-things with an originary perceptual activity in the mind. His inversion of Tooke's false etymology has again become an algorithm for idealist epistemological play.

Coleridge was philosophically interested in puns; and in an 1810 Notebook entry that mentions "my intended Essay in defence of Punning," he appears to be on the point of devoting sustained attention to the phonetic, if not the graphic or economic, materiality of language in one of its conspicuously arbitrary dimensions. Again, though, his concern with words-as-things veers off in another direction—this time in a direction signaled by one "Mr Whiter of Clare Hall," who attempted to show, Coleridge says, "that words are not mere symbols of things & thoughts, but themselves things—and that any harmony in the things symbolized will perforce be presented to us more easily as well as with additional beauty by a correspondent harmony of the Symbols with each other" (*Notebooks* III, #3762; 1810). This is more than a familiar-sounding speculation on verbal mimesis. Coleridge is inspired here by Walter Whiter's *Etymologicon Magnum or Universal Etymological Dictionary* (1800) and its introductory argument that phonetic patterns, even when they do not imitate properties of things as in onomatopoeia, still correspond to the ordering of things in nature. From this, Coleridge develops a notion that words become things because they correspond to them, not according to older Adamic or Cratylean theories of linguistic mimesis, but according to principles of harmony simultaneously and congruently at work in the physical world and in language. Words are things in this sense because they operate according to principles of order that also govern things, principles that ultimately derive from the structure of the creative mind. It is as if the rules governing the deep structures of language in the Chomskyan sense were transformations of the laws of physics. Words-as-things thus get swept up in the grand theoretical project of the Coleridgean Logos: the infinite mind of God externalizes or embodies itself in a created natural world that is the text of divine utterance, capable of being read by the finite human mind with its imperfect linguistic resources. As Coleridge promises his infant son in *Frost at Midnight*,

> so shalt thou see and hear
> The lovely shapes and sounds intelligible
> Of that eternal language, which thy God
> Utters, who from eternity doth teach
> Himself in all, and all things in himself.[27]
>
> (58–62)

Things cogently perceived through the senses are the words of God; God's words are "intelligible" things. This is not what the Byron of *Don Juan* 3 has in mind.

To say that Coleridge's position on words-as-things resembles in several respects the Renaissance order of things as characterized by Foucault is to recognize one of the ways in which nineteenth-century thinking about language looks backward rather than forward. In American writing Emerson continues and amplifies the Coleridgean vision, with some additional help from Swedenborg, when he says in "Nature" that "the use of the outer creation [is] to give us language for the beings and changes of the inward creation. . . . It is not words only that are emblematic; it is things which are emblematic."[28] Though the roots of this conception of language—in opposition to the Lockean emphasis on language as a humanly constructed system of arbitrary signs—are essentially theological, it has in spite of itself led to rich speculation on the power of material things as constituents of or constraints on verbal meaning.

A remarkable late experiment in the Coleridgean-Emersonian vein is Kenneth Burke's quirkily insightful essay, first published in the 1962 number of *Anthropological Linguistics* and collected in *Language as Symbolic Action*, called "What Are the Signs of What? A Theory of 'Entitlement.'" "What might be discovered," Burke asks, "if we tried inverting [the customary view that 'words are the signs of things'], and upholding instead the proposition 'that things are the signs of words'?"[29] Burke discovers, via his conjectural inversion, that "things of the world become material exemplars of the values which the tribal idiom has placed upon them." There are, as Burke is aware, curious logical difficulties with the procedure he entertains, particularly with what happens to the phrase "signs of" (things can be thought of as "signs of" words only if they are already discursive constructs). Still, his analysis of how things or "thing-situations" may come to function as abbreviations or summaries of verbal expressions can help us understand an important aspect of social figuration in Romantic writing. It can help us grasp the force of that late remark by the conservative Coleridge in *Table Talk* that ironically anticipates, as Heinzelman observes in quoting it, Marx's ideas of alienation and human reification: "It is not uncommon for 100,000 *operatives* (mark this word, for words *in this sense* are things) to be out of employment at once in the cotton districts, and, thrown upon parochial relief, to be dependent upon hard-hearted task-masters for food."[30] The word "operatives" has become a thing because the workers to whom it was applied in early industrialized Britain are treated as things, as mechanical functions. In Burke's terms, these workers stand as signs, "material exemplars," of the social relations implicit in the "tribal idiom" of early nineteenth-century capitalism.

3.

In Coleridge and Wordsworth the belief that words are, or may become, things reveals contradictory ties between the political and the linguistic in their ideologies of the poetic—ties that idealize but also expose the limits of British "nature" and British national culture as independent sources of value. When we turn to Blake and Shelley, we have to contend with quite different relations of words to things, differences that arise from their respective and distinctive couplings of visionary idealism and radical politics.

Blake's feeling for what other writers mean when they say that "words are things" springs from a belief in the Logos that is at once discursively simpler than Coleridge's—it never has to be articulated in the language of "Kanto–Fichtian, Fichto-Schellingian" metaphysics—and more intricate in its practical consequences. A passage from the "Annotations to Lavater's *Aphorisms on Man*" (1788) sets out Blake's fundamental attitude: "For let it be remembered that creation is. God descending according to the weakness of man for our Lord is the word of God & every thing on earth is the word of God & in its essence is God" (*CPPWB*, 599).[31] "Creation" is an act both of God and of the artist whose imagination allows him (always and resolutely him, in Blake) to become God. More violently and decisively than Coleridge, Blake rejects the Lockean doctrine of arbitrary, humanly instituted signs with its double removal of words from the things to which they refer. For him, words need to be distinguished from things only when exposing the shallowness of discourse, like Sir Joshua Reynolds's, that takes the traditional distinction for granted. Reynolds says in Discourse VII: "We apply the term TASTE to that act of mind by which we like or dislike, whatever be the subject.... We are obliged to take words as we find them; all we can do is to distinguish the THINGS to which they are applied." To which Blake objects: "This is False the Fault is not in Words. but in Things Locke's Opinions of Words & their Fallaciousness are Artful Opinions & Fallacious also" (*CPPWB*, 659). As Nelson Hilton says, "Blake must reject Locke's contention that words are the arbitrary 'signs of our ideas only,' since for Blake words are living beings: 'The Holy Word / That walk'd among the ancient trees'" ("Introduction," *Songs of Experience*, 4–5).[32]

The relation of Blake's artistic practice to his vision of words-as-"living beings" presents two kinds of critical complication for a reader concerned with the materiality of language. First, mystical influences from Boehme's conception of "the Language of Nature" and Swedenborg's doctrine of "Correspondences" ironically produce in Blake, as Hilton and Robert Essick both demonstrate, an astonishing attentiveness to the phonetic, graphic, and etymological properties of words. Blake's mind was "extraordinarily attuned to the richness of the word as sign" (*Literal Imagination*, 14), despite his rejection of prevailing theories of the sign. Beyond this, the fusion of verbal and pictorial impulses in Blake's work means that the distinction between linguistic and nonlinguistic materiality is made extremely, at times deliberately, ambiguous. Hilton reproduces a line from plate 25, Copy C, of *The Marriage of Heaven and Hell* in which the words "the Devil utter'd these words" is immediately followed by the form of a flower executed in the same linear style and ink-color as the words of the text; the flower is immediately followed by forms, again in the same linear style and ink-color, that look indeterminately like writing, like organic shapes, and like playfully arbitrary abstract decoration (*Literal Imagination*, 3). Such textual events as these substantiate Essick's argument that "Blake's critique of the dominant sign theories of the eighteenth century" cleared the space in his artistic practice for a "semiotic of play," for a "unique method of relief etching" that "provided a medium for . . . radical experiments in the interweaving of graphic conception and execution." The "experiments" included a "willingness to incorporate the contingent in verbal production," "the pleasures and significance of chance."[33]

So in Blake's work as in no other contemporary writing, words become things in relation to his distinctive version of the belief that "every thing on earth is the word of God," and as the result of an artistic process that produces words as unique graphic phenomena within unique physical objects. To recognize this is not to endorse all that Essick claims on behalf of a Blakean Logos that transcends or subsumes the arbitrariness of language. Essick sees Blake's demonstrable "belief in the unity of conception and execution" (163) as inviting a phenomenological reading committed to the "constitutive proliferations of language as performance" (102), to "a sense of language as prolific activity in which the desire to act encompasses, but overflows, the desire to mean" (159). Understanding language as "act" or "performance" enables us to see it as "motivated" — but not "motivated" in that sense opposed to "arbitrary" in modern semiotic discourse or in Johnson's sense of "Despotick; absolute; . . . following the will without restraint" (in Johnson's *Dictionary* "arbitrary" conspicuously names a kind of all-powerful motivation). Essick acknowledges this limit on the linguistic dimension of the Blakean prolific in describing "acts of writing that [Blake] felt to be motivated even if the signs he used were arbitrary" (185). At the level of physical production, words as "act" or "performance" become special kinds of Blakean things that still depend importantly on arbitrary signs to generate acts and performances by Blake's readers.

The problem of knowing what in Blake's composite art counts as language is intricately connected to a second, economic problem concerning the status of Blake's art as commodity. Heinzelman argues that Blake confronted the commodification of his art head on by imagining a regenerated exchange, through the body of the poem, between his own visionary labor and that of the reader, an exchange requiring "no commercial representation beyond that which the artistic product . . . embodies"

(*Economics of the Imagination*, 133). Clifford Siskin addresses the issue by looking at Blake "the pragmatic technician whose 1793 prospectus for works of a special kind at a 'fair Price'" advertised "a method of Printing both Letter-press and Engraving" that "produces works at less than one fourth of the expense."[34] Whatever Blake's visionary or practical intentions, his mode of production could only ever result in small numbers of hand-made artifacts. Twenty-four copies of *Songs of Innocence and Experience* are known to exist; nine of *The Marriage of Heaven and Hell*; seventeen of *America: A Prophecy* (only four of these ever colored); seventeen of *Visions of the Daughters of Albion*. Blake's work enters the realm of economic materiality on very different terms from Wordsworth's or Coleridge's, not to mention Byron's. These terms, as distinct from those set by his subsequent publishers, are such that Blake the artisan was bound to sell the products of his labor less to any reading public than to the collecting connoisseurs.[35] As economic "things" produced by a process developed partly in resistance to the commodification of art, Blake's works make his words into objects whose broader material as well as strictly physical mode of existence cannot be adequately grasped in terms of his distinctive version of the Logos.

Despite obvious political affinities—and in keeping with less obvious political differences—Blake and Percy Shelley diverge sharply in their assumptions about words and things. In the technical philosophical sense Shelley's idealism is more radical than Blake's and develops out of a completely different intellectual orientation toward Enlightenment theories of language. Where Blake relentlessly repudiates the Lockean division of words from things, Shelley—except in a few self-consciously utopian moments—either accepts and confirms it, or finds its collapse cause for dismay. In the essay "On Life," things are seen to function like words ("almost all familiar objects are signs, standing not for themselves but for others"), and "things" get dissolved into "thoughts" ("By the word *things* is to be understood ... any thought upon which any other thought is employed, with an apprehension of distinction"; *SPP*, 507–8). But language never fully coincides with the mind's perceptions of the world or of itself: "How vain is it to think that words can penetrate the mystery of our being" (*SPP*, 506.) Shelley bases his most exuberant celebration of language in the *Defence of Poetry*, as we have seen, on the principle that "language is arbitrarily produced by the Imagination and has relation to thoughts alone," whereas "all other materials, instruments and conditions of art, have relations among each other, which limit and interpose between conception and expression" (*SPP*, 513). This means that when Shelley attends theoretically to the physical aspect of language, he places it in an order semiotically connected to, but never identical with, the "thought" a word signifies: "Sounds as well as thoughts have relation both between each other and towards that which they represent, and [in poetry] a perception of the order of those relations has always been found connected with a perception of the order of the relations of thoughts" (*SPP*, 514). While Shelley privileges "sounds" rather than graphic markings in this sentence from the *Defence*, the conceptual logic of a double relational order also underlies moments in his poetry when "thoughts" materialize as writing. Insofar as words become things for Shelley, they are things that remain split between different orders, different registers, of experience.

The irreducible difference or split in the constitution of words reflects, and is a reflection of, a split in the constitution of Shelleyan subjectivity. Paul Fry remarked some time ago that there is in Percy Shelley's writing "what could be called a Lacanian psycholinguistics in embryo."[36] Of the several critical attempts to bring Fry's conjecture to bear upon the relevance to Shelley of what the Lacanian tradition calls the "materiality of the signifier," the most interesting from the perspective of my argument insists on rethinking Mary Shelley's response to Percy Shelley's writing. In her chapter on *Frankenstein* in *Bearing the Word*, Margaret Homans uses her compelling premise—that "Lacan's account of language . . . provides the most explicit and compelling contemporary formulation of a myth that was . . . already at the heart of nineteenth-century culture"[37]—to read *Frankenstein* as a critique of Percy Shelley's poetic response to the subject self-divided by and in language. In her account, Victor Frankenstein's demon is the distorted "literalization" or (a better term) "reification" of its creator's desire to usurp both the creative word of God and the procreative act of bearing children. The various images of language-acquisition and writing in the novel suggest to Homans that "Shelley knew she was writing a criticism . . . of the gendered myth of language" (110), according to which vital linguistic tropes substitute for the experience of being at one with objects of desire, and ultimately for the loss of the mother. Repeatedly regarded not as a human being but as a monstrous thing, the creature initially tries to generate language but produces semiotic failures that parody Rousseau's and other eighteenth-century conjectures about the emotive genesis of natural signs:

> His jaws opened, and he muttered some inarticulate sounds, while a grin wrinkled his cheek. He might have spoken, but I did not hear . . . (1.5.57)[38]
>
> 'Sometimes I wished to express my sensations in my own mode, but the uncouth and inarticulate sounds which broke from me frightened me into silence again.' (2.3.100)

The creature's inability to communicate and "'express'" his "'sensations'" registers the creator's isolated, distorting, and substitutive act of creation and his subsequent refusal to regard the creature as anything other than a thing alien to humanity. This makes it difficult, though not impossible, for the creature to comprehend writing: "'I conjectured . . . that he found on the paper signs for speech which he understood, and I ardently longed to comprehend these also; but how was that possible when I did not even understand the sounds for which they stood as signs?'" (2.4.110) The creature overcomes this difficulty by discovering and acting on an impulse toward social communication that Victor Frankenstein has either forgotten or denied: "'I ought not to make the attempt [to present himself to the De Lacy family] until I had first become master of their language, which knowledge might enable me to make them overlook the deformity of my figure'" (2.4.110). The creature's reference to "'my figure'" here and elsewhere projects his sense of his own thing-ness, a condition he labors to modulate/negotiate by words he has emphatically *not* acquired through any act of parenting or care-giving. Homans sees Mary Shelley's novel as enacting "the vanishing of the referent . . . to be replaced by language as figuration that never quite touches its objects" (110). We might usefully turn this by saying that the creature has himself been made both "figure" and "referent," sign and thing, in a process that denies him the social matrix in which figuration and reference can answer to the need for meaning and value—and human touch. Created as a figure of Victor's self-involved imagination, he is made to exist as an object of fear and contempt. It is significant in this regard that the first book he learns to read is Volney's *Ruins of Empire*, with its opening scene of reading the decaying vestiges of ancient arbitrary power: "When the whole earth, in chains and silence, was yet crouching under the rod of tyrants, you had already proclaimed the truths which they abhor."[39]

Homans's reading of *Frankenstein* shares basic theoretical terms with Peter Brooks's Lacanian account in "'Godlike Science/Unhallowed Arts': Language, Nature, and Monstrosity." Brooks uses the Lacanian categories of the "imaginary" versus the "symbolic order" to argue that under the terms of the former—until he has acquired language—"the Monster will always be the 'filthy mass,'" unrecognizable as a human subject.[40] As he enters with great difficulty the symbolic order of language, Brooks says, the "Monster . . . uncovers the larger question of the arbitrariness, or immotivation, of the linguistic sign" (209) and with this the recognition that the possibilities of subjectivity depend on the linguistic order of culture, on what the the creature himself refers to as a "'chain of existence and events'" (*Frankenstein*, 2.9.143) that is apprehended in and through language. But the creature's material "'figure'" places him outside the cultural order of the human, condemns him to an order of "monstrosity" that his linguistic competence can never overcome. He is himself, for Brooks, "a kind of accursed signifier" (218). Homans's dissent from Brooks on this point articulates the novel's grim thematizing of the materiality of language: "in its materiality and its failure to acquire an object of desire, the demon enters the symbolic primarily as the (dreaded) referent, not as signifier. The negative picture of the demon's materiality is a product of its female place in the symbolic. . . . the novel presents, not a vision of the condition of human signification, but a targeted criticism of those in whose interest the symbolic order constitutes itself in the ways that it does" (304–5). The creature's heroic acquisition of language is doomed to fail under the conditions set by Victor's tyrannically reflexive and obsessive self-projection; he has to live on as the horrible reification of his creator's "interest" and ambition. So it is that in Homans's *Frankenstein*, the word as monstrous "living thing" eventually destroys its fictive speaker/creator and, in the 1831 Preface, comes to be identified with the book itself as the "hideous progeny" produced by Mary Shelley in her attempt to participate in a literary competition dominated by Percy Shelley and Lord Byron.

In chapter 5 I will more closely question Percy Shelley's positioning of women's writing in relation to Romantic "myths" and theories of language. Homans's argument provokes a fresh realization that he imagines, more fully than Homans herself allows, the destructive consequences of the abandoned and abused subject's attempts to overcome its self-division and insufficiency. The potential for such destruction is there even in the most metaphysically universalized of Shelleyan poetic contexts. "The everlasting universe of things" in *Mont Blanc* "Flows through [a] mind" whose desire forever exceeds the mind's capacity to accommodate itself to things through words. While Shelley's radical philosophical idealism, like the radical materialism with which he experimented early in his career, springs from a deep political as well as intellectual aversion to dualistic separations and subordinations of mind and nature, thoughts and things, the separation persists as the incommensurability between imaginative desire and a historical actuality that includes the "vulgar" language of common use. For Shelley as for Blake, although for very different epistemological and linguistic reasons, political resistance precludes any accommodation of words to what Godwin calls, in the title of the novel we know as *Caleb Williams*, "things as they are." Poetic language preserves an intimacy with thought in necessary opposition to things—to the natural world as it is habitually experienced, to social life as it is customarily lived. Both Blake and Shelley envision worlds in which things will be transformed by the liberated imagination into a condition of unalienated oneness with thoughts. It is such a world that Shelley celebrates in the great utopian lyrics of *Prometheus Unbound*, with their image of language as a "perpetual Orphic song." But the immediate historical and material conditions of life generate a radical idealist resistance in Shelley. The power of his writing springs from a relentlessly experimental effort both to reclaim words from "things as they are" and to transform while acknowledging writing's necessary and inevitable belonging to the realm of materiality.

4.

"I have not loved the world, nor the world me,— / But let us part fair foes" Byron wrote in that summer of 1816, when Mary Shelley was conceiving in words her monstrous "living thing," and Percy Shelley was speculating in the verse of *Mont Blanc* on how "The everlasting universe of things flows through the mind." Byron continues,

> I do believe,
> Though I have found them not, that there may be
> Words which are things . . .
> (*Childe Harold* 3. 1059–61)

This is the most striking occasion in Byron's writing when the claim that "words are things" seems to fail him, at least for the moment; it is revealing that it comes in a text where the relation of words to things is made so much a matter of isolated psychic expression and projection into nature, rather than of pragmatic social and cultural efficacy. These lines near the end of *Childe Harold* 3 echo, of course, the climactic anticlimax of the storm on the Lake of Geneva seventeen stanzas earlier, and specifically Byron's professed inability to "throw / Soul, heart, mind, passions, feelings . . . into *one* word, / And that one word were Lightning" (3. 906–11). The only "thing" fit to be identified with Byron's "word" at this moment is lightning, and Byron makes high drama of the fact that his words here can only name and refer to, not become, that thing.

But as the Byron of *Don Juan* 3 realizes, written and printed words become things in senses unintended by their author, unacknowledged by the words themselves. In John Murray's 1832–1833 ottavo edition of *The Works of Lord Byron*, an engraved facsimile of stanza 92 of *Childe Harold* 3, where the Alpine thunder and lightning is said to give "every mountain . . . a tongue," is offered to the purchaser as having been "dashed off by Lord Byron, in June, 1816, during one of his evening excursions on the Lake of Geneva." The facsimile appears not in volume 8, which contains the text of *Childe Harold*, but at the beginning of volume 9, along with engraved scenes of Petrarch's tomb and of Seville, as an artifact whose value no longer depends on its original poetic context. We are directed by the editor, Thomas Moore, to look back at volume 8 for

Sir Walter Scott's praise of this "thunder-storm . . . described in verse almost as vivid as its lightnings." Scott's "almost" indicates that he accepts Byron's claim not to have found "one word" that was "Lightning." Yet Byron's words about lightning have become a thing with a material and economic life of its own.

Prior to the momentary and strategic demurral at the end of *Childe Harold* 3, Byron twice invokes "words are things" as a maxim he approves of in contexts that are overtly political and social. On 16 November 1813, he writes in his journal about attending a performance of *Antony and Cleopatra* the previous night with Monk Lewis. Byron is clearly, though somewhat defensively, partial to Antony:

> why do they abuse him for cutting off that poltroon Cicero's head? Did not Tully tell Brutus it was a pity to have spared Antony? and did he not speak the Philippics? and are not *"word*[s] *things?"* and such *"words"* very pestilent *"things"* too? If he had had a hundred heads, they deserved (from Antony) a rostrum (his was stuck up there) apiece — though, after all, he might as well have pardoned him, for the credit of the thing. (*BLJ* 3:207)

A year after he had made his own maiden speech in the House of Lords opposing the death penalty called for in the Frame-Breaking Bill, Byron is obviously fascinated by political oratory on the subject of capital punishment that is "performative" and "illocutionary" (to use Austin's terms): Cicero's accusations against Antony, Antony's potential pardon and actual order of execution — these are classic instances of words as acts, deeds, "things" of state. Subsequent references to Madame de Staël (who *"talks* folios") and Sheridan (whose talk kept Byron, Rogers, and Moore entertained "without one yawn from six till one in the morning") link this journal entry to a letter to Samuel Rogers dated 27 February 1814(?). The occasion is Byron's making an excuse for not attending one of Madame de Staël's soirées: "I believe that I need not add one [an excuse] for not accepting Mr. Sheridan's invitation on Wednesday, which I fancy both you and I understand in the same sense: — with him the saying of Mirabeau, that *'words* are *things,'* is not to be taken literally" (*BLJ* 4: 74). Byron liked Sheridan and had admired his famous Parliamentary speeches — but "Poor dear Sherry!" had become a drunken parody of the great orator. The maxim Byron associates with Cicero and Mirabeau is pathetically deflated in the joke he shares with the impeccably self-possessed Rogers: even Sheridan's dinner invitations are no longer to be treated as real things.[41]

I have paused over these early instances of Byron's thinking of words as things because their emphasis on political and social speech contrasts pointedly with the emphasis on writing in Canto 3 of *Don Juan*. The attitude toward language in Canto 3 implicates both the predatory mercantilism of Lambro's piracy and the sumptuous, fetishized materiality of the feast indulged in by Juan and Haidée while Lambro is away. On his way home, we learn in stanza 15, Lambro

> had chain'd
> His prisoners, dividing them like chapters
> In number'd lots; they all had cuffs and collars,
> And averaged each from ten to a hundred dollars.
> (3.117–20)

Lambro deals with his prisoners as if they were texts, things made of words to be ordered and numbered in acts of authorial agency. Yet he himself is "a man who seldom used a word / Too much," we are told, preferring instead to move men "with the sword." The odd way in which "word" gets taken up into "sword" in this stanza and yet rhymes with it only to the eye, not to the ear, bears a diacritical relation to the "ink" / "think" rhyme in *Don Juan* 3, stanza 88 (and to *Childe Harold* 3, stanza 97, where "word" also gets taken up into "sword" but to quite different effect). The imagery of language and writing carries over into the lush decoration of the hall where Haidée's feast has been laid. The room is hung with damask tapestries, and above these

> The upper border, richly wrought, display'd,
>   Embroider'd delicately o'er with blue,
> Soft Persian sentences, in lilac letters,
> From poets, or the moralists their betters.
>
> These oriental writings on the wall,
>   Quite common in those countries, are a kind
> Of monitors adapted to recall,
>   Like skulls at Memphian banquets, to the mind
> The words which shook Belshazzar in his hall,
>   And took his kingdom from him . . .
> (3. 509–18)

These lines critically anticipate "The isles of Greece" lyric sung by Lambro's minstrel, and the narrator's "But words are things" comment on it. In the hall's embroidered border, words are literally, opulently materialized; at first the physical qualities of the "Soft Persian sentences" appear to make any semantic content beside the point. But whether he reads Persian or not, Byron knows that such "oriental writings" may pronounce a death sentence on the very sensuousness they embody—as in the account of Belshazzar's feast in the book of Daniel, to which Byron alludes: "They drank wine, and praised the gods of gold, and of silver, of brass, of iron, of wood, and of stone. In the same hour came forth fingers of a man's hand, and wrote over against the candlestick upon the plaster of the wall of the king's palace. . . . Then the king's countenance was changed, and his thoughts troubled him" (Daniel 5: 4–6).

The stanzas that precede the performance of Lambro's minstrel should alert us to troubling strains in the "But words are things" passage that follow it. So should the reference to Cadmus in the minstrel's song itself: "You have the letters Cadmus gave— / Think ye he meant them for a slave?" ("The Isles of Greece," st. 10). Writing and luxurious consumption, writing and moral warning, writing and political decay: all these connections inform the lines following "But words are things." I quote the key stanzas in full now:

> But words are things, and a small drop of ink,
>   Falling like dew, upon a thought, produces
> That which makes thousands, perhaps millions, think;
>   'Tis strange, the shortest letter which man uses
> Instead of speech, may form a lasting link
>   Of ages; to what straits old Time reduces
> Frail man, when paper—even a rag like this,
> Survives himself, his tomb, and all that's his.
>
> And when his bones are dust, his grave a blank,
>   His station, generation, even his nation,
> Become a thing, or nothing, save to rank
>   In chronological commemoration,
> Some dull MS oblivion long has sank,
>   Or graven stone found in a barrack's station
> In digging the foundation of a closet,
> May turn his name up, as a rare deposit.
>   (3. 793–808)

When Byron wrote *Don Juan* 3, hundreds of thousands of copies of his words had been reproduced and sold; for more than two years he had forgone his earlier disdain for authors who wrote to make a living and—to cover the cost of indulgences that Belshazzar would have enjoyed—had accepted payments from the publisher he was making rich.[42] If ever a writer appreciated the force of words-as-things in the full social, cultural, commercial meaning of this phrase, it was the Byron of *Don Juan* 3. And if he is astonished by the power of "ink" to make "thousands, perhaps millions, think," he is also appalled by the economic dispersal of his own thinking, his own identity, on material terms over which he has no control. In ways that ironically connect him with Lambro's prisoners and with the soldiers in the War Cantos whose identities are reduced to "Three lines of the despatch" (7. 158) or citation in "a *bulletin*" (7. 162), Byron has no choice but to consign what Walter Benjamin would call his "aura" to "a rag like this," like *Don Juan*, and to the interests of those who will read him and write about him.

It is the aristocratic and enormously popular Lord Byron who, at the very moment when he is about to earn profits from his writing, articulates a more developed awareness of the reification of words than any of his contemporaries. This awareness permeates much of Byron's later work and continues to evolve in ways that carry complex political implications. Jerome Christensen has used Marcel Mauss's analysis of gifts-as-things to link the public and commercial appropriation of Byron's writing to other appropriations of his social identity: "Lord Byron bestows gifts . . . he gives because he is obliged by the thing given him, his title, which compels his return and in turn makes him a compelling thing."[43] This strikingly glosses the movement from "words are things" to the writer as "thing" in *Don Juan* 3, stanzas 88–89. Though the writer in these stanzas is imagined to be dead, the possibility that the living poet's very self and voice will be arbitrarily reified—transformed by publishers, booksellers, book-buyers into a fetishized commodity—is a real threat. The social character of Byron's poetry can survive the impositions of market forces only for readers who recognize, as he did, its inevitable vulnerability to them.

Near the outset of *Lord Byron's Strength*, Christensen defines "Byronism" as "the literary system . . . which was collaboratively organized in the second decade of the nineteenth century by coding the residual affective charge that still clung to the paraphernalia of aristocracy in order to reproduce it in commodities that could be vended to a reading public avid for glamor" (xvi). Christensen's perspective is explicitly Nietzschean and postmodernist: Byron's was an "age," he writes, "when the grounds of authority have been disclosed as being no more than nominal" (xvii).

What the arguments of this chapter and this book are beginning to show, I hope, is that seeing the "grounds of authority" as "nominal" and multiply arbitrary takes us back into, rather than away from or beyond, the historical determinations of class and of economic production and consumption. Christensen's reading of Byron's literary and social self-production acquires a broader and a deeper relevance to British Romantic writing, I believe, when rethought from the perspective of Eagleton's *The Ideology of the Aesthetic*: on the one hand Eagleton invites us to grasp "the aesthetic as a kind of incipient materialism," as an attempt to establish a discourse of the bodily and the sensuous in a bourgeois culture needing to privilege "mind" or "spirit"; on the other, he summons us to see the commodity, with Marx, as a "grisly caricature of the authentic [aesthetic] artifact."[44] Even without the force and aura of aristocratic "glamor," writing enters the early nineteenth-century marketplace of literary commodities on intensely contradictory terms. The desire that words be things, and conversely the anxiety that they already are things or have accommodated themselves to things as they are, constitute specific instances within Romantic poetics and poetry of what Eagleton reveals about an increasingly hegemonic discourse of the aesthetic. Attending to the ways in which Romantic writing represents, enacts, resists its status as physical and economic "thing" can help continue the critical work of understanding how our own traditions of valuing this writing remain implicated in the cultural ideologies of the late eighteenth and early nineteenth century. It can help us use recognitions of the specific historical materiality of writing to reveal the contradictory workings of power both through and beyond conscious human agency, individual and collective.

3

THE POLITICS OF RHYME

THE MANIFOLD connections between the exercise of political power in society and the production of meaning in language are foregrounded in the making and breaking of formalized cultural practices, especially in those practices that we designate "aesthetic" or "literary." Such practices always carry the imprint of ideological dominance disguised as what is natural and normative. At the same time, however, disruptions and reworkings of form may be motivated by and communicative of deep social pressures. It is at this level that the formal conventions of art and literature become especially worth studying as phenomena of materialist history.

Within literary history, no category of formal convention has proven to be both more contentious and more often taken for granted than rhyme. In the early modern period the term "rhyme" had become so nearly synonymous with "poetry" itself that Milton resorts to considerable rhetorical violence in justifying the ways of God to men in an epic poem that "rhymes not." A century and a half later, at the end of an era of revolution and restoration more extensive than the one Milton lived through, rhyme again emerges as a distinctively contested dimension of poetic discourse. Why and how this should be so is the problem I want to explore here, with reference to two sustained examples. A founding assumption throughout will be that rhyme—the usually accidental phonetic correspondence between or among different words—dramatizes the principle of linguistic arbitrariness as no other formal convention does, and that as an organizing feature of verse it projects its arbitrariness into very extensive and fundamental structures of meaning, including political meaning.

1.

Keats's couplet writing in the *Poems* of 1817 and in *Endymion* of 1818 still embarrasses many readers, even some who understand that embarrassment is one of the great Keatsian subjects. The conspicuous influence of Leigh Hunt, together with the Tory attacks on Keats's "Cockney style" largely provoked by that influence, make it possible to reconstruct a more detailed political context for this poetry than for any other text or moment in Keats's career. The political implications of Keats's "Cockney style" have been recognized for some time: by John Hayden and Theodore Redpath in the late 1960s; more recently by Jerome McGann, Marjorie Levinson, Nicholas Roe, Susan Wolfson, Jeffrey Cox, and Richard Cronin.[1] My concern is to investigate one aspect of those implications more intensively, speculating along the way about the difficulties as well as the possibilities of doing so. And I want to suggest that whatever readers think about the couplets in *Sleep and Poetry* or *Endymion*, the critical questions they encourage are never entirely dissolved in Keats's later stylistic achievements. McGann was right to say that "the significance of this Cockney style . . . is not very widely recognized," especially (I would add) its significance for Keats's own subsequent development.[2]

In late July, 1818, on a visit to Scotland, Benjamin Bailey dined at the house of Bishop George Glieg, his future father-in-law, and there met John Gibson Lockhart, one of the main contributors to the new magazine recently founded by the Tory publisher and bookseller William Blackwood.[3] In August, Bailey wrote to Keats's new publisher, John Taylor, about this meeting: "[Lockhart] abused poor Keats in a way that, although it was at the Bishop's table, I could hardly keep my temper. I said I supposed then [Keats] would be attacked in Blackwood's. He replied 'not by *me*'; which would carry the insinuation he would by some one *else*. The objections he stated were frivolous in the extreme. They chiefly respected the *rhymes*."[4] As it turned out, of course, Lockhart—and possibly his cohort John Wilson—did attack Keats in *Blackwood's Magazine*, in the last of a series of abusive articles begun in October 1817 on the "Cockney School of Poetry." For "Z," as the *Blackwood's* reviewers signed themselves, Keats's rhyme in his 1817 and 1818 volumes was not a frivolous matter at all. It epitomized the corruption of what *Blackwood's* called "the Cockney school of versification, morality, and politics": "[T]his romance is meant to be written in English heroic rhyme. To those who have read any of Hunt's poems, this hint might indeed be needless. Mr Keats has adopted the loose, nerveless versification, and Cockney rhymes of the poet of Rimini."[5] Lockhart's implication is clear: Keats's loose liberal couplets are a stylistic analogue of the loose liberal politics he had imbibed from Hunt. Near the end of the review Lockhart quotes twenty-two lines (exactly half of them enjambed) from Keats's denunciation of those "who lord it o'er their fellow-men / With most prevailing tinsel" at the beginning of Book 3 of *Endymion*.[6] He introduces this quotation by saying: "We had almost forgotten to mention, that Keats belongs to the Cockney School of Politics, as well as the Cockney School of Poetry."[7]

The same linking of politics and versification marks John Wilson Croker's attack on *Endymion* in the arch-Tory *Quarterly Review*:

At first it appeared to us, that Mr. Keats had been amusing himself and wearying his readers with an immeasureable game at *bouts-rimés*. . . . He seems to us to write a line at random, and then he follows not the thought excited by this line, but that suggested by the *rhyme* with which it concludes. There is hardly a complete couplet inclosing a complete idea in the whole book.[8]

For Croker, Keats's Cockney couplets are an affront to the orthodoxy of the closed Augustan couplet and to the social and moral traditions it symbolizes. Croker's reference to the game of *bouts-rimés*, though it does not exactly fit the compositional process he thinks he sees in Keats, is politically significant. Addison had defined the game in attacking its eighteenth-century vogue in one of his *Spectator* essays (No. 60) on forms of "False Wit": "They were a List of Words that rhyme to one another, drawn up by another Hand, and given to a Poet, who was to make a Poem to the Rhymes in the same Order that they were placed upon the List."[9] That this game was still fashionable in Regency society is evident from Byron's delightfully macaronic couplet in Canto 16 of *Don Juan*, where we hear about the Duchess of FitzFulke's taste in poetry: "But of all verse, what most ensured her praise / Were sonnets to herself, or 'Bouts rimés'"[10] (16. 447–48). In accusing Keats of playing at *bouts rimés*, Croker insinuates that this low-born London "neophyte" of Leigh Hunt is abusing Pope by taking seriously a parlor game with which his aristocratic betters merely while away their time on country week-ends. Like *Blackwood's* "Z," Croker ridicules other features of Keats's Cockney style as well: the meter, the diction, the erotic imagery. But it is the "Cockney rhymes" that most obviously betray what these Tory reviewers see as Keats's inseparable poetical and political vices.

Keats was caught up, then, in a squabble between Tory traditionalists, for whom the balanced and closed Augustan couplet had become something of a cultural fetish, and the liberal reformers who set out to establish "a freer spirit of versification," as Hunt says in the Preface to *The Story of Rimini*, along with a freer society.[11] So far this picture of the politics of Keats's "Cockney style" would seem to be fairly predictable. But that is because it is still misleadingly simple.[12] Consider, for instance, the political ramifications of Hunt's developing the couplet, not blank verse, as an antithesis to what he saw as the monotonous regularity of "Pope and the French school of versification" (Preface, *The Story of Rimini*). Hunt's effort to retain and reform the heroic couplet is the very image of his moderate reformist politics. There is a later formulation in Hunt's essay "What is Poetry?" (1844) that could characterize his ideal society almost as easily as his ideal couplet: "Poetry shapes this modulation into uniformity for its outline, and variety for its parts, because it thus realizes the last idea of beauty itself, which includes the charm of diversity within the flowing round of habit and ease."¹³ Hunt loves "the flowing round of habit and ease" that marks the couplet as long as it is internally varied, diverse. There is an undeniably conservative impulse in his desire, as he says in the Preface to the second edition of *The Feast of the Poets*, "to bring back the real harmonies of the English heroic, and to restore to it half the true principle of its music—variety."¹⁴

But there may also be a specifically political anticonservative impulse in Hunt's—and initially Keats's, before the un-Cockney Miltonic experiments of the first *Hyperion*—avoidance of blank verse. For by 1817–1818, blank verse had come to be associated with Wordsworth, whose political conservatism Hunt frequently criticized even as he made efforts to align himself with Wordsworth's power as a poet of nature.¹⁵ We should note in this regard that when the *Blackwood's* review defends Pope against Keats's attack on "rocking horse" couplets in *Sleep and Poetry*, it does so by proclaiming that "to deny [Pope's] genius, is just as absurd as to dispute that of Wordsworth, or to believe in that of Hunt."¹⁶ Hunt and Keats may not have shared Shelley's judgment that the author of *The Excursion* was "a slave" (Shelley himself countered *The Excursion* in *Alastor* by taking on its verse form as well as its argument), but their staying away from blank verse may have had a political motivation all the same.¹⁷ It was in the summer of 1818—the summer of the *Blackwood's* and *Quarterly Review* attacks—that Keats tried to visit Wordsworth at Rydal Mount, only to hear that he was out campaigning for the Tory William Lowther against the liberal Henry Brougham in the Westmoreland elections.¹⁸

While Keats praises Wordsworth in that section in *Sleep and Poetry* on the current state of English verse, he does so as part of a performance that suggests anything but a writer naive about or unaware of the politics of style. It is not just that twenty-eight of the forty-nine lines in these two verse paragraphs are enjambed, in open defiance of the closed couplets savored by the likes of Croker. At several points Keats's couplets mock by mimicking the poetic conventions under scrutiny:

> with a puling infant's force
> They sway'd about upon a rocking horse,
> And thought it Pegasus. Ah dismal soul'd!
> (185–87)

The rhythm of "They sway'd about upon a rocking horse" rocks childishly along in satirical harmony with the rhyme ("infant's force" / "rocking horse"), and then comes to an abrupt halt at the medial full-stop after "And thought it Pegasus."¹⁹ Keats knew what he was about in attacking Pope's couplets with couplets of his own devising:

> But ye were dead
> To things ye knew not of,—were closely wed
> To musty laws lined out with wretched rule
> And compass vile: so that ye taught a school
> Of dolts to smooth, inlay, and clip, and fit,
> Till, like the certain wands of Jacob's wit,
> Their verses tallied. Easy was the task:
> (193–99)

Here Keats flouts the "wretched rules" of Augustan verse formally as well as argumentatively by refusing to pause grammatically for four consecutive line-endings (the doubly unstopped "rule" / "school" couplet is an act of open unruliness)—until he moves into the mincing steps of "to smooth, inlay, and clip, and fit," where he prosodically parodies the process he names. It was shrewd of Byron, in what we may take to be the first of his contributions to the "Pope controversy," to attack Keats's attack on Pope by referring sarcastically to Mr. Keats's "new 'Essay on Criticism.'"[20] Byron recognized Keats's polemical exploitation of making "The sound . . . seem an Echo to the sense" (*Essay on Criticism* 2. 365), and he knew that Keats learned to do that sort of thing from Pope himself.

Byron's response to Keats's parody of Pope's couplets suggests just how complicated and even contradictory the politics of poetic style could become during the Regency. He first mocks Keats's mockery in "Some Observations upon an Article in *Blackwood's Edinburgh Magazine*," the rambling piece quoted above written in March 1820 and sent to Murray for immediate publication (Murray held it back, however, and did not publish it until 1833—without the commentary on Keats).[21] The *Blackwood's* article in question, published in August 1819, had nothing directly to do with Pope—it was a moralizing denunciation of Byron's private life as reflected in *Don Juan*. Byron thought that the *Blackwood's* piece was authored by John Wilson, who the previous summer had very likely collaborated in the attack on Hunt and Keats.[22] So Byron's initial denunciation of Keats's writing appears as part of his assault on the same Tory magazine that had first derided Keats's "Cockney rhymes." The ironic political crossings get even more intricate. Byron dedicated his unpublished "Observations" to Isaac D'Israeli, who just four months later defended Pope in a long review of two competing editions of Joseph Spence's *Anecdotes* and of William Lisle Bowles's *The Invariable Principles of Poetry* in *The Quarterly Review*, which had of course published Croker's savaging of *Endymion*.[23] "They support Pope I see in the Quarterly," he wrote to Murray in November 1820. "Let them continue to do so."[24] It was D'Israeli's review that elicited Byron's first public entry into the "Pope controversy" (the first, that is, since *English Bards and Scotch*

Reviewers), the *Letter to **** ****** [John Murray], on the Rev. W. L. Bowles' Strictures on the Life and Writings of Pope*. Byron now sides openly with the *Quarterly*'s position in the "Pope controversy" and has another go at Keats (or "Ketch," as he calls him)—this time as part of a condescending dismissal of "my friend Leigh Hunt" and what "some one has maliciously called the 'Cockney School.'"[25]

Byron's willingness to side with the Tories in the "Pope controversy" against the liberal poetics of Hunt and Keats reflects interestingly on the politics of his own couplet style. As Peter Manning has shown in two excellent articles on the political context and significance of *The Corsair*, Byron's writing appealed strongly to reformist and even to radical readers.[26] Conrad's "anti-authoritarian" and "anarchic" behavior led to his being invoked as the type of Jeremiah Brandreth, one of the leaders of the Pentridge uprising of June 1817, and to a popular prose adaptation of *The Corsair* by the radical publisher William Hone. Byron himself had indicated his own ties to the reformist Whigs in the dedicatory letter to Thomas Moore that prefaced the first edition of *The Corsair* in 1814. By referring to "the wrongs of your own country" and "the magnificent and fiery spirit of her sons,"[27] Byron reaffirms his passionate appeal for Catholic emancipation in his second speech before the House of Lords (21 April 1813).[28] At the same time, as Manning demonstrates, there was much about *The Corsair* that contradicted its reformist implications and made it appeal to conservative bourgeois readers: the volume's expensive production, the learned epigraphs and notes, the urbane authorial voice adopted in those notes and in the letter to Moore—and the versification, which Byron advertises as "the best adapted measure to our language, the good old and now neglected heroic couplet."

The couplets of *The Corsair* provide a striking contemporary contrast to Keats's Cockney couplets in *Sleep and Poetry* and *Endymion*—though, as Susan Wolfson demonstrates, the reviewers were divided as to whether Byron's style, in relation to his poem's narrative, extended or violated Augustan practice.[29] Enjambment is rare; only two lines in the poem's opening 42-line section, for example, are not strongly end-stopped. Croker could have found in Byron's couplets just what he missed in Keats's: "a complete couplet inclosing a complete idea." And the relation between couplet form and idea in *The Corsair* is politically suggestive in ways inventively elaborated by Wolfson. Consider the couplet that begins the opening song of Conrad's pirates: "'O'er the glad waters of the dark blue sea, / Our thoughts as boundless, and our souls as free'," (1. 1–2). Conrad and his followers may have "'thoughts'" that are "'boundless'" and "'souls'" that are "'free,'" but the couplet that celebrates this spirit is neither—it is as carefully bounded and closed as a couplet from *The Essay on Man*. An even more arresting instance of the way in which Byron's heroic couplets check—and also give contrasting point to—the poem's appeal to a restless, rebellious energy appears later in this opening section, as the pirates distinguish their lives on the open sea from "'him who crawls enamoured of decay'": "'While gasp by gasp he faulters forth his soul, / Ours with one pang—one bound—escapes controul.'" (1. 31–2). "'Escapes controul'" comes sharply up against the controlling closure of that full-stop. Manning's work on *The Corsair* helps us see that however anti-authoritarian and anarchic Byron's hero may be, he performs within stylistic terms as familiar and congenial to many genteel Regency readers as Keats's Cockney couplets were strange and rebarbative.

Keats knew what he wanted to do in his 1817 Cockney couplets, and he knew how far beyond the "flowing round of habit and ease" characteristic of Hunt's liberal reform couplets he wanted to go. The *Blackwood's* review is right, given its basic assumption, to assert that "the defects of [Hunt's] system are tenfold more conspicuous in his disciple's work than in his own."[30] Tenfold may be an exaggeration, but anyone interested in the statistical evidence for just how much further Keats went than Hunt in breaking the metrical and grammatical conventions of the Augustan couplet can look such evidence up in the older and still important studies of M. R. Ridley and W. J. Bate.[31] Hunt himself had complained about the excesses of Keats's couplet experiments in his *Examiner* review of the 1817 *Poems*: "Mr. Keats' . . . fault, the one in his versification, arises from . . . contradicting over-zealously the fault on the opposite side. It is this which provokes him now and then into mere roughness and discords for their own sake, but not for that of variety and contrasted harmony."[32] Keats's friend John Hamilton Reynolds had made much the same complaint a few months earlier in his unsigned review for the progressively liberal *Champion* (9 March 1817).[33] In fact the liberal reviewers, though quite favorably disposed towards Keats's early poems, had almost as many reservations about the couplets as their Tory counterparts. P. G. Patmore in *The London Magazine* (April 1820) praised the "freedom, sweetness, and variety" of Keats's rhythms in *Endymion* but admitted that "the verse frequently runs riot, and loses itself in air."[34]

Such responses ought to make us ask to what extent, and in just what ways, the stylistic choices and performances of the 1817 and 1818 volumes *are* political choices and performances. And there are even more fundamental theoretical implications: some of the Regency critics are asking whether Keats's performances in verse are based on real choice at all, and their doing so sometimes merges with current postmodernist skepticism about both discursive and political agency: Keats's lines appear to write him, to produce him as callow Cockney reformer—or as a follower of Hunt whose verse has gone over the edge and "run . . . riot." The broad relevance of a highly politicized context to Keats's early style is clear, but no one would want to argue that his extravagant experiments in couplet-writing are in themselves expressive of political convictions more radical and anarchic than those of liberals like Hunt. If anything, Keats's stylistic extravagance might appear to be radically antipolitical in its tendency to produce lines that, as Hunt said in 1832 of the more disciplined couplets of *Lamia*, "seem to take pleasure in the progress of their own beauty."[35] Have we arrived at a point where the explanatory usefulness of the political context for Keats's early couplet style breaks down? Or have that context and Keats's stylistic response to it only complicated themselves beyond the level at which we usually work when we study what McGann designates "the specific ways in which certain stylistic forms intersect and join with certain factual and cognitive points of reference."[36]

As a way of continuing to explore such intersections and joinings, I want to turn to another moderately liberal reviewer, Francis Jeffrey, writing belatedly about *Endymion* in the August 1820 number of *The Edinburgh Review*. Jeffrey sees that if Keats is playing at *bouts rimés* in the couplets of *Endymion*, he is doing so in a distinctive and at least potentially fruitful way:

> A great part of the work indeed, is written in the strangest and most fantastical manner that can be imagined. It seems as if the author had ventured every thing that occurred to him in the shape of a glittering image or striking expression—taken the first word that presented itself to make up a rhyme, and then made that word the germ of a new cluster of images—a hint for a new excursion of the fancy—and so wandered on, equally forgetful whence he came, and heedless whither he was going, till he had covered his pages with an interminable arabesque of connected and incongruous figures, that multiplied as they extended, and were only harmonized by the brightness of their tints, and the graces of their forms.[37]

Some of Jeffrey's response is vaguely generalizing, but the part worth holding onto for the moment is the suggestion that Keats allows himself to be led (and also misled) by the rhyme as it generates a need for connection and development, as it provokes and then gives unexpected shape to figurative elaborations. At times in *Endymion* and in the 1817 volume, Keats seems to be doing just this, and with an air of self-delighting curiosity as to the consequences. There is an extraordinary moment in *I Stood Tip-toe* when the speaker wanders off into a daydream occasioned by the couplet that precedes it:

> Were I in such a place, I sure should pray
> That nought less sweet might call my thoughts away,
> Than the soft rustle of a maiden's gown
> Fanning away the dandelion's down;
>
> (93–96)

He follows this figure for four more couplets before reluctantly letting her depart:

> And as she leaves me may she often turn
> Her fair eyes looking through her locks aubùrne.
>
> What next? A tuft of evening primroses,
> O'er which the mind may hover till it dozes;
> (105–8)

"What next?" is winning in its way: it produces an effect of genial audacity that is hard not to read as the writer's—the fictional speaker-as-writer's—exclamation about having gotten by with a rhyme like "turn" / "aubùrne," as well as an indication that he is letting himself be surprised by what turns up next. The gesture projects both that anti-aristocratic "ease" in Cockney writing that, as Cronin observes, "always implies the perplexities of its readers," and an opportunism that is at once stylistic and social.[38]

The serious critical issue here is the extent to which Keats is willing to let the pressures and possibilities of rhyming—and thus of contending with arbitrary phonetic and semantic convergences—shape the development of his poem. Is this an issue with political implications, amenable to historical and political understanding? Or have we passed beyond the level at which politics and form intersect? It is one thing to accept P. N. Medvedev's principle that "a linguistic form is only real in the concrete speech performance, in the social utterance," or David Simpson's insistence "on the historical grounds of [a] play of possibilities rendered into language."[39] It is quite another to make good on McGann's claim that "only by reading [Keats's Cockney poetry] in a sharply specified historical frame of reference are we able to see . . . and hence to describe precisely not merely the abstract *characteristics*, but the felt *qualities* of its poetic structure."[40] Some of those "felt *qualities*," as we have seen, yield amply to being understood "in a sharply specified historical" and political "frame of reference." But what about the quality Jeffrey felt in observing that Keats often allows the first rhyme-word in a couplet to become "the germ of a new cluster of images—a hint for a new excursion of the fancy"?

One initial response to these questions ought to be that they cannot be settled theoretically, or simply as points of principle. The degree to which historical and political circumstances are precisely useful in understanding matters of style, or the level at which they cease to become useful, is not decidable in advance of our actually trying to think about a particular stylistic feature from a historical and political point of view. With this in mind, it is instructive to look briefly at rhyme-induced figurative "excursions" from Keats's later poetry. That such "excursions" grow out of the sort of verbal opportunism in Keats's "Cockney style" that upset Tory and liberal Whig reviewers alike was inadvertently demonstrated years ago by Kingsley Amis, in the inaugural volume of *Essays in Criticism*. Amis complained that Keats's "hopelessly inadequate" rhyming of "my sole self" and "deceiving elf" in the last stanza of *Ode to a Nightingale* has its origin in one of the Cockney couplets of *Endymion*, when the narrator laments "The journey homeward to habitual self! / A mad-pursuing of the fog-born elf," (2. 276–77). Readers more interested than Amis apparently was in Keats's broodings about the self as a construct at once deceiving in its significance and yet hauntingly, inescapably persistent may find that the rhyming precipitation of "elf" out of "self" (it is like a miniature of Blake's "spectre" and "emanation"), far from being "hopelessly inadequate," is intrinsic to Keats's working through the issues of poetic subjectivity. His attitude toward authorial identity, as Marjorie Levinson helps us see, is implicitly political in ways that are about a Cockney writer's struggle for social and cultural recognition. Cockney rhyming slang was only beginning to emerge in the speech culture of the City and the East End in Keats's day, and its most likely sources—"navvy gangs building canals and railways" and petty thieves trying to confuse the police—were not the formative social influences in Keats's immediate environment.

Yet this tradition of hiding the identity of a word in a rhyming phrase whose relation to the word is flagrantly arbitrary may well be indirectly connected to impulses in the Cockney middle-class discourse to which Keats was orienting and reorienting himself as a writer.[41] The accidents and the opportunism of rhyme became distinctive resources for speakers and writers who had both something to hide and something to reveal, and who had to make up their discursive identities as they went along, challenging stylistic norms in the process of establishing their place in the culture. For a poet accused of being a Cockney upstart, the fortuitous discovery that a "deceiving elf" hides inside "self" may be seen as especially pertinent to ending a poetic reverie in the garden of a genteel friend on the edge of Hampstead Heath.

Consider another example that raises immediate questions about the politics of style and impinges directly on the debate initially provoked by McGann's political reading of *To Autumn*. Here are the last seven lines of the poem's opening stanza, beginning with the second of that stanza's opulent infinitive clauses:

> To bend with apples the moss'd cottage-trees,
>   And fill all fruit with ripeness to the core;
> To swell the gourd, and plump the hazel shells

> With a sweet kernel; to set budding more,
> And still more, later flowers for the bees,
> Until they think warm days will never cease,
> For summer has o'er-brimm'd their clammy cells.
>
> (5–11)

In this stanza of *To Autumn*, where all is made to feel so inevitable, we feel an inevitable resistance to recognizing that anything as overtly arbitrary as the exigencies of rhyme could be involved in generating that culminating image. Yet the "bees" in "their clammy cells" are there in part to rhyme with "cottage-trees" and "hazel shells." And these very rhymes appear in *Endymion*, in Cockney couplets like the ones attacked by *Blackwood's* and the *Quarterly*:

> Just when the light of morn, with hum of bees,
> Stole through its verdurous matting of fresh trees.
>
> (3. 419–20)

> And gather up all fancifullest shells
> For thee to tumble into Naiads' cells,
>
> (1. 271–72)

It is plausible to think that Keats was led to the "cluster of images" that concludes the first stanza of *To Autumn* by, among other concerns, the suggestive pressure of rhyme, and by his recalling his own Cockney versification. But is there anything political about his being thus led?

Keats had already used a reference to bees to distinctive political effect in "Robin Hood" (1818), where it is followed in rhyming position by an aggressively Cockney couplet linking "honey" to "money" (45–48). We know from a letter to Bailey shortly after his moving to Winchester that however pleased Keats may have been with this quiet retreat into solitude, the class-based slurs on his Cockney writing were still very much in his mind: "One of my Ambitions is . . . to upset the drawling of the blue stocking literary world" (14 August 1819).[42] Keats was avidly keeping up with the current political turmoil in the country. He had gone back to London from Winchester for a few days (to try to arrange financial help for his brother George in America) just in time to see Orator Hunt's tumultuous return from Manchester and Peterloo. The *Examiner*'s reports on Peterloo, which Keats read during his Winchester stay, provide a dark backdrop to the "Season of mists and mellow fruitfulness" celebrated in *To Autumn*. The number for Sunday, 5 September—the last number Keats would have seen before his trip to London—contains a particularly important linking of the month's political and literary significance. Following a series of letters reporting on the aftermath of Peterloo, including letters from Henry Hunt himself on his Manchester trial, and immediately following a piece entitled "Return of the Killed and Wounded at Manchester. Letter from Mr. Pearson," is an entry called "Calendar of Nature. (From the Literary Pocket-Book.) September." This item begins with the September stanza from the procession of the months in Spenser's Mutability Cantos (*The Faerie Queene* 7.7.38), a stanza that contains iconographical details to which Keats was clearly responding in *To Autumn*.[43] Even more suggestive, however, are the details in the *Examiner*'s gloss on Spenser's stanza:

> The poet still takes advantage of the exuberance of harvest and the sign of the Zodiac in this month, to read us a lesson on justice. Autumn has now arrived. This is the month of the migration of birds, of the finished harvest, of nut-gathering, of cyder and perry-making. . . . The swallows . . . disappear for the warmer climates, leaving only a few stragglers behind, probably from weakness or sickness. . . . September, though its mornings and evenings are apt to be chill and foggy, and therefore not wholesome to those who either do not or cannot guard against them, is generally a serene and pleasant month, partaking of the warmth of summer and the vigour of autumn. . . . The feast, as the philosophic poet says on a higher occasion . . .[44]

Here the *Examiner* quotes a Spenserian stanza from Canto 5 of Shelley's *The Revolt of Islam* (Hunt's extended enthusiastic review of the poem had appeared in February and March 1818) describing a victory feast held by the forces of liberation. The stanza is slightly misquoted to make it fit with the *Examiner*'s prose:

> The feast is such as earth, the general mother,
>   Pours from her fairest bosom, when she smiles
> In the embrace of Autumn. To each other
>   As some fond parent fondly reconciles
>   Her warring children, she their wrath beguiles
> With their own sustenance; they, relenting, weep.
>   Such is this festival, which from their isles,
>   And continents, and winds, and oceans deep,
> All shapes may throng to share, that fly, or walk, or creep.
>   (5. 2209–2307)

Is this Autumn's "lesson on justice," this image of a momentary natural bounty that "beguiles" the "wrath" of people previously oppressed? Hunt had not quoted the stanza in his review of Shelley's poem, but his summary of this phase of the narrative is pertinent: "a festival is held at which *Cythna* presides like a visible angel, and every thing seems happiness and security. The Revolters however are suddenly assailed by the allies of the tyrant; and the fortune of the contest is changed."[45]

All this contextual material may seem remote from Keats's bees in *To*

Autumn, but the *Examiner*'s quoting of Shelley suggests one way in which it may be pointedly relevant. When in his "Song to the Men of England" (1819) Shelley asks the "Bees of England" why they allow "these stingless drones" to "spoil / The forced produce of your toil" (the "spoil" / "toil" rhyme, incidentally, appears in the stanza from Spenser quoted in the *Examiner*), he is drawing upon a figurative tradition common in radical political writing of the later eighteenth and early nineteenth centuries.⁴⁶ True, Keats's imagery has an important Virgilian source, as editors have pointed out: even the rhyme-word "cells" has its antecedents in the "cellas" of Virgil's famous simile.⁴⁷ But knowing this need not preclude our thinking politically about Keats's image. On the contrary: Virgil's early summer image ("aestate nova") of Dido's subjects joyfully laboring to build Carthage has complicated political resonances of its own, resonances carried over but transformed in Keats's early autumnal image of worker-bees whose momentary abundance makes them "*think* warm days will never cease" (emphasis added), and whose "o'er-brimm'd ... cells" are disturbingly "clammy." A reader in 1819–1820 familiar with popular political pamphlets and songs might have found Keats's image of laboring bees political in ways of which no "bluestocking" would have approved.

I am not arguing that all references to bees in Romantic poems ask to be read politically, or that Keats's stylistic practices led him deliberately to focus his own and his readers' attention in these lines on the living conditions of real English gleaners in the autumn of 1819. But I am arguing that here as elsewhere, *To Autumn* presents us with an idealized, mythologized image of culminated, and therefore death-set, fruition that is never merely escapist precisely because it fends off but cannot finally exclude a conflicted historical actuality with which Keats was certainly in touch. Chandler has argued that *To Autumn* is written out of an "acute historical self-consciousness" and reads it as a "neopagan hymn" designed to counter what Keats himself refers to in a letter to his brother and sister-in-law of 18 September 1819 as the "horrid superstition against all innovation" that, in the form of dominant Christian ideology, prevailed in Britain after the failure of the French Revolution (*England in 1819*, 425–32). In support of this argument one could also cite Keats's December 1816 sonnet "Written in Disgust of Vulgar Superstitions," which hears the binding of human progress and creativity in the "black spell" of "church bells" that "toll a melancholy round, / Calling the people to some other prayers, / Some other gloominess" (1–6). Chandler's reading of *To Autumn* is more politically affirmative and consolidated than the one I am suggesting—and yet it leaves open the question of what kind of political meaning and value to attribute to a poetic attempt to find "some *form* of refashioned post-Enlightenment *form* of religion" (429; emphasis added). I prefer to hold on to the explicitly averting impulse in *To Autumn's* concluding "Think not of them" (24) and to believe that Keats's writing movingly fails to free itself from either the political reality or the political language that many critics, in opposite ways, insist that he wants to avoid.

Even at a level of performance where the specific political context of Keats's Cockney couplets ceases to be immediately instructive, the stylistic instincts encouraged and shaped by that context may produce writing with an important though momentarily suppressed or concealed dimension of class politics. If our engagement with the "richer entanglements" of Keats's poetry is going to continue to expand to include a fresh sense of this political dimension, we will need to make ourselves newly alert to the ways in which acts of writing and reading may be subject to historical and political circumstances quite remote from a poem's most immediate field of reference.

2.

On 12 July 1822, Byron wrote to Thomas Moore: "I wish to know (and request an answer to *that* point) what became of the stanzas to Wellington (intended to open a canto of Don Juan with) which I sent you several months ago. If they have fallen into Murray's hands, he and the Tories will suppress them, as those lines rate that hero at his real value" (*BLJ* 9: 182–83). The stanzas Byron was concerned about are as politically provocative as anything he ever wrote:

> Oh, Wellington! (or "Vilainton"—for Fame
> Sounds the heroic syllables both ways;
> France could not even conquer your great name,
> But punned it down to this facetious phrase—
> Beating or beaten she will laugh the same)—
> (9. 1–5)

Byron's readers have sounded the political syllables of his poetry, including the syllables of *Don Juan*, both ways—and with good reason.[48] He was right to worry that the Wellington stanzas would have been suppressed by Murray and his Tory friends; he himself had agreed to suppress them when they were part of Canto 3, which Murray had published in 1821, saving them for the opening of Canto 9 (the second of the War Cantos), which John Hunt would publish in 1823.[49] Yet Murray's Tory friends—particularly John Hookham Frere and William Stewart Rose—were prominent influences on Byron's syllables: it was through their writing that he began to see what the *ottava rima* of Pulci, Boiardo, Berni,

Ariosto, and Casti could become in English. I want to look here at the political context of the *ottava rima* from which Byron learned, and then use that context to say something about instances when his own *ottava rima* sounds the political syllables both ways. As in the previous reading of Keats's Cockney couplets, I will be working from two assumptions: first, that stylistic options are often charged or inflected with political and social significance; second, that establishing the political and social aura of a stylistic convention such as a stanza form is one thing, reading the politics of a specific passage in which that convention is deployed quite another. We have to be prepared to recognize that a stanza may contradict or elude the principle of political association we have established for it—especially in Byron. Whether or not contradiction or elusiveness themselves point to further principles of political understanding then becomes a hard and important question.

One associate of Murray's who would not have liked the Wellington stanzas was John Hookham Frere. His burlesque Arthurian poem in *ottava rima*, "*Prospectus and Specimen of an Intended National Work*, by William and Robert Whistlecraft," published by Murray in 1817 and 1818, was by Byron's own acknowledgement the direct stylistic forerunner of *Beppo*. "Whistlecraft was *my* immediate *model*," Byron wrote to Murray in March, 1818 (*BLJ* 6: 24). Frere's connection with Murray was long-standing and based in part on Tory alignments.[50] In 1797–1798 he had joined George Canning and William Gifford in founding and contributing regularly to the *Anti-Jacobin*. He followed Canning as undersecretary of state in the foreign office in 1799. Soon after, he began a diplomatic career in Portugal and Spain that ended in 1808 when, as minister to the Junta during the Peninsular War, he gave advice to a commander of British forces that resulted in a disastrous advantage for Napoleon. In a cancelled stanza to Canto 1 of *Childe Harold*, Byron joined popular opinion in attacking "blundering Frere," along with "vaunting Wellesley" (Wellington in his pre-duke days), for English losses in Spain.[51]

Frere returned to England in 1809, just in time to lend his support to Murray's project of establishing a Tory rival to *The Edinburgh Review*—*The Quarterly Review*. And Frere turned to writing verse again. His facility with *ottava rima* helped Byron find the stylistic idiom of his greatest poetry, and Byron suggested to Murray that Frere be consulted about the publication of the early cantos of *Don Juan*, and then of his translation of Pulci's *Morgante Maggiore* (*BLJ* 6: 74 and 7: 46).[52] But it is not surprising that Frere took a dim view of most of what Byron came to do with Pulci's stanza. Of *Don Juan*, he is reported to have said—not unobservantly—"it is strange . . . he [Byron] should think there is any connection between patriotism and profligacy." He told his nephews that he decided not to continue with his *ottava rima* burlesque in part because of "the sort of stigma which at first attached to the metre after the publication of 'Don Juan.'"

Byron first read Frere's *Prospectus and Specimen* (more often referred to as *The Monks and the Giants*) in September 1817, in a copy from Murray which may have been brought to him in Venice by William Stewart Rose.[53] Rose was another associate of Murray's with strong Tory credentials, though he was also on good literary terms with prominent Whig politicians like Henry Hallam and Lord Holland. He was the son of George Rose, the old political ally of Pitt. In 1800 he had been nominated by his father to be reading clerk of the House of Lords and served in that capacity for more than a decade. It may have been in the House of Lords that Byron first made Rose's acquaintance—or if not there, then in Murray's office in Albemarle Street. By this time Rose had developed a passion for medieval romance, and partly on this basis, a strong friendship with Scott. After the peace of 1814 he went to live in Italy, but remained in close contact with Murray. His literary importance to Byron has principally to do with his imitations of the late eighteenth-century Italian satirist Giambattista Casti, and apparently with his knowing more about the poetry of Pulci and Berni than anyone else in England. Byron saw a good deal of Rose between September 1817 and June 1818, and there can be little doubt that Rose was a critical spur, along with his friend Frere, to Byron's intensive study of Italian *ottava rima* writing.[54]

As for Casti, Byron had already read and admired his satirical *ottava rima* renderings of narratives mainly from Boccaccio, the *Novelle Galanti*, in the summer of 1816.[55] Peter Vassallo has insisted that Casti's Italian, not Frere's English, was the key influence on the style of *Beppo*,[56] but it seems more likely that Byron's familiarity with Casti prepared him to see the possibilities in what Frere—and Rose—were doing in "*that there* sort of writing."[57] In March 1818 Murray sent Byron a copy of Rose's English adaptation of Casti's satirical beast fable, the *Animali Parlanti*. Byron thought it "excellent" (*BLJ* 6: 24). The *Animali* is written in *sesta rima* or sixains, rather than *ottava rima*; Rose's adaptation must have sharpened Byron's sense of the difference the two additional lines make to the pace and rhetorical scope of otherwise identical stanzaic patterns.

Before saying more about the political satire in Rose's version of Casti, it will be helpful to introduce into the discussion a third member of what Jerome McGann refers to as "the circle of wits . . . that congregated at Murray's," John Herman Merivale.[58] His background was different from Frere's and Rose's: he was not an Etonian, and he had left Cambridge before taking a degree to study and practice law in London, and to write scholarly poetry.[59] Politically he seems to have been something of a reformer in legal affairs. In December 1819, under the pseudonym

"Metrodorus," he defended the first two cantos of *Don Juan* in a letter to the editor of *Blackwood's* entitled "Remarks on some of our Late Numbers; by a Liberal Whig." Merivale complains in this letter that "in the present days, the grand question of politics absorbs every other; and, if a man be neither a Radical nor an Alarmist, he must find himself (generally speaking) in a very awkward and graceless predicament, much like that ancient worthy of whom the proverb runs,—'Between two stools,' &c. This is my own case."[60] A *Blackwood's* editor—presumably John Wilson ("Christopher North"), to whom the letter was addressed—took eager advantage of Merivale's political moderation and commented that "we . . . can scarcely believe it possible that METRODORUS can be a Whig." Merivale wrote regularly for the *Quarterly*, so his relations with Tory writers were obviously cordial.

Byron knew Merivale early in his career, and in *English Bards and Scotch Reviewers* praises the volume of *Translations Chiefly from the Greek Anthology* (1806), to which Merivale was a major contributor. He also admired Merivale's imitation of Pulci, the *Orlando in Roncevalles*, published in 1814. Addressing himself to "the much-contested question whether the 'Morgante Maggiore' ought to be regarded as a burlesque poem," Merivale was eager to show that Pulci is not "a mere buffoon," and his translations and imitations emphasize the serious chivalric aspect of Pulci's writing.[61] This makes all the more interesting McGann's suggestion that Merivale's *ottava rima* performance may have inspired what looks like Byron's first experiment with the stanza, twenty lines of manuscript verse written late in 1813, on the subject of Southey's laureateship:

> Bob now no more the sapphic patriot [warbles,]
>   And up to Pye's Parnassus he may climb—
> George gives him what—God knows he wanted—laurels,
>   And spares him what—he never spared us—rhyme.[62]
>   (7–10)

This draft shows Byron already taking Merivale's Pulcian stanza in the direction of the anti-Tory satire of the suppressed dedication to *Don Juan* and of *The Vision of Judgement*.

Byron came to *ottava rima*, then, primarily through the work of three literati with close ties to Murray, and with political and social alignments running from the *Anti-Jacobin* to *The Quarterly Review*. Yet Frere's and Rose's poetry, and certainly Merivale's, is far from being mere Tory propaganda in verse. These writers too sound the political syllables both ways. Just what their poetry amounts to politically is a complicated matter; such critical attention as has been paid to it has come to nothing like a consensus. Vassallo says that Frere departed from his Italian models, Pulci and Berni, into "authorial digression and intrusion" in order to make "carefully veiled allusions to prominent generals and politicians of the moment."[63] But he is never specific about these allusions, and concludes that "Frere's satire was too vague and mild to be effective." This is essentially in agreement with what Southey said to Murray in February, 1820: "What [Frere] produced was too good in itself and too inoffensive to become popular; for it attacked nothing and nobody."[64] Frere himself complained years after the publication of *The Monks and the Giants* that "most people who read it at the time it was published, would not take the work in any merely humorous sense; they would imagine it was some political satire, and went on hunting for a political meaning."[65] We are to believe, it would seem, that Frere's Arthurian burlesque either has no intended political meaning at all, or a political meaning so mild and sporadic as to count for little.

This view of Frere's poem obscures the kind of political interest it may have held for Byron. Frere's pseudonymous authors, William and Robert Whistlecraft, are designated on the title-page as "Harness and Collar-makers" from Suffolk, and there is unmistakable though intermittent social satire in this working man's view of chivalric legend. The point was not lost on Ugo Foscolo, who wrote in his long piece on "Narrative and Romantic Poems of the Italians" in the *Quarterly* that "sometimes" the poet "is *really* Mr. Whistlecraft, the harness and collar-maker," and on such occasions Frere gives us "an exquisite transcript of the sensations and ideas of a working man" — a "transcript," one hardly needs to add, written by a bemused Tory litterateur.[66] For at times Frere's own political experience and perspective clearly show themselves in his manipulations of Whistlecraft's sense of chivalric values:

> In form and figure far above the rest,
>   Sir LAUNCELOT was chief of all the train,
> In Arthur's Court an ever welcome guest;
>   Britain will never see his like again.
> Of all the Knights she ever had the best,
>   Except, perhaps, Lord Wellington in Spain:[67]
>   (Canto 1, stanza 13)

That Spain had been the setting for a low point in his own diplomatic career ("blundering Frere") does not deter him from celebrating it as a high point in Wellington's ("vaunting Wellesley"). Whistlecraft's rhyming allusion here must certainly have caught Byron's eye. When R. D. Waller says in his edition of *The Monks and the Giants* that such references to contemporary persons or interests were "a hint which Byron was quick to follow," he fails to suggest what kind of hint this one was, or the degree to which Byron would intensify it.[68]

Rose's version of Casti raises more difficult questions about Byron's political relation to his *ottava rima* forerunners. McGann refers to Casti's "biting liberal satire," but such a characterization does not do justice to the cynicism of Casti's exposure of corruption not only in court and government circles, but in popular political movements, too.⁶⁹ There is a telling moment in Vassallo's book when he imagines that the *Animali Parlanti* might have struck a chord with Byron because "the abortive Neapolitan uprising in 1820" and "the re-establishing of absolute monarchy by the Austrians in Naples and Piedmont a year later . . . made Byron aware of the woeful insufficiency of the common people."⁷⁰ Here Vassallo quotes Byron's well-known diary entry for 1 May 1821: "It is still more difficult to say which form of Government is the *worst*—all are so bad.—As for democracy it is the worst of the whole—for *what is (in fact)* democracy? an Aristocracy of Blackguards.—" (*BLJ* 8: 107). Casti, for all his attacks on the corruption of European court life, had been a kind of court poet: his satire is indebted to Voltaire and the French Enlightenment, but also to his worldly intimacy with members of the ruling families and high government officials. As Roberto Benaglia-Sangiorgi has pointed out, he "recited his tales to entertain and amuse the courts of Europe."⁷¹ In this respect he may be said to have inherited the perspective of Renaissance court poets like Pulci, Berni, and Ariosto, with their medievalizing romantic fictions and dependence on aristocratic patronage on the one hand, and their irreverent, ironic sense of personal and historical corruptibility on the other. One imagines that Rose and Frere understood very well the sociopolitical circumstances out of which the *ottava rima* tradition came, and that they in part identified it with their own: erudite poets/scholars/translators, deeply attached to the Tory establishment and given to satirizing it gently, carefully, from a privileged inside position.

Late in life Rose recalled that Byron had "said he should have inscribed 'Beppo' to [Frere] that had served him as a model, if he had been sure it would not have been disagreeable. Supposing (as I concluded) that some passages in it might have offended him."⁷² Which passages of *Beppo* did Rose have in mind? Although Byron told Murray that *Beppo* "has politics and ferocity, & won't do for your Isthmus of a Journal" (*BLJ* 6: 9), the first of Byron's *ottava rima* triumphs appears to be the least overtly political, a poem in which Byron's understanding of the Italian way of doing things—an understanding that he thought he especially shared with Rose, by the way ("a fine fellow—and one of the few English who understand *Italy*" [*BLJ* 6: 38])—stands in funny, unferocious contrast to English social conventions: "But Heaven preserve Old England from such courses! / Or what becomes of damage and divorces?" (295–96). There is nothing in lines like these that Murray and the Tories would want to suppress. On the contrary, the narrator's plea to "preserve Old

England" sounds too patriotic to be plausible for Byron. But this is the tack Byron takes in *Beppo*, just at those moments when English matters that might rub Murray or Frere or Rose the wrong way come up:

> "England! with all thy faults I love thee still,"
>   I said at Calais, and have not forgot it;
> I like to speak and lucubrate my fill;
>   I like the government (but that is not it);
> I like the freedom of the press and quill;
>   I like the Habeas Corpus (when we've got it);
> I like a parliamentary debate,
> Particularly when 'tis not too late;
> . . . .
> And so God save the Regent, Church, and King!
> Which means that I like all and every thing.
>   (369–84)

These stanzas give us, I would suggest, Byron momentarily posing as patriotic satirist, edging toward parody throughout the passage, and at times toward a different kind of satire altogether.[73] "I like the Habeas Corpus (when we've got it)": Habeas Corpus, very recently suspended for a time in 1817–1818, had of course been more notoriously suspended from 1794 to 1801, when Rose's father was Pitt's loyal supporter in the House of Commons, and when Frere was collaborating with Canning and Gifford on the *Anti-Jacobin*.

The stanza that follows in *Beppo* extends this pose of the patriotic traditionalist abroad, only slightly discomforted by the way things are going back home:

> Our standing army, and disbanded seamen,
>   Poor's rate, Reform, my own, the nation's debt,
> Our little riots just to show we are free men,
>   Our trifling bankruptcies in the Gazette,
> Our cloudy climate, and our chilly women,
>   All these I can forgive, and those forget,
> And greatly venerate our recent glories,
> And wish they were not owing to the Tories.
>   (385–92)

How do we read Byron's positioning himself in that final couplet? It is possible to hear the aristocratic reformist Whig, now older and wiser, venerating his country's glorious victories over the French and wishing that his own party had been in power to take credit for them. But it is more consistent with Byron's strategy in this sequence of stanzas, I think, to hear the narrator as a Tory, loyal to "Regent, Church, and King" but a little ashamed as well as proud of "our recent glories." It is a strategy meant to appeal to, even as it congenially makes fun of, Byron's Tory friends whose work had led him to the style he was working out in *Beppo*. No wonder that when the poem first appeared anonymously, Frere had to be persuaded that Rose was not the author.[74] And no wonder that Murray was so delighted with *Beppo*—"an extraordinary effort," he called it, "written in two nights, in consequence of reading Whistlecraft."[75]

The response of Murray and his coterie to Byron's *ottava rima* satire was soon to change. Within eight or nine months after the publication of *Beppo* (in late February 1818), Whistlecraft was arguing with Murray against publishing Byron's new poem, *Don Juan*.[76] Byron must have felt particularly irked that the very writer who had helped him discover the idiom of *Beppo* and *Don Juan*, and whom he had made a point of asking Murray to consult about his new project, was now retreating into fastidious conservatism. Byron's disgust with Murray "and the Tories" in his letter to Moore about the Wellington stanzas derives, at least in part, from his remembering that he would never have written that kind of stanza without the help of Frere, Rose, and Merivale.

Written in July 1819, the Wellington stanzas show how far Byron's *ottava rima* writing had moved politically since the jovial parody of expatriot patriotism in *Beppo*. Yet Byron's tone in these stanzas is still importantly connected to the tack of "'England! with all thy faults I love thee still!'" of the *Beppo* passage. The narrator's political pose in *Beppo* is not rejected; rather, it gets turned into an irony at once fiercer and more complexly poised. The pretense of venerating "our recent glories" is still part of the posture:

> You have obtained great pensions and much praise;
> Glory like yours should any dare gainsay,
> Humanity would rise, and thunder "Nay!"
>
> (9. 6–8)

This stanza begins by sounding the syllables of Wellington's name both ways: "Wellington" and "Vilainton," English and French, heroic nobleman and ill-bred butcher.[77] It ends by thinking, not sounding—and in several, not just "both"—ways the single syllable that is at once the English negation and the French name of the military commander whom Wellington had defeated at Waterloo. "'Nay,'" the spelling Byron finally settled on, pretends to repudiate any who might "gainsay" Wellington's "Glory," and yet does this so emphatically that it is impossible not to feel "Humanity's" repudiation directed against Wellington himself. "Ney," the name of Napoleon's field marshall, and a spelling Byron played with in the manuscript, might seem to name one of Wellington's conquered foes as a punning, rhyming denial of those who would gainsay his greatness. But this way of thinking that syllable's sound also invites us to join with France in remembering Ney's bravery and laughing in defeat at the contingency of Wellington's fame—or infamy ("Beating or beaten she will laugh the same").[78] There is no doubt that Byron is out to attack Wellington here. His way of proceeding, however, is not to call him a "'bloody blustering booby'" (BLJ 7: 228) or a "Miscreant . . . Cub of Fortune" (BLJ 9: 49), as he does in his letters, but to sound the syllables both ways, heroic as well as mock-heroic.

There is an important link back from the Wellington stanzas to the satiric manner of *Beppo*, with its own links back to the verse of Frere and Rose. At the beginning of his career, as Elizabeth Boyd reminds us, *English Bards and Scotch Reviewers* had "aligned [Byron] with Gifford, Frere and Canning, and the Tory Quarterly Reviewers."[79] Certain aspects of that alignment continued to play a part in the *ottava rima* writing of what McGann refers to as Byron's "revisionist project" from *Beppo* onward.[80] In the work of Frere and Rose and in the Italian poetry they admired, imitated, and adapted, *ottava rima* had already sounded the heroic syllables both ways. Southey complained to Landor in 1820 that Frere's handling of the stanza "had the fault of his Italian models, that the transition from what is serious to what is burlesque was capricious. Lord Byron immediately followed."[81] This "transition from what is serious to what is burlesque" is an aspect of the *ottava rima* tradition that Byron was always reluctant to give up, even when taking a political line that was bound to offend not just his Tory enemy Southey, who called *Don Juan* "an act of high treason on English poetry," but his Tory friends, who had pointed him toward "*that there* kind of writing" in the first place. No writer in English raises more pointedly the question of whether sounding the syllables both ways is an act of evasive political cynicism or provocative political integrity.

When Southey complains that the "transition from what is serious to what is burlesque" is "capricious" in Byron's Tory predecessors in *ottava rima* writing, he accuses an entire formal tradition of being *arbitrary* in the second sense noted by Johnson's *Dictionary*. When Byron self-parodically vaunts from within this formal tradition that he "Was reckoned a considerable time / The grand Napoleon of the realms of rhyme" (*Don Juan* 11. 439–40), he links himself to the greatest political exemplar of Johnson's first definition ("Despotick; absolute; bound by no law; following the will without restraint") while treating this link as a function of what "foolscap subjects" among his Regency readers momentarily "reckoned" him to be. The couplet rhyming of "rhyme" with "time" is emblematic of how the willfully powerful and the capricious play themselves out both in the realm of local and generic stylistic gesture and in the realm of national and international political and cultural history.

4

VULGAR IDIOMS

> I should like to see that word *vulgar* properly defined, and its meaning limited—at present it is the most arbitrary word in the language.
> —Medon in Anna Jameson, *Characteristics of Women: Moral, Poetical, and Historical,* 1835

1.

PERCY SHELLEY wrote to Leigh Hunt on 15 August 1819, asking him to give the manuscript of *Julian and Maddalo* to Charles Ollier for publication. In this poem, Shelley says, "I have employed a certain familiar style of language to express the actual way in which people talk with each other whom education and a certain refinement of sentiment have placed above the use of vulgar idioms" (*LPBS* 2: 108). This letter and the poem it refers to provoke difficult questions about the connection of Shelley's awareness of class to the reformist and radical aspects of his politics. More specifically, they provoke questions about the social register (as it were) of a particular stylistic ideal—an ideal not usually associated with Shelley or with Romantic attempts to bring the language of verse close to "the real language of men." More broadly, Shelley's terms make us think about the social identities and stylistic practices of other writers who were among his immediate and most discerning readers—Hunt himself, Byron, Hazlitt, Keats. These terms mark fundamental points of intersection between the politics of class and the politics of style, and they lead out to some basic considerations about how we locate, describe, analyze such intersections.

I want to set these basic considerations more decisively in motion before coming back to Shelley's letter to Hunt and to *Julian and Maddalo*. It is telling that the first serious evaluation of Shelley's attempt to represent—or "express," as he says—a class-specific colloquial idiom came not from a Marxist or historicist critic, but from a conservative writer working to find in late eighteenth- and nineteenth-century poetry principles of stylistic integrity for British poetry of the 1950s. In the chapter called "Shelley's Urbanity" in *Purity of Diction in English Verse* (1952), Donald Davie praises *Julian and Maddalo* as an instance of the "mean" or middle style, as an "accurate" representation of the "civilized" and civilizing decorum of gentlemanly conversation (apart from the maniac's speech, which for Davie no less than for Harold Bloom is an "excrescence").[1] Davie's way of taking seriously Shelley's aim to write colloquially and yet "above the use of vulgar idioms" is still instructive. But as Kelvin Everest has shown, Davie's equation "of civilizing virtues and values with 'the habit of gentlemen,'" and especially his inattentiveness to the pressure the poem comes to put on its urbane dialogue, limit "Shelley's Urbanity" even as an initial posing of critical issues.[2]

The sociolinguistic resources to which we might instinctively turn in thinking analytically and theoretically about the questions posed by Shelley's passage provide only limited help with the concepts of the "vulgar" and of "idiom."[3] In its theorizing of "carnival," the work of Bakhtin and his circle offers the most productive account available of "vulgar" cultural practices and institutions. And in his powerful insistence on the social differentiation of language and on the dialogic structure of all texts, Bakhtin provides useful techniques for grasping the social implications of the rhetorical structure in *Julian and Maddalo*, with its celebrated dialogue that is both framed by and centered around monologue (Julian's, and the maniac's).[4] Such a reading of the poem, which I do not undertake in this chapter, would have to overcome the Bakhtinian privileging of speech over writing, and of prose fiction over poetry. It would also have to provide the kind of detailed account of the social and historical forces acting on and through Shelley's stylistic aims and practices that we find in, say, David Simpson's readings of Wordsworth, or Peter Manning's of Byron, or Marjorie Levinson's of Keats, or John Barrell's of Clare.[5]

Thinking through the key terms of Shelley's stylistic project as he conveyed it to Hunt is one way of beginning to develop the detailed social and historical account for which I am calling. It is also a way of drawing attention to insufficiently examined complications in just those theoretical perspectives that seem most relevant to such an undertaking. When Davie deplores the stylistic "barbarities" of Shelley's *The Cloud*, or admires the "base" style of the *Letter to Maria Gisborne*, or condemns the "vicious diction" in *To Jane. the Recollection*, he is quite straightforward about the social and moral significance of his terms. Many readers will not agree with the value he gives them, but we know perfectly well what he means by "barbarities," "base," and "vicious," and we know why he uses them. But do we know with comparable clarity why Marx speaks of "vulgar economics"?[6] Or, following Marx more or less directly, why Simpson or Jameson speak of "vulgar materialism"?[7] Or, to shift to a different theoretical tradition, why Derrida says that "the linearity of language entails [a] vulgar and mundane concept of temporality"?[8]

It is not that Marx has no specific historical development in mind when he refers, in the Afterword to the second German edition of *Capital*, to the "vulgarising" of David Ricardo's theories of political economy in England between 1820 and 1830. Nor, to refocus the question somewhat, is Marx or the classical Marxist tradition uncritical of sentimental tendencies simply to identify the experiences or beliefs of the "common" people with historical truth or with revolutionary consciousness. And it is not that Derrida fails to be explicit about the "vulgar . . . concept of temporality" he seeks to expose and undo in *Of Grammatology* ("homogeneous, dominated by the form of the now and the ideal of continuous movement, straight or circular . . . which Heidegger shows to be the intrinsic determining concept of all ontology from Aristotle to Hegel").

The problem is that Marx in his way, and Derrida in his, disregard the most rudimentary social meaning of the word "vulgar": "Plebeian; suiting to the common people; practised among the common people," as Samuel Johnson begins by defining it in the *Dictionary*. It could of course be argued that Marx and Derrida are merely using "vulgar" in its familiar extended senses to mean, simultaneously, "widespread" or "familiar" and therefore "crude," "reductive," "simplified." But what does it mean tacitly to accept these extensions, to ignore the implicit identification of what is "crude" and "reductive" with what is "practised among the common people"? I focus on this deracination of "vulgar" from its reference to a particular social class because, as we will see, a version of this process is ideologically and rhetorically conspicuous in Shelley and his contemporaries, and because it is inconspicuously, silently, and therefore deceptively taken for granted by many of the writers on whom we rely for theoretical orientation in thinking about style as a registering of social and political forces.

The social basis and historical functions of the "vulgar" are not, however, taken for granted by Bourdieu. On the contrary, one of the fundamental arguments of *Distinction* is that "[i]n contrast to the detachment and disinterestedness which aesthetic theory regards as the only way of recognizing the work of art for what it is, i.e., autonomous, *selbständig*, the 'popular aesthetic' ignores or refuses the refusal of 'facile' involvement and 'vulgar' enjoyment, a refusal which is the basis of the taste for formal experiment."[9] Since aesthetic theory generally and Kant's *Critique of Judgment* in particular are foundational constituents of the international formation we call "Romanticism," Bourdieu's massive sociological account of the ways in which "art and cultural consumption are predisposed, consciously and deliberately or not, to fulfil a social function of legitimating social difference" (7) contains much that is enabling for our understanding of how "the distinguished and the vulgar" operate in Romantic discourse. Bourdieu's "Postscript: Towards a 'Vulgar' Critique of

'Pure' Critiques" is especially suggestive on matters addressed in this and the preceding chapter. His scrutiny of aesthetic theory's "Disgust at the 'Facile'" and at "easy" pleasure (486) is sharply pertinent to Cronin's observations about Cockney stylistic "ease" (*The Politics of Romantic Poetry*, 185). And his comments on the ways in which Derrida's reading of the *Critique of Judgment* "remains subject to the censorships of the pure reading" and reproduces Kant's own "distance from all 'vulgar' discourses" (494, 495) demonstrate how even the most rigorously self-critical and self-questioning analysis depends on maintaining "distinctions" that work to exclude critical engagement with the vulgar. These insights are available also in the essays that make up *Language and Symbolic Power*—in "The Production and Reproduction of Legitimate Language," for instance, when Bourdieu notes that "during the Romantic period" writers reject "a language censored and purged of all popular usages" but then "invoke genius against the rule," thereby reinstating the opposition of "distinction" against "vulgarity" (59).

What Bourdieu leaves insufficiently examined, and—for my purposes in this chapter—insufficiently historicized, are important questions about the relation of the "vulgar" to the "common" and the "popular." He cites the following passage from the *Critique of Judgment* as an instance of aesthetic theory's relentless antagonism to "simple aesthesis," of its characteristic "disgust" understood as "the ambivalent experience of the horrible seduction of the disgusting and of enjoyment, which performs a sort of reduction to animality, corporeality, the belly and sex, that is, to what is common and therefore vulgar" (*Distinction*, 489):

> *Common human understanding* . . . has therefore the doubtful honour of having the name of common sense (*sensus communis*) bestowed upon it; and bestowed, too, in an acceptation of the word *common* (not merely in our own language, where it actually has a double meaning, but also in many others) which makes it amount to what is *vulgar* [*das Vulgäre*]—what is everywhere to be met with—a quality which by no means confers credit or distinction upon its possessor. (Part 1, Book 2, sec. 40)[10]

Kant's reference to the "double meaning" of *common* (*gemein* is Kant's German adjective: "what is generally practiced among ordinary people" but also "low," "crude") presents an opportunity for commenting on the related but not identical doubleness of *vulgar*—an opportunity that Bourdieu not only misses but erases as opportunity by repeating the very equation Kant invites us to think about: "reduction . . . to what is common and therefore vulgar." Bourdieu's "therefore" joins an analogous but asymmetrical doubleness in both "common" and "vulgar" through a logic that much of his book invites us to interrogate.

Bourdieu implicitly interrogates this logic in "The Production and Reproduction of Legitimate Language," in the passage quoted earlier where he glances at the Romantic period. Considering how it is that the "struggles among writers over the legitimate art of writing contribute, through their very existence, to producing both the legitimate language, defined by its distance from the 'common' language, and belief in its legitimacy," Bourdieu says that

> it is a question of the contribution [writers, grammarians or teachers] make, independently of any intentional pursuit of distinction, to the production, consecration and imposition of a distinct and distinctive language. In the collective labour which is pursued through the struggles for what Horace called *arbitrium et jus et norma loquendi,* writers—more or less authorized authors—have to reckon with the grammarians . . . who take upon themselves the power to set up and impose norms . . . by . . . fixing a language censored and purged of all popular usages. . . . (*Language and Symbolic Power,* 58–59)

It is important to allow here for the centralization and rationalization of discursive authority in French society. That being said, Bourdieu's representation of what he goes on to call "a social function of distinction in the relations between classes and in the struggles they wage on the terrain of language" has important implications for any analysis of "vulgar idioms." His citing a canonical Latin phrase from Horace's *Ars Poetica* (72) performs a version of the very "pursuit of distinction" in the social process of establishing linguistic and stylistic norms that is under discussion. Bourdieu sees this process as a "collective" but not "common" "labour" designed to control "popular usages." Interestingly, in this part of the *Ars Poetica* Horace is defending "popular usages," asserting the poet's right to use "words stamped with the mint-mark of the day" (*signatum praesente nota . . . nomen,* 59).[11] But "usage" itself, invested by Horace with a will of its own (*si volet usus,* 71), turns out to exert selective constraints that reproduce society's patterns of domination and subordination. Horace's *arbitrium,* cited in Lewis and Short as an example of the broader social meanings of "judgment, opinion, decision" that the word acquired as it came to be transferred from the narrower "sphere of judicial proceedings," contains within it just those veiled contradictions of the collective and the exclusive, the rational and the willful, that make the maintaining of linguistic and stylistic standards in any class-divided society an exercise in arbitrary power.

Though I have called this chapter "Vulgar Idioms," it is more precisely about Romantic resistance to the vulgar, about the desire to be above or beyond vulgarity. The resistance is various and pervasive, even in Blake and Wordsworth, in whose writing we expect and often find an openness to what is "practised among the common people." I focus here on a network of textual instances characteristic of relations between the upper-class ex-patriots Shelley and Byron and the middle-class London liberals Hunt and Hazlitt. The chapter does not explore in detail the actual connections between any of these writers and literally "vulgar" readers (in the sense of readers among the "common people" and among the emergent working class). To do so would mean extending and rethinking the equation of the "vulgar" and the "vernacular" in Olivia Smith's indispensable *The Politics of Language 1791–1819*, and it would mean taking issue with Jerome Christensen's recent account of "demotic speech" as the equivalent of English "Jacobin" discourse—as an "anachronistic," "prepolitical" language of "insurrectionary" hope—in *Romanticism at the End of History*.[12] It would also mean taking a fresh look at transgressive print-culture events such as William Hone's unauthorized prose adaptation of Byron's *The Corsair* in 1817, William Clarke's and William Benbow's pirated editions of Shelley's *Queen Mab* in 1821, or Richard Carlile's numerous cheap editions of the same poem from 1822 on.[13] My immediate concern is with the interaction between social and stylistic preoccupations among middle- and upper-class writers at a time when "the society of the text," as Jon Klancher calls it, had become increasingly volatile and unpredictable.[14]

2.

I return now to Shelley's letter to Hunt and look at the sentence quoted earlier in its fuller context. The paragraph it comes from is remarkable as a contradictory enactment of the principles it announces:

> I send you a little Poem to give to Ollier for publication but *without my Name*. Peacock will correct the proofs. I wrote it out with the idea of offering it to the Examiner, but I find that it is too long. It was composed last year at Este; two of the characters you will recognize; the third is also in some degree a painting from nature, but, with respect to time and place, ideal. You will find the little piece, I think, in some degree consistent with your own ideas of the manner in which Poetry ought to be written. I have employed a certain familiar style of language to express the actual way in which people talk with each other whom education and a certain refinement of sentiment have placed above the use of vulgar idioms. I use the word *vulgar* in its most extensive sense; the vulgarity of rank and fashion is as gross in its way as that of Poverty, and its cant terms equally expressive of bare conceptions, and therefore equally unfit for Poetry. Not that the familiar style is to be admitted in the treatment of a subject wholly ideal, or in that part of any subject which relates to common life, where the passion exceeding a certain

limit touches the boundaries of that which is ideal. Strong passion expresses itself in metaphor borrowed from objects alike remote or near, and casts over all the shadow of its own greatness. But what am I about. If my grandmother sucks eggs, was it I who taught her.

With its insistence on anonymous publication, its urbane self-deprecation (a text of more than 600 lines is "a little Poem," "the little piece"), and its reliance on phrases conveying unspoken nuances of judgment ("in some degree" and "a certain" both appear twice), this paragraph itself begins as the performance of someone "whom education and a certain refinement of sentiment have placed above the use of vulgar idioms." It ends with a vulgar idiom, sophisticatedly turned and ambiguous in what it conveys about Shelley's attitude towards Hunt. The *OED* lists it under "Egg . . . proverbial phrases of obvious meaning . . . *teach your grandmother to suck eggs*: said to those who presume to offer advice to others who are more experienced." Since the word "egg" dwells etymologically inside the word "cockney" (the *OED* offers "Cockney: egg: lit. 'cocks' egg'"), Shelley may be alluding to Hunt's reputation among the Tory reviewers as King of the Cockneys. In between these gestures, Shelley's characterization of his poem involves delicate negotiating between his own literary and social position and that of Hunt, Cockney poet and journalist. As it turns out, the *Examiner* may not have been the right place for *Julian and Maddalo* for reasons other than that it was simply "too long."

It is striking that Shelley claims to have represented the talk of those who are "above the use of vulgar idioms" in a letter to Hunt, whom he believes—even more strikingly—will find *Julian and Maddalo* "consistent with your own ideas of the manner in which poetry ought to be written." Hunt's poetry had been repeatedly attacked in *The Quarterly Review* and in *Blackwood's* for being vulgar: the word chimes through the four articles in *Blackwood's* on the "Cockney School of Poetry" that ran from May through August of 1818—that is, through the summer before Shelley's visit to Byron in Venice. In addressing himself to "the potent and august King of the Cockneys" in the first of these articles, "Z" (Lockhart and Wilson) says he will "occasionally depart from that respectful language which the vulgar prejudices of the ignorant may think due to majesty."[15] In the third article he expresses his "hatred and contempt" for "that loathsome vulgarity which clings around him [Hunt] like a vermined garment from St. Giles."[16] Keats is drawn into this class-centered denunciatory rhetoric in the fourth article, which emphasizes the influence of Hunt—"the meanest, the filthiest, and the most vulgar of Cockney poetasters"—on the "prurient and vulgar lines" of Keats's 1817 *Poems*, some of which "Z" imagines are "evidently meant for some young lady east of Temple-bar."¹⁷ Shelley's assertion that his objectives in *Julian and Maddalo* are "in some degree consistent" with Hunt's "own ideas" is already hedgingly calibrated; it seems even more so when he slides from "in some degree consistent" to a position "above the use of vulgar idioms."

This is where the Tory reviewers themselves positioned Shelley: above the vulgar. "He also is of the 'COCKNEY SCHOOL', so far as his opinions are concerned," wrote Lockhart in the *Blackwood's* review of *The Revolt of Islam*, "but the base opinions of the sect have not as yet been able entirely to obscure in him the character, or take away from him the privileges of the genius born within him." "Mr Shelly [sic], whatever his errors may have been, is a scholar, a gentleman, and a poet; and he must therefore despise from his soul the only eulogies to which he has hitherto been accustomed—paragraphs from the Examiner, and sonnets from Johnny Keats. He has it in his power to select better companions."¹⁸ John Taylor Coleridge took up this line in his piece on *The Revolt of Islam* for the *Quarterly*: "[Shelley] has never yet exhibited the bustling vulgarity, the ludicrous affectation, the factious flippancy, or the selfish heartlessness" of "his friend and leader Mr. Hunt."¹⁹ Shelley's aristocratic birth and education placed him above the vulgarity of the Cockneys, whatever his ties to them of politics and principle may have been. "Mr Shelley . . . is not merely superior, either to Mr Hunt, or to Mr Keats," wrote the *Blackwood's* reviewer of the *Prometheus Unbound* volume, "but altogether out of their sphere and totally incapable of ever being brought into the most distant comparison with either of them. It is very possible that Mr Shelley himself might not be inclined to place himself so high above these men as we do, but that is his affair, not ours."²⁰

Shelley was of course not inclined to follow the class bigotry exercised on his behalf by the Tory reviewers. But he was inclined, in the letter to Hunt, to place himself "in some degree" above as well as on the same level as the friend and intermediary to whom he wrote. In the months that followed, he continued to connect Hunt with his "little piece" in the "familiar style." "Have you seen my poem, *Julian and Maddalo*?" he writes to Ollier in December 1819. "Suppose you print that in the manner of Hunt's *Hero and Leander*" (*LPBS* 2: 164). Shelley kept worrying about his poem's stylistic decorum. He insists in May of 1820 that Ollier not print *Julian and Maddalo* with *Prometheus Unbound*, and in doing so appears to demote the former to a stylistic category lower than the middle or "familiar": "It is an attempt in a different style, in which I am not yet sure of myself, a *sermo pedestris* way of treating human nature quite opposed to the idealism of that drama. If you print *Julian and Maddalo*, I wish it to be printed in some unostentatious form . . . and I particularly desire that my name be not annexed to the first edition of it"

(*LPBS* 2: 196). Part of Shelley's anxiety seems to have been that his attempt at the *sermo pedestris*, though "above the use of vulgar idioms" and sanctioned by classical precedent, might be associated with kinds of writing that were vulgar. A letter of 29 October 1820 bears revealingly on the matter. Addressed to Marianne Hunt, it praises Keats's first *Hyperion* as an indication "that he is destined to become one of the first writers of the age."

> His other things are imperfect enough, & what is worse written in the bad sort of style which is becoming fashionable among those who fancy that they are imitating Hunt & Wordsworth.— But of all these things nothing is worse than a volume by Barry Cornwall [Bryan Waller Procter] entitled the Sicilian story. The Sicilian story *itself* is pretty enough, but the other things in the volume, I hope that Hunt thinks abominable, in spite of his extracting the only three good stanzas from Gyges with his usual good nature in the Examiner. Indeed *I* ought not to complain of Hunt's good nature for no one owes so much to it.— Is not the vulgarity of these wretched imitations of Lord Byron carried to a pitch of the sublime? (*LPBS* 2: 239)

The movement here from Keats's version of Hunt's "Cockney" experiments through imitations of Wordsworth's *Lyrical Ballads* manner to "Barry Cornwall"'s attempts at Byronic *ottava rima* span a range of "vulgar" fashions that Shelley urgently puts at a distance. Yet *Julian and Maddalo*, which is "in some degree consistent" with Hunt's poetic aims and at the same time an attempt to express Lord Byron's very self and voice, runs a double risk of lapsing into, rather than rising above, vulgarity.

The pressure of Byron's influence on Shelley's writing, always tense and complicated, is especially so in *Julian and Maddalo*. Though he inadvertently and suggestively left behind in England the copy of *Beppo* sent to him by Murray at Byron's request in the spring of 1818 (see *LPBS* 2: 13), Shelley makes clear in a letter to Peacock that he had read the poem by the time of his visit to Byron in Venice in late August (*LPBS* 2: 42). Something of what *Beppo* may have meant to the style of *Julian and Maddalo* is hinted at in Francis Jeffrey's unsigned review of Byron's poem:

> The great charm is in the simplicity and naturalness of the language—the free but guarded use of all polite idioms, and even of all phrases of temporary currency that have the stamp of good company upon them. . . . The unknown writer [*Beppo* was first published anonymously] . . . has furnished us with an example, unique we rather think in our language, of about one hundred stanzas of good verse, entirely composed of common words, in their common places; never presenting us with one sprig of what is called poetical diction . . . but running on in an inexhaustible series of good easy colloquial phrases, and finding them fall into verse by some unaccountable and

happy fatality. . . . the greater part is very pleasant, amiable, and gentleman-like.[21]

Jeffrey's Whig poetics, as full of their own kind of class politics as the sneers of the Tory reviewers, bear a clarifying relation to Shelley's aims as expressed in the letter to Hunt. In *Beppo* Byron has managed to write colloquially and yet above the use of vulgar, though not (apparently) of politely "common," idioms. Byron's poetry, more positively than Hunt's, may have been in Shelley's mind when he wrote about his visit to Byron. Had he talked to Byron about Hunt? Would Byron have spoken about Hunt to Shelley as he did to Thomas Moore in the letter quoted below, written just three months earlier?

> Hunt's letter [to Moore, criticizing *Lalla Rookh*] is the exact piece of vulgar coxcombry you might expect from his situation. He is a good man, with some poetical elements in his chaos; but spoilt by the Christ-Church Hospital and a Sunday newspaper, — to say nothing of the Surrey Jail, which conceited him into a martyr. But he is a good man. When I saw "Rimini" in MSS., I told him that I deemed it good poetry at bottom, disfigured only by a strange style. His answer was, that his style was a system, or *upon system*, or some such cant; and, when a man talks of system, his case is hopeless. . . .
> He believes his trash of vulgar phrases tortured into compound barbarisms to be *old* English. . . . He sent out his "Foliage" by Percy Shelley * * *, and of all the ineffable Centaurs that were ever begotten by Selflove upon a Night-mare, I think this monstrous Sagittary the most prodigious. *He* (Leigh H.) is an honest Charlatan, who has persuaded himself into a belief of his own impostures, and talks Punch in pure simplicity of heart. . . . But Leigh Hunt is a good man, and a good father — see his Odes to all the Masters Hunt; — a good husband — see his Sonnet to Mrs. Hunt; — a good friend — see his Epistles to different people; — and a great coxcomb and a very vulgar person in every thing about him. But that's not his fault, but of circumstance. (*BLJ* 6: 46–47)

A sense of Byron's condescending mockery was surely an influence on Shelley when he wrote to Hunt about the poem that dramatized his own friendship with Byron. When Byron hastens to make clear to Moore that the "*He*" who "is an honest Charlatan" is Hunt and not Shelley, as the previous sentence might suggest, we get a glimpse of what was at issue for Shelley in coming under Byron's judgment. Being around "Lord Byron," as he always referred to him, made him feel that he needed to keep his social as well as his stylistic differences from Hunt clear — especially, perhaps, when acknowledging "in some degree" a stylistic connection with Hunt in a poem in which Byron figures so prominently.

And what about Hunt's own perspective on the Shelleyan postures and gestures we have been looking at? Shelley's "manners . . . were any thing but vulgar," Hunt says in *Lord Byron and Some of His Contemporaries*. "They could be, if he pleased, in the most received style of his rank. He was not incapable, when pestered with moral vulgarity, of assuming even an air of aristocratic pride and remoteness."[22] Though he had developed a thick skin to withstand Tory charges that he was a vulgar Cockney, Hunt must have winced a bit at being asked to deliver a poem depicting a conversation between those "whom education and a certain refinement of sentiment have placed above the use of vulgar idioms." Hunt's vulnerability was not so great as Keats's, who complained to his brother and sister-in-law (as Sonia Hofkosh reminds us) that "my name with the literary fashionables is vulgar—I am a weaver boy to them."[23] The threat of being regarded as a maker of textiles rather than of texts was quite real—Keats's allusion here to the Manchester cotton-spinner's strike of the previous year opens onto an entirely different social and political scene. His very name could become the target of class-based derision. "The Edinburgh praises Jack Keats or Ketch or whatever his names are," Byron wrote to his Tory publisher Murray; "why his is the *Onanism* of Poetry—something like the pleasure an Italian fiddler extracted out of being suspended daily by a Street Walker in Drury Lane" (*BLJ* 7: 217).[24] Hunt was never abused in social terms as rough as these. What he had to contend with was the Tory image of him as a presumptuous middle-class radical and poetaster from "east of Temple-bar" or, just as bad, from the suburbs.

When he first met him in 1811, Shelley found Hunt "a man of cultivated mind" (*LPBS* 1: 77) and he would no doubt have objected to Byron's calling him a "good man" but vulgar. But Shelley would not have included his good friend among "those whom education and a certain refinement of sentiment have placed above the use of vulgar idioms." Hunt himself was under no illusion about that.

3.

So far I have tried to unfold the implications of Shelley's saying that he and Byron were "above the use of vulgar idioms" by assuming that "vulgar" in his sentence refers to social class. And of course it does, though Shelley's emphasis on "education and a certain refinement of sentiment" is not the same as an explicit emphasis on, say, inherited rank and property. But in the very next sentence Shelley wants to detach "vulgar" from its exclusively lower-class references. "I use the word *vulgar* in its most extensive sense," he writes; "the vulgarity of rank and fashion is as gross in its way as that of Poverty, and its cant terms . . . equally unfit for Poetry." This extension of "vulgar" to include upper- as well as lower-class behavior and language anticipates modern uses of the word that are not meant to be class-specific or class-restrictive. What is at issue is not that hesitation "between matter-of-fact description and disapproval" in the use of "vulgar" (the hesitation is more evident with "common" and "ordinary") noted by Susie Tucker in her study of eighteenth-century vocabulary.[25] Shelley, like Marx and Derrida, uses "vulgar" disapprovingly, not neutrally or matter-of-factly. But the disapproval has attached itself to qualities or characteristics no longer confined "to the common people," as Johnson puts it. Yet a sense of these qualities or characteristics as nonetheless rooted in social class remains conspicuous in Shelley, as it does not in many of the modern instances I looked at earlier. "Rank and fashion" may be vulgarly "gross"; so may "Poverty." The "cant terms" of the former, no less than the unrefined patois of the latter, are "unfit for Poetry."

Shelley's extension of "vulgar" to include the full spectrum of social class and economic status, though it serves in the letter to Hunt the distinctive purpose of qualifying his previous claim to be "above the use of vulgar idioms," is characteristic of radical reformist writing in the late eighteenth and early nineteenth centuries. The extension is there in Paine's *Rights of Man*, when he accuses Burke of having "libelled . . . in the grossest style of the most vulgar abuse, the whole representative authority of France," and then asks only a few pages later "How then is it that such vast classes of mankind as are distinguished by the appellation of the vulgar, or the ignorant mob, are so numerous in all old countries?"[26] And it is there even more dramatically in Wollstonecraft's second *Vindication*:

> In this metropolis a number of lurking leeches infamously gain a subsistence by practising on the credulity of women, pretending to cast nativities, to use the technical phrase; and many females who, proud of their rank and fortune, look down on the vulgar with sovereign contempt, shew by their credulity, that the distinction is arbitrary, and that they have not sufficiently cultivated their minds to rise above vulgar prejudices.[27]

Mary Poovey observes that "the rich and poor alike stand condemned by Wollstonecraft's epithet 'vulgar.' "[28] The movement of "vulgar" from the ignorant poor to people of rank and fortune and back again, made possible by a recognition "that the distinction" between common vulgarity and "rank and fortune" is "arbitrary," is a mark of Paine's and Wollstonecraft's positions as radical middle-class reformers. In their writing "vulgar" becomes unfixed in its social designation not by being neutralized, but by having its pejorative connotations (here of irrational prejudice and superstition) extended to apply to those above as well as below. It is through this unfixing that Wollstonecraft can accuse those who "look down on the vulgar with sovereign contempt" of failing to rise above "vulgar prejudice." Fanny Burney deploys this perspective as a principle of satirical dramatic rhetoric in *A Busy Day* (written 1800–1802), a play about the collision between the obvious "vulgarity" of Cockney merchants and the differently obvious "vulgarity" of gentry boors.[29]

The unfixed, extended reference of "vulgarity" has an evolved afterlife in early Victorian culture. It is at work in Hunt's Preface to the first edition of *The Masque of Anarchy* (1832), a poem written in a different "lax and familiar measure," as Hunt puts it.[30] It is striking that Hunt feels called upon to deny that Shelley's writing in *The Masque* is condescending, that Shelley was "an aristocrat by disposition as well as by birth."[31] What bothers Hunt about such a view of Shelley—which he admits is "natural enough even with intelligent men, who have been bred among aristocratical influences"—is that it will "confirm inferior understandings in a similar delusion, and . . . make the vulgarity of would-be refinement still more confident in its assumptions" (xvi). Here, as in *Lord Byron and Some of His Contemporaries*, Hunt insists that "Mr. Shelley's mind was not to be measured by common rules,—not even by such as the vulgar, great and small, take for uncommon ones." Again he reports: "I have seen him indeed draw himself up with a sort of irrepressible air of dignified objection, when moral vulgarity was betrayed in his presence, whatever might have been the rank of the betrayer" (xvii–xviii). Hunt's effort is to convert social into moral discrimination, the "quintessence of gentlemanly demeanour . . . observable in Mr. Shelley, in drawing-rooms, when he was not over-thoughtful," into "an exquisite combination of sense, moral grace, and habitual sympathy," into "an aristocracy of intellect and morals" (xix–xx). But the class-specific dimension of Shelley's being above vulgarity persists in Hunt's very attempts to dismiss it. "It was finely said one day in my hearing by Mr. Hazlitt, when asked why he could not temporise a little now and then, or make a compromise with an untruth, that it was 'not worth his while.' It was not worth Mr. Shelley's while to be an aristocrat." This last sentence could be read as registering, on Shelley's behalf, a quintessentially aristocratic disdain for keeping up appearances.

What it registers on Hunt's own behalf is less obvious. His invocation of Hazlitt is pertinent: the most vivid elaboration of the "extensive sense" of the vulgar in Romantic writing is Hazlitt's essay in *Table-Talk* (1821–1822) "On Vulgarity and Affectation." The coupling of terms in Hazlitt's title signals the preoccupation with false or failed social mobility that I want to emphasize. "Vulgar" and "vulgarity" are themselves mobile, constantly on the move, in this essay. At first "vulgar" applies to the foolishly aspiring lower classes: "I hardly know which is to be regarded with most distaste, the vulgar aping the genteel, or the genteel constantly sneering at and endeavouring to distinguish themselves from the vulgar."³² In the next paragraph, this "sneering at ... the vulgar" provokes Hazlitt's own extension of the word to the upper classes: "Gentility is only a more select and artificial kind of vulgarity" (8: 157). "A coronation," Hazlitt argues, is "a vulgar ceremony" that "delights equally the greatest monarch and ... the vilest of the rabble. For what degree of refinement, of capacity, of virtue is required in the individual who is so distinguished, or is necessary to his enjoying this idle and imposing parade of his person?" (8: 159). "Refinement," which was essential to Shelley's sense of being "above the use of vulgar idioms" ("a certain refinement of sentiment"), is also crucial to Hazlitt's way of defining the "essence" of vulgarity: "It is coarseness or shallowness of taste arising from want of individual refinement, together with the confidence and presumption inspired by example and numbers. It may be defined to be a prostitution of the mind or body to ape the more or less obvious defects of others, because by so doing we shall secure the suffrages of those we associate with" (8: 161). Hazlitt's definition is at once essentialist—of the "essence" and not subject to social or historical constraints—and intensely political, a matter of individual independence that is imagined to be free from "example and numbers," from "the suffrages of those we associate with." So while he goes on to insist that "a thing is not vulgar because it is common"—that "grossness is not vulgarity, ignorance is not vulgarity, awkwardness is not vulgarity" but only become so "when they are affected and shewn off on the authority of others"—he retains a strong conviction that such affectation and imitation are appallingly prevalent among the lower classes. "Cobbett is coarse enough, but he is not vulgar. He does not belong to the herd" (8: 161).³³ "There is a well-dressed and an ill-dressed mob, both which I hate," he asserts, and then quotes Horace, the classical voice of refined urbanity: "*Odi profanum vulgus, et arceo*" (8: 163). Hazlitt's disposition toward "the word *vulgar* in its most extensive sense" is as selectively democratic in its way as Shelley's. People in all classes may be vulgar when they act collectively to assert their class identities, rather than individually to assert what is "natural," "real," "original."

This preference for individual independence over social collectivity becomes contradictory, as it often does in Romantic writing, when Hazlitt turns from behavior and judgment to language. He says that "all slang phrases are ... vulgar; but there is nothing vulgar in the common English idiom," on the principle that slang "is not the offspring of untutored nature but of bad habits" (8: 162). The Yorkshireman Tyke in Thomas Morton's *The School for Reform* is vulgar because he is full of "the cant and gibberish, the cunning and low life of a particular district"; "A cockney is a vulgar character, whose imagination [and presumably whose talk] cannot wander beyond the suburbs of the metropolis" (8: 162). More broadly, "If there are watchwords for the rabble, have not the polite and fashionable their hackneyed phrases, their fulsome unmeaning jargon as well? Both are to me anathema!" (8: 164). Hazlitt is very close to Shelley here, despite his different class perspective. But his appeal to "the common English idiom" presents a difficulty that does not arise in Shelley's letter to Hunt. The "common English idiom" that Hazlitt wants to distinguish from "vulgar" provincial slang is itself a matter of habit rather than of "untutored nature"; it is a mode of socially sanctioned collective behavior that conflicts with the commitment elsewhere in the essay to individual taste and independent judgment. On this point Hazlitt is more idealizing than Shelley or even than Jeffrey, for whom Byron's deployment of "common words, in their common places" consists in "the free but guarded use of all polite idioms, . . . all phrases of temporary currency that have the stamp of good company upon them."

To bring Hazlitt's remarks on vulgarity more directly to bear on Shelley's effort in "a certain familiar style of language," we may turn to the essay later in *Table-Talk* "On Familiar Style." There Hazlitt begins by sounding surprisingly like Donald Davie, as well as like Shelley: "Many people mistake a familiar for a vulgar style, and suppose that to write without affectation is to write at random. On the contrary, there is nothing that requires more precision, and, if I may so say, purity of expression, than the style I am speaking of. It utterly rejects not only all unmeaning pomp, but all low, cant phrases" (8: 242). Hazlitt is referring here to prose rather than verse, and there are critical distinctions to be made about what "familiar style" means to each that I will return to. For now, it is worth remembering that the Latin term Shelley attaches to the style of *Julian and Maddalo* in his letter to Ollier, *sermo pedestris*, usually applies in classical rhetorical discourse to prose. Where Hazlitt most notably diverges from Shelley, again, is in his appeal to a "common English idiom." "Common" is a recurrent term for Hazlitt as it is not for Shelley, and his use of it makes us see how much more readily it sheds its pejorative senses than does "vulgar": "It is not to take the first word that offers, but the best word in common use; . . . to follow and avail ourselves of the true idiom of the language. To write in a genuine familiar or truly English style, is to write as one would speak in common conversation" (8: 242). Hazlitt's masters of familiar prose, like the speakers Shelley wants to represent in *Julian and Maddalo*, are "above the use of vulgar idioms." You are not at liberty, Hazlitt says, "to resort to vulgar dialect or clownish pronunciation. You must steer a middle course." But this course is not easy, because the "common" and the "vulgar" are not so easily separated in practice as in principle:

It is clear you cannot use a vulgar English word, if you never use a common English word at all. A fine tact is shewn in adhering to those which are perfectly common, and yet never falling into any expressions which are debased by disgusting circumstances, or which owe their signification and point to technical or professional allusions. A truly natural or familiar style can never be quaint or vulgar, for this reason, that it is of universal force and applicability, and that quaintness and vulgarity arise out of the immediate connection of certain words with coarse and disagreeable, or with confined ideas. The last form what we understand by *cant* or *slang* phrases. (8: 243)

Much of Shelley's sense of the decorum of familiar style is here, but with a thoroughly middle-class belief in the universal force and applicability of such a style instead of Shelley's implications of an uncommon familiarity based on elite education and "refinement of sentiments." Refinement for Hazlitt means the "fine tact" necessary to negotiate what was for him a narrower and more uncertain separation between the "common" and the "vulgar," or the "common" and the "technical or professional." "I have been (I know) loudly accused of revelling in vulgarisms and broken English. I cannot speak to that point: but so far I plead guilty to the determined use of acknowledged idioms and common elliptical expressions. . . . As an author I endeavour to employ plain words and popular modes of construction, as were I a chapman and dealer, I should common weights and measures" (8: 244). How to be a "determined" "chapman and dealer" in prose without being either "vulgar" or merely "technical or professional"—this is the problem Hazlitt faces, and it is a problem distinct from the risks Shelley believes he runs in experimenting with a familiar style in verse, however much their attitudes toward what counts as "vulgar" may have in common.

4.

Most poets write bad prose because the constraints of verse corrupt their feeling for the rhythms of "spirited conversation"—so Hazlitt argues in "On the Prose-Style of Poets." "[A] poet will be at a loss, and flounder about for the common or (as we understand it) *natural* order of words in prose-composition" (12: 7–8). But what about the poet who aims to follow the cadences and syntax of colloquial, conversational prose in verse itself, in what Shelley calls "a *sermo pedestris* way of treating human nature"? Hazlitt's remarks on Hunt, the only prose-writer other than Burke and Southey whom he approves of in this essay, imply yet another stylistic tie between Hunt and Shelley. "To my taste," Hazlitt observes, "the author of Rimini, and the Editor of the Examiner, is among the best and least corrupted of our poetic prose-writers":

> In his light but well supported columns we find the raciness, the sharpness, and sparkling effect of poetry, with little that is extravagant or far-fetched, and no turgidity or pompous pretension. Perhaps there is too much the appearance of relaxation and trifling (as if he had escaped the shackles of rhyme), a caprice, a levity, and a disposition to innovate in words and ideas. Still the genuine master-spirit of the prose-writer is there; the tone of lively, sensible conversation . . . (12: 16)

Hazlitt hints at, without really exploring, connections between Hunt's writing when he is bound by "the shackles of rhyme" in *The Story of Rimini*, and when he has "escaped" those "shackles" in the columns of the *Examiner*. These connections pertain indirectly to the style of *Julian and Maddalo*.

What is most impressive about Shelley's "familiar style" in this poem subtitled "A Conversation" is its distinctive counterpointing of idiomatic diction, prose syntax, and the constraints of couplet structure:

> I rode one evening with Count Maddalo
> Upon the bank of land which breaks the flow
> Of Adria towards Venice:—
>
> (1–3)

The opening couplet directs and accents but does not break the flow of Julian's reminiscence with its rhyme on Maddalo's name. The effect of such counterpointing is wonderfully varied, particularly in the dialogue.

> "Where is the love, beauty and truth we seek
> But in our mind? and if we were not weak
> Should we be less in deed than in desire?"
> "Ay, if we were not weak—and we aspire
> How vainly to be strong!" said Maddalo:
> "You talk Utopia." "It remains to know,"
> I then rejoined, "and those who try may find
> How strong the chains are which our spirit bind;
> Brittle perchance as straw . . ."
>
> (174–82)

Shelley's model for such flexibly enjambed couplets, according to one late Victorian editor of Hunt's writing, is obvious: "The 'Julian and Maddalo' . . . showed at once in a very signal manner how great had been the effect on him of Leigh Hunt's exultant revival, or readaptation, in 'The Story of Rimini,' of the resonant versification of Chaucer, and the ringing triplets of Dryden."[34] Now even a cursory look at *The Story of Rimini* will show that Shelley's couplet-writing is in fact as different from Hunt's as it is from Byron's (to whom, ironically given his low opinion of it, Hunt's poem was dedicated). Yet the example of Hunt's couplet style may well have been an element in Shelley's sense of what it would mean to write a colloquial, familiar poem that was "above the use of vulgar idioms." Shelley had to be aware that his experiment in the *sermo pedestris* might be associated with what *Blackwood's* called "the loose, nerveless versification and Cockney rhymes of the poet of Rimini."[35]

Shelley's couplets are intrinsic to the politics of style in *Julian and Maddalo*. Their importance indicates why a Bakhtinian analysis of contending "voices" or discourses—unless amplified to take in poetic conventions and traditions that *The Formal Method in Literary Scholarship* actually tends to dissociate from their cultural contexts—fails to account for the relation of social and stylistic values represented in the poem. That Shelley's couplets might be thought to have been indebted to Hunt—rather than or even in addition to Chaucer or Dryden or Byron—invites us to rethink Everest's observation that Shelley's writing "appears to operate from within a literary culture that is the possession and medium of the ruling class that his revolutionary critique is directed towards."[36]

So what are the precedents for Shelley's couplets in *Julian and Maddalo*? How does the decorum they evoke—or violate—pertain to a familiar style that means to remain "above the use of vulgar idioms"? Hazlitt's commentary on the poem in his review of the 1824 *Posthumous Poems* (which was published by Hunt's brother and nephew, John and Henry Hunt, and opened with *Julian and Maddalo*) addresses these questions in ways that are at once discerning and perplexing. He likes *Julian and Maddalo* more than he does most of Shelley: it is "full of thoughtful and romantic humanity" and written "in Mr. Shelley's best and *least mannered* manner," despite its falling at times under "the veil of shadowy or of glittering obscurity which distinguished [his] writing."[37] As for what Hazlitt calls the "metre," that "too, will not be pleasing to every body." "It is in the antique taste of the rhyming parts of Beaumont and Fletcher and Ben Jonson—blank verse in its freedom and unbroken flow, falling into rhymes that appear altogether accidental—very colloquial in the diction—and sometimes sufficiently prosaic." For Hazlitt this is uncommonly noncommittal—curiously so, given his consistent praise elsewhere of Jonson and especially of Beaumont and Fletcher. While the stylistic influence he implies is apt enough with respect to the formal features he singles out, there is little additional evidence to support it. Percy's letters and Mary's journal show that Shelley read many of the plays Hazlitt would have had in mind, but in his only reference to Beaumont and Fletcher he compares them unfavorably to Calderón, and the single reference to Jonson commends to Peacock's attention a passage, in prose, from *Every*

Man in His Humour (it later appeared as an epigraph to *Nightmare Abbey*) (*LPBS* 2: 27, 120).

What is of interest in this part of Hazlitt's commentary is his connecting the style of *Julian and Maddalo* with a tradition in Renaissance dramatic writing notable for its integrated representations of urbane wit and urban vulgarity. Hazlitt's essay on "Vulgarity and Affectation" concludes with an extended comment on and quotation from *Eastward hoe*, written jointly by Jonson, Chapman, and Marston; it is one of the richest Jacobean examples, as Hazlitt points out, of an incipiently "Hogarthian . . . view of vulgar and genteel life" (8: 164–65). Hazlitt focuses particularly on the character of Gertrude in this play, who "rises into the air of gentility from the ground of city life" (8: 165), and he quotes with relish her appeal to Sir Petronel Flash: "Sweet knight, as soon as ever we are married, take me to thy mercy, out of this miserable city. . . . carry me out of the scent of Newcastle coal and the hearing of Bow-bell." This is the comic prose above which rise the elegant yet "very colloquial" and "sometimes sufficiently prosaic" "rhyming parts" of Jacobean city comedy that Hazlitt is reminded of by the verse of *Julian and Maddalo*, a poem far removed from any scent of Newcastle coal and the Cockney sound of Bow Bells.

But Hazlitt is reminded of other parallels, too, when he quotes three extended passages from the first third of the poem—parallels that follow very oddly on the references to Jonson, Beaumont, and Fletcher. The third passage Hazlitt quotes describes Julian's and Maddalo's somber return across the lagoon at dusk, after they have paused to look at the madhouse:

> The broad star
> Of day meanwhile had sunk behind the hill
> And the black bell became invisible
> And the red tower looked grey, and all between
> The churches, ships and palaces were seen
> Huddled in gloom;—into the purple sea
> The orange hues of heaven sunk silently.
> We hardly spoke, and soon the gondola
> Conveyed me to my lodging by the way.
> (132–40)

These lines punctuate a critical stage in the exchange between Julian and his host—I will return to the significance of "We hardly spoke" in a moment. Hazlitt disregards the "swift thought, / Winging itself with laughter" (28–29) and the ecstatic description of the Venetian sunset in his first two quoted extracts and concentrates entirely on the return home: "The march of these lines is, it must be confessed, slow, solemn, sad: . . . There is something . . . that reminds us of the arid style and matter of Crabbe's versification, or that apes the labour and throes of parturition of Wordsworth's blank-verse." Is there any poet less likely to remind one of Crabbe than Shelley? True, there are distant ties between the "matter" of *Julian and Maddalo* and Crabbe's most famous tale of guilt and insanity, *Peter Grimes*, from which Hazlitt quotes in *The Spirit of the Age*. But the movement of Shelley's strange additive syntax across the muted couplet rhymes here is nothing at all like the grimly closed couplets of the Crabbe passage that Hazlitt quotes. And as for Shelley's "aping" Wordsworth's blank verse, the observation is illuminating mainly because of Hazlitt's having to swing so completely away from Crabbe's neoclassical rhyming to verse that does not rhyme at all.

Jonson, Beaumont and Fletcher, Crabbe, Wordsworth—Hazlitt's far-flung effort to characterize the versification of *Julian and Maddalo* finally testifies to the singularity of a prosodic idiom that willfully distances itself from Hunt on the one side and Byron on the other, from Crabbe and certainly from Wordsworth. This formal idiom is intricately bound up with the voice that, in recalling, also contains not only Julian's memories and responses but the dialogue with Maddalo and the lyrical ravings of the maniac. All the represented voices in the poem are, rhetorically, ventriloquistic inflections of Julian's voice, however much we may imagine that voice as having been determined or constituted by other voices to which the poem's fiction gives us only mediated, indirect access. Shelley's idiosyncratic couplets are the formal signature of that rhetorical inclusiveness. As such, they are integral to a performance through which he represents himself as being above vulgar idioms, on a stylistic level appropriate not just to representing, but to exerting a self-defining control over, his familiar talk with Lord Byron.

5.

But there is more to be represented in *Julian and Maddalo* than Shelley's recollections of noble Italophile hospitality, however prominent "conversation" may be in the subtitle and in the text itself. In the last part of that key paragraph in the letter to Hunt, Shelley turns to the limits of the "familiar style" he has just defined: "Not that the familiar style is to be admitted in the treatment of a subject wholly ideal, or in that part of any subject which relates to common life, where the passion exceeding a certain limit touches the boundaries of that which is ideal. Strong passion expresses itself in metaphor borrowed from objects alike remote or near, and casts over all the shadow of its own greatness."[38] This, presumably, is the principle of which Shelley suddenly acknowledges Hunt to be already aware with his urbanely self-deprecating turn on the old proverb about teaching one's grandmother to suck eggs. One may be "above the use of vulgar idioms" and yet below a discourse in which "strong passion" in "common life" verges on—converges with?—the "ideal." This conviction points to moments in *Julian and Maddalo* articulated on the margins of the sophisticated give-and-take between the title figures, like Julian's rapt description of the setting sun (54 ff.), and also to instances when urbane sociability modulates fleetingly into meditative isolation:

> I love all waste
> And solitary places; where we taste
> The pleasure of believing what we see
> Is boundless, as we wish our souls to be:
> And such was this wide ocean, and this shore
> More barren than its billows . . .
> (14–19)

Julian's desire for the "boundless" here is self-consciously indulgent and can only hint at the kind of "passion" that "exceeding a certain limit touches the boundaries of that which is ideal." Still, this and other passages show "strong passion" and the "ideal" to be continually active in *Julian and Maddalo*, stressing a familiar idiom that cannot open itself to such forces—even indirectly, ironically, dialogically—without putting its own social, emotional, and formal integrity at risk.

The madman's discourse is central in this regard, both structurally and as an ambiguous indication of what cannot be said in the familiar idiom that surrounds it. Even before we encounter his "eloquence of passion" (284), however, the expressive limitations of upper-class talk appear as silences or acknowledged distortions in the flow of Julian's narrative. He quotes Maddalo's dark rejoinder to his own dismissal of the lunatics' vespers and adds:

> I recall
> The sense of what he said, although I mar
> The force of his expressions.
> (132–33)

On the way home after this exchange, "We hardly spoke" (139). Both moments anticipate Maddalo's reactions to Julian's altruistic idealism when their conversation resumes the next day.[39] "You talk Utopia" (179); "I think you might / Make such a system refutation-tight / As far as words go" (193–95). Shelley sets the poem's prevailing gentlemanly idiom against itself before subjecting it to passions that contort it beyond intelligibility, and yet produce a deeply compelling "melody" (265).

In contrast to his previous inability to represent fully the "force" of

Maddalo's "expressions," Julian says of the maniac's discourse: "I yet remember what he said / Distinctly: such impression his words made" (298–99). What Julian records is a speech that, in its lyric formality and elevation, rises still further "above the use of vulgar idioms," despite its being fragmented, in some places even shattered, by brutally visceral recollections and impulses. And yet the maniac is apprehensive that his suffering will cut him off from the "few" who can understand him:[40]

> "Ye few by whom my nature has been weighed
> In friendship, let me not that name degrade
> By placing on your hearts the secret load
> Which crushes mine to dust. . . .
> Nor dream that I will join the vulgar cry,
> Or with my silence sanction tyranny,
> Or seek a moment's shelter from my pain
> In any madness which the world calls gain."
> (344–65)

Though he is presumably oblivious to his immediate audience, the madman here addresses just those interrelations of the social, the emotional, and the discursive that concern Julian elsewhere in the poem—and Shelley outside it. His speech is represented in the same couplet form that Julian uses to articulate his own and Maddalo's discourse. The couplets are a counterforce to passion so strong that it has exceeded not only "a certain limit" but the "boundaries" of a fully comprehensible "ideal." They are also a sign that in representing what he recalls so "distinctly," Julian tries to accommodate violent suffering to the poem's established formal idiom. If the madman's emotional extremity makes such accommodation difficult, even impossible, his social and cultural position facilitates it ("He was evidently a very amiable and cultivated person," the Preface tells us). Like Julian he had himself conversed with Count Maddalo (195–97); "fame / Said he was wealthy, or he had been so" (233–34); he knew how to take familiar pleasure in the "busts and books and urns for flowers . . . And instruments of music" that Maddalo had sent to "Those rooms beside the sea" that "I fitted up for him" (252–56). The madman's speech challenges the poem as much from within as from beyond its socially determined stylistic norms.

At the end of the madman's speech, Julian recalls that he and Maddalo "Wept without shame in his society" (516). For the moment tears have replaced words—"our argument was quite forgot" (520). When talk resumes after dinner late that evening, "argument" gives way to empathic agreement about what little could be understood of the madman's situation, and about the survival in him of what Shelley described to Hunt as "a certain refinement of sentiment":

>   he had store
> Of friends and fortune once, as we could guess
> From his nice habits and his gentleness;
> These were now lost . . . it were a grief indeed
> If he had changed one unsustaining reed
> For all that such a man might else adorn.
> The colours of his mind seemed yet unworn;
> For the wild language of his grief was high,
> Such as in measure were called poetry;
>   (534–42)

The last line asks us to believe that Julian has supplied the "measure"—his measure—for the wildly elevated language of someone whose "nice habits and . . . gentleness" correspond to his own. Social continuity and familiarity underwrite, for the moment, a stylistic accommodation. Julian imagines never having to leave "sweet Venice" (545), where he could continue to delight in Maddalo's "subtle talk" (560) and at the same time patiently study to "reclaim" the maniac "from his *dark estate*" (574; emphasis added). The phrase Shelley echoes here from Pope's "The Universal Prayer" seems socially, even economically, appropriate in its new setting.[41] Julian thinks he could bring the maniac back into possession of his proper estate of bright and "subtle talk." While the maniac's discourse calls into question Julian's reformist idealism and the comfortable colloquial intimacy he enjoys with Maddalo, it also remains attached to the social and verbal hierarchies that define Julian's situation.

At the same time, the maniac's tortured grief moves him to "high language" that hovers between wild eloquence and inarticulacy, that is not just above the familiar idiom of his sympathetic aristocratic listeners but on the border of, and partly at odds with, idiom altogether. Or, we might say, the maniac's speech radically returns idiom to its etymological source in Greek *idios*, "own, personal, private," and *idioesthai*, "to make one's own"—to a condition of the discursive so embedded in private subjectivity that it threatens to turn sociolect into idiolect.[42] What brings tears to Julian's and Maddalo's eyes is language that wants to function as sublime emotional music, and only sporadically exists as intelligible social and historical discourse. Shelley is confronting, not just idealizing or sentimentalizing, an impulse in his own writing that for many readers, then as now, threatens or limits communication.

The eventual consequences of this impulse for the social and discursive world that *Julian and Maddalo* represents are very dark. A poem that celebrates familiar speech—"the actual way in which people talk with each other"—ends in a defiant refusal to speak and to be familiar. Because he was not "an unconnected man" (547), Julian had to leave Venice for

London. "After many years / And many changes" (583–84) he returns to find the discursive scene itself fundamentally altered. Maddalo's "subtle talk" is no longer there to be shared: he "was travelling far away / Among the mountains of Armenia" (586–87). If, as Shelley's editors tell us, this is an allusion to Byron's studying the Armenian language at the monastery on the island of San Lazzaro, we are being offered an image of linguistic removal and retreat. Maddalo's daughter is home to remind Julian of the old days, and of their passing, as she receives him "with a manner beyond courtesy" (594). Also "beyond courtesy" is what she reluctantly tells Julian about the maniac's momentary revival, subsequent collapse, and death: "I urged and questioned still, she told me how / All happened—but the cold world shall not know" (616–17).

Julian's refusal to communicate to the world what has been confidingly communicated to him recalls the maniac's own frantic refusal to "join the vulgar cry," his defiance of a capitulation "which the world calls gain" (362–65). The gesture is as negative socially as it is discursively. If Julian's earlier love of "all waste / And solitary places" seemed a trivial posture beside his pleasure in Maddalo's company and his "faith" in human self-liberation, it now returns as an apt figure for what it means to be "above the use of vulgar idioms" and yet cut off from any "high" language of "passion" strong enough to touch "the boundaries of that which is ideal." Within the terms of its rhetorical fiction, a poem that begins in communicative intimacy and shared imaginative pleasure ends in defiant self-silencing. Julian places himself not just above vulgarity but out of touch with the "world" altogether.

6.

Julian and Maddalo is, as Everest argues, a politically self-critical poem, the fullest expression we have of Shelley's perception of his own conflicted situation as an upper-class radical reformer and—sometime—revolutionary. But the style of the self-criticism reveals the social "boundaries" of Shelley's political imagination. The social reality enacted in the poem is criticized not by a less circumscribed social alternative, but by an encounter with "strong passion" that is idealized and defined in terms that minimize the risk to those "whom education and a certain refinement of sentiment have placed above the use of vulgar idioms." "Conversation," the "actual way in which people talk with each other," remains class-bound in *Julian and Maddalo*; it gives way only before the "high" language of sublime emotion and the silence of discursive despair.

The boundaries of Shelley's self-criticism are further delineated by the appearance of the feminine in the poem. The voice of Maddalo's daughter at the end seems at first to mediate the disjunction between the "familiar style" of urbane conversation and the fractured sublimity of "strong passion." This mediatory potential is evident in the indirect discourse produced when her voice is momentarily taken inside Julian's:

> and when I asked
> Of the lorn maniac, she her memory tasked
> And told as she had heard the mournful tale:
> That the poor sufferer's health began to fail
> Two years from my departure . . .
> (594–98)

But her mediation is incomplete because she is herself part of a rhetorical fiction that is about to fail. She supplements and ultimately reinforces, rather than displaces, the dominant masculine triangle of Julian, Maddalo, and the maniac. She first appears in the text as a child without a voice worth recording, a lovely "toy" of nature: "A serious, subtle, wild, yet gentle being, / Graceful without design and unforeseeing" (145–46). Yet even at this stage she is casually and charmingly drawn into the social ambience of her father and his friend: "For after her first shyness was worn out / We sate there, rolling billiard balls about" (156–57). When Julian encounters her years later on his return to Venice, she has become

> A woman; such as it has been my doom
> To meet with few, a wonder of the earth
> Where there is little of transcendent worth,
> Like one of Shakespeare's women:
> (589–92)

Julian's fondly idealizing simile, skewed by that ominous rhyme-word "doom" three lines before, may ironically remind us that "Shakespeare's women" are inescapably determined by the masculine structures of authority dominant in the plays. It may remind us that both Portia and Desdemona reveal their "transcendent worth" in Venetian dramatic contexts where even the most intelligent and risk-taking women face the constraints of patriarchal family and state rule.

The simile carries other implications as well, many of them thrown into relief by an exchange on Shakespeare's women in the explicitly dialogical Introduction to Anna Jameson's *Characteristics of Women: Moral, Poetical, and Historical* (1832). "Alda" explains to her skeptical male interlocutor "Medon" that Shakespeare's

> women of wit and humour are not introduced for the sole purpose of saying brilliant things, and displaying the wit of the author; they are, as I will show you, real, natural women, in whom *wit* is only a particular and oc-

casional modification of intellect. They are all, in the first place, affectionate, thinking beings, and moral agents; and *then* witty, as if by accident.... I allow that the humour is more or less vulgar; but a humorous woman, whether in high or low life, has always a tinge of vulgarity.

MEDON: I should like to see that word *vulgar* properly defined, and its meaning limited—at present it is the most arbitrary word in the language.

ALDA: Yes, like the word romantic, it is a convenient "exploding word," and in its general application signifies nothing more than "see how much finer I am than other people!" but in literature and character I shall adhere to the definition of Madame de Staël, who uses the word *vulgar* as the reverse of *poetical*. Vulgarity (as I wish to apply the word) is the *negative* in all things. In literature, it is the total absence of elevation and depth in the ideas, and of elegance and delicacy in the expression of them.[43]

For Shelley's Julian, being "like one of Shakespeare's women" means being "of transcendent worth" and beyond worldly vulgarity; for Jameson's Alda, Shakespeare's "women of wit and humour" bear an inescapable "tinge of vulgarity," as if it were the mark, the coloring, of their existence as "real, natural women," "affectionate, thinking beings, and moral agents." Jameson may be thinking positively here of Johnson's remark in the *Preface to Shakespeare* on the proximity of vulgarity and sublimity, a remark noted by A. W. Schlegel in his *Lectures on Dramatic Art and Literature* (1808): "Johnson founds the justification of the species of drama in which seriousness and mirth are mixed, on this, that in real life the vulgar is found close to the sublime."[44] Or she may be thinking negatively of Coleridge's comments on Mistress Quickly in *The Friend*, which, as Barrell shows, characteristically confound class and gender in judgments of style and intellectual self-representation.[45] Momentarily, contradictorily, and with a distinctive emphasis on the gendering of Shakespearean comedy, Jameson opens literature up to the force of the vulgar—something Shelley is unable to do in *Julian and Maddalo*. Then she abruptly appears to close it off, countering the kind of arbitrary power in the word "vulgar" that Wollstonecraft had noted by adhering to Madame de Staël's equally arbitrary—and un-Shakespearean—antithesis of "vulgar" and "poetical." Having become, "like the word romantic, ... a convenient 'exploding word,'" "vulgar" cannot be allowed to explode inconveniently. To be "like one of Shakespeare's women" is to be either above the vulgar or below the poetical: an idea of the feminine that transgresses the separation between those spheres is finally unacceptable to Jameson, as it is to Shelley.

Yet Jameson's dialogue puts both "vulgar" and "romantic" under pressures that reveal hidden, unresolved assumptions about the social power and cultural configurations on which these concepts depend. Class and gender converge around the question of what it means to regard Shakespeare's women as "affectionate, thinking beings, and moral agents," and the convergence alerts us to what is missing from Julian's fond declaration that he is conversing with "a wonder of the earth." Alda may follow Madame de Staël in perpetuating an entirely negative valuing of the "vulgar" and in finally driving it apart from the "poetical," but Jameson has produced a dialogic space in which an opposing process can begin to emerge. "[W]omen of wit and humour" in Shakespeare may be "tinged" with vulgarity as a sign of their connection to common humanity and of an always embattled agency that challenges our sense of what "poetical" as well as "romantic" can mean. More broadly, Jameson makes us aware that the anxiety to exclude the vulgar from what is "poetical" and "romantic," along with the inclination to represent the figure of woman as alternatively removed from and the bearer of this excluded vulgarity, are defining gestures in early nineteenth-century literary culture.

The various ways in which Shelley and his contemporaries place themselves discursively above, at a distance from, or in an insistently revised relation to the vulgar reveal tensions that mark a period of uneven change and deep class conflict in British society. These tensions mark radical as well as conservative ideologies, bourgeois as well as aristocratic positions. Their manifestations across the spectrum of established literary culture are increasingly affected by the demands of working-class writers and readers whose relation "to what is common and therefore vulgar" (Bourdieu) is at odds with Hunt and Hazlitt as well as with Shelley and Byron. When Anna Jameson, middle-class Irishwoman consolidating her career as a London writer in the year of the First Reform Bill and of the delayed publication of *The Mask of Anarchy*, has Alda explain that "vulgar" and "romantic" are " 'exploding word[s]' " aggressively deployed to assert social superiority, she may well have had an eye on political explosions of the kind that *The Mask of Anarchy* envisions and that the Reform Bill was meant to forestall.[46] An increasingly hegemonic bourgeoisie was still a minority class in nineteenth-century Britain; the cultural "explosions" generated as it claimed more political and cultural power could extend the discourse of vulgarity across the entire social spectrum, but they could not explode the identification of what is "practised among the common people" with what is crude, coarse, intellectually reductive.

5

"'A SUBTLER LANGUAGE WITHIN LANGUAGE'"

1.

SHELLEY'S IMAGINING of a communicative engagement between men "whom education and a certain refinement of sentiment have placed above the use of vulgar idioms" meets, at its dramatic center and at its framing margin, the figure of a woman speaking. This figure elicits passion and madness as well as affectionate admiration—and silence: "I urged and questioned still, she told me how / All happened—but the cold world shall not know" (616–17). The gesture with which *Julian and Maddalo* closes is indicative of a larger pattern in Shelley's writing, and in Romantic poetry more generally, having to do with representations of women's discursive and political authority. My particular concern in this chapter is with the contradictions and limits of male feminism as it was historically constituted (at least incipiently) during the Romantic period—and the related but distinct issue of male writers imagining themselves as, or in the condition of, women. Such imaginings take on a fluctuating political significance in the wake of the French Revolution, when women acted, for a time at least, with unprecedented consequence and were followed—as in the march on Versailles in October 1789—by men dressed as women.[1] They also situate questions about the "arbitrary imposition" of linguistic institution and use within a new set of social and psycholinguistic frames of reference.

My point of departure and of reference throughout much of the chapter is a remarkable moment from a Shelley poem that seems antithetical to *Julian and Maddalo* in its thematic and stylistic emphases. It is the scene of writing in Canto 7 of *Laon and Cythna* (or *The Revolt of Islam*, as the poem was retitled in its revised version), a scene set in an underwater cave where the revolutionary heroine Cythna has been isolated and imprisoned. At the center of this episode is Shelley's representation of a woman transforming the conditions of solitary confinement into possibilities of liberation. From this representation emerges a series of interrelated questions. What does Cythna mean when she says "'I resumed my ancient powers at length'" (7. 3075)? How are we to read the connection between her effort to communicate, through something like natural signs, with a sea-eagle who brings her food "'By intercourse of mutual imagery / Of objects'" (7. 3087–88) and that assertively reflexive discursive exploration in which her own mind takes the place of the very cave where she is confined?

> 'My mind became the book through which I grew
> Wise in all human wisdom, and its cave,
> Which like a mine I rifled through and through,
> To me the keeping of its secrets gave—'
> (7. 3100–103)

What does it mean for Cythna to extend such self-generated knowledge through writing that registers liberating transformations worked from within, rather than from outside or on the borders of, existing language—even as this writing recalls a literary tradition that makes it vulnerable to erasure by the waters of change and oblivion?

> 'And on the sand would I make signs to range
> These woofs, as they were woven, of my thought;
> Clear, elemental shapes, whose smallest change
> A subtler language within language wrought.'
> (7. 3109–12)

And finally: what difference does it make that in the first printings of both versions of the poem, though not in the drafts contained in the Bodleian notebook manuscripts, the stanzas of Cythna's narration are set off by quotation punctuation, unlike the stanzas of Laon's narration?[2]

To pursue these questions we must move beyond the point at which Earl Wasserman left off in his influential 1959 book, *The Subtler Language*, noticing as we do that by substituting the definite article—at once restrictive and universalizing—for Cythna's indefinite and open-ended *a*—"'A subtler language'"—and especially by eliminating the subsequent phrase that situates Cythna's discovery of linguistic power within a larger sphere of discursive potentiality, Wasserman was appropriating Cythna's words on behalf of an ideology and an aesthetic for which he was a formidable advocate. We must move beyond this appropriation and take up the findings of feminist critics who have discerned remarkable convergences between Shelley's representations of women's access to linguistic agency and current theories of language acquisition and performance. We will also need to explore the intertextual complications of Shelley's most ambitious poem before *Prometheus Unbound*. The figure of Cythna was in part produced, I will argue, out of Shelley's reading of Mary Wollstonecraft's two *Vindications* and her *Historical and Moral View of the Origin and Progress of the French Revolution*, and of Robert Southey's *Joan of Arc*. Shelley's representation of Cythna's access to discursive and political power needs to be understood as a rethinking simultaneously of Wollstonecraft's key interventions in the political debates of the early

1790s, and of Joan of Arc's relation to the voices of visionary prophecy in Southey's epic. The intertextual organization of the argument in this chapter will mirror, in important respects, the intertextual and rhetorical structures of Shelley's writing; my belief is that in this case such a procedure can enable, rather than weaken, a critical analysis of a male writer's attempts to represent a woman speaking and writing and acting politically. The necessary historical context for these lines of inquiry is the shifting and contradictory role of women during the French Revolution. Shelley's retrospective understanding of this role, at once critical and visionary, is fundamental to his effort to address and transform the "panic which, like an epidemic transport, seized upon all classes of men during the excesses consequent upon the French Revolution" (Preface, *The Revolt of Islam*).

2.

It has been evident for some time now that Shelley's speculations on the formation of human subjectivity through prelinguistic and linguistic phases anticipate influential developments in recent psycholinguistic theory. In chapter 2 I quoted a sentence from a 1979 review essay by Paul Fry in which, using a suggestive gestational figure, he claimed: "In the *Defence*, and everywhere in the poetry too, there is much that could be called a Lacanian psycholinguistics in embryo."[3] Fry's observation turned out to have been predictive, particularly of the application to Shelley's writing of feminist revisions of Lacanian theory. Jerrold Hogle, William Ulmer, Laura Claridge, Barbara Gelpi—and, from a quite different and more negatively judgmental feminist angle, Margaret Homans—all explore ways in which a gender-inflected critique of the Lacanian paradigm of an infant's entry into language can be brought to bear on Shelley's representations of the desiring subject's reflexive, specular construction of an inevitably divided and unstable identity.[4]

The most ambitious of these efforts, Gelpi's *Shelley's Goddess: Maternity, Language, Subjectivity*, positions the Lacanian model in dialectical opposition to alternative accounts of language acquisition and subject formation and situates its argument historically in relation to late eighteenth- and early nineteenth-century accounts of maternity, childrearing, and education. Gelpi's chief textual focus is *Prometheus Unbound*; she devotes only passing attention to other poems, including *The Revolt of Islam*. But her effort to shift analytical emphasis toward the maternal and the feminine in Shelley's great epic drama reveals much about the status of these issues in his prior work.

Gelpi's opening chapter is called "Infancy Narratives," and we may begin to assess its relevance to *The Revolt of Islam* by reminding ourselves that in Canto 7 Cythna is confined, by command of the tyrant Othman, in a womb-like cave in which she not only gives birth to a daughter but becomes, figuratively, her own mother. As William Ulmer puts it, "Carrying a baby in her womb, Cythna is herself carried in a kind of womb" (*Shelleyan Eros*, 67). The cave in Canto 7 figures the double tradition summarized by Sandra Gilbert and Susan Gubar in "The Parables of the Cave": in the course of the episode the patriarchal cave of anatomical destiny in which "woman is a prisoner of her own nature" comes to be refigured as the "place of female power, the *umbilicus mundi,* one of the great antechambers of the mysteries of transformation."[5] The transformative power comes from Cythna herself as she enacts a textual version of the mythical role of Weaver Woman, one of "those 'great weavers' who determine destiny" ("'. . . I make signs to range / These woofs, as they were woven, of my thought'").

This episode in Shelley's epic of revolutionary vision resonates with, while never entirely conforming to, Gelpi's dialectical psycholinguistic matrix, and it may be helpful to summarize that matrix before moving further into Shelley's mythopoeic configurations. There is, on the one hand, what Gelpi calls the "Lacanian-Kristevan Narrative," with its image of the mother as "'mirror' for the formation of [the infant's] sense of a coherent and bounded subjectivity," its synaesthetic account of the mother's voice as an "acoustic mirror" provoking and shaping the infant's earliest utterances, and its alternatives of a subject divided as the necessary condition of its entry into the "symbolic" order—or potentially sustained in a condition of pleasure and play through a "semiotic" (in Kristeva's unusual sense of this term) relation to the mother's corporeal aura (*Shelley's Goddess*, 7–12). In anticipation of her extended reading of *Prometheus Unbound*, Gelpi argues that "Lacanian theory works as a remarkably apt gloss for the Jupiterean [perception of the way in which speech "creates" thought; see *Prometheus Unbound* 2.4.72]. The subject, driven by the desire to fill a loss of something, a lack, and thus experiencing subjectivity as emptiness, finds itself at the same time filled, inscribed—and simultaneously annihilated—because it helplessly mirrors an Other" (16).

Yet it is in part because the Lacanian account of subject-formation is ineluctably masculinist and privative that Gelpi counterposes to it another infancy narrative that "more adequately captures Shelley's positive understanding of the link between the experience of being mothered and the acquisition of language" (17). This is "The Interpersonal Narrative" that derives most notably (as Gelpi develops it) from Daniel Stern's analysis of the first fifteen months of an infant's emotional, cognitive, and linguistic development. Stern understands this development in terms of four "domains" (rather than Lacanian "stages") of "relatedness": "emergent," "core," "intersubjective," and "verbal" "relatedness."[6] His approach is emphatically social and material: the infant's subjectivity emerges not as an illusory construct produced by Lacanian mirroring, but through an intensely interactive engagement, both immediate and recollected, with the mother and with other people. Crucial to this process in Stern's account is "affect attunement," "the intersubjective behavior between mothers and infants" in which the mother "show[s] the infant that she shares the feeling of a moment . . . not by mimicking the infant's acts or facial expressions but by a virtually instantaneous response in another sensory modality" (*Shelley's Goddess*, 19). Gelpi continues: "While not a shared system of arbitrary verbal signs, affect attunement functions as a language in that it involves communication about a common referent—the infant's experience at that moment." It is, in Stern's words, "the predominant way to commune with or indicate sharing of internal states" (*Interpersonal World of the Infant*, 142).

Building on this interactive and fundamentally social model of language acquisition, Gelpi extends Stern's references to the Marxist psychologist L. S. Vygotsky's inquiry into how children develop a sense of "'mutually negotiated meanings (*we* meanings)' for the arbitrary symbols" of language (*Interpersonal World of the Infant*, 170). From the beginning, Vygotsky insists, speech is "for others." This is true even of what Piaget identified as a child's "egocentric speech": "Three- to five-year-olds while playing together often speak only to themselves. What looks like a conversation turns out to be a collective monologue. But even such a monologue . . . actually reveals the social engagement of the child's psyche."[7] In a sense radically different from the Lacanian account, the Vygotskian paradigm gives us subject-formation within language that is always "for others." Underlying the entire cognitive-linguistic process as Vygotsky understands it are "desires and needs, . . . interests and emotions"—in other words, "an affective-volitional tendency" that is inherently social and communicative (*Thought and Language*, 252). At the same time, verbal signs themselves take on a distinctive materiality for the infant, who associates their "mutually negotiated meanings" with the mother's bodily production of responsive speech: "the word is a property, rather than the symbol of the object; a child grasps the external structure of a word-as-object earlier than the inner symbolic structure" (*Thought and Language*, 92). Here the Vygotskian account anticipates some features of the Kristevan "semiotic" but offers a materialist rather than idealist and mythopoeic analysis of them.

While Gelpi's "Interpersonal Narrative" emphasizes social and material relations as preconditions for the infant's entry into the linguistic order and thus offers a way out of Lacan's inescapably alienated and divided model of subject formation, the narrative that emerges from the work of Stern and Vygotsky does not preclude "elements of loss and alienation." The infant's early access to "amodal experience" and "nonverbal affect attunement" subsides or withers away as the price paid for acquiring a socially "normal" capacity to respond to and use the arbitrary signs and grammatical structures of adult language. What Gelpi adds is the critical dimension of gender formation: insofar as the mother is distinctively associated with social interrelationships that are presupposed and then left behind in the mutually constitutive process of language acquisition and subject formation, language eventually "takes the place of or stands in for the state of being-with-the mother" (*Shelley's Goddess*, 26). The very power and importance of the mother's role in enabling a child to realize its innate capacity to acquire language become tokens of loss and separation, of that state of being prior to full subjectivity. Whether this irony is a necessary and essential dimension of subject formation, or instead a historically contingent and changeable feature of "things as they are," is still disputed in modern and postmodern psycholinguistic theory. It is also recurrently posed by and in Shelley's writing. Through quotations from Shelley's speculative prose, and in her reading of *Prometheus Unbound*, Gelpi demonstrates the extent to which Shelley was beginning to articulate and explore questions that remain central to—and unresolved in—psycholinguistics today. These questions are also thematically and structurally central to *The Revolt of Islam*, where they emerge in a context that dramatizes their broader implications for Shelley's understanding of gender and political agency.

Cythna's narrative in Canto 7 begins with a recollection of imprisonment and madness, and of an experience of mothering indeterminately suspended between the actual and the fantasized or specular. The infant daughter of Cythna's " 'dream' " begins to mark the play of light entering the cave where they are confined through a process that conforms closely to what the French psycholinguist Bénédicte de Boysson-Bardies designates as one of the "initial conditions for the development of language": as a precondition for their being able to "process the acoustic characteristics of the sounds that constitute speech," "children must be able to organize sensory information" by deploying a genetically encoded ability to "segment it, categorize it, and organize its variations according to their semantic value."[8] In his own terms Shelley is figuring conditions of language acquisition and production that, for the child, precede the use of arbitrary signs—and for the mother turn out to change profoundly her relation to the doubly arbitrary language of tyrannical oppression. The infant daughter turns to Cythna in prelinguistic responses that elicit just that kind of "affect attunement" theorized by Stern:

> 'Methought her looks began to talk with me;
> And no articulate sounds, but something sweet
> Her lips would frame,—so sweet it could not be,
> That it was meaningless; her touch would meet
> Mine, and our pulses calmly flow and beat
> In response while we slept;'
>
> (7. 3010–15)

Suddenly in the following stanza the "'dream'"-daughter vanishes, leaving Cythna alone, hollow. Yet her mind and the cave of her confinement have been transformatively activated by the memory of reciprocal mother-daughter "response":

> 'all that cave and all its shapes possessed
> By thoughts which could not fade, renewed each one
> Some smile, some look, some gesture which had blessed
> Me heretofore:'
>
> (7. 3050–53)

The preverbal and protoverbal connections between mother and daughter are resources that eventually enable Cythna herself to resume her "'ancient powers'" and see the cave not simply as a place of imprisonment but as an enabling figure for her own mental life, as a repository of potential freedom kept alive through recollections of affective communication with her "'dream'"-daughter.

As Cythna's ontologically ambiguous memory of bearing, nurturing, communicating with a daughter gives way to loss and renewed isolation, the roles of mother and child begin to collapse and converge:

> 'We, on the earth, like sister twins lay down
> On one fair mother's bosom:—from that night
> She fled;—'
>
> (7. 3021–23)

This evanescent and precarious fusion of parent-child with sibling relationships—Cythna is momentarily her own daughter's twin sister, sharing with her a privileged access to "'one fair mother's bosom'"—glances deep into the political as well as the psychosexual implications of the poem's incest thematics. It is the recollected vanishing of her "'dream'"-daughter that produces this fantasized image of sororal-maternal mingling and that necessitates an extraordinary process of self-liberation:

> 'We live in our own world, and mine was made
> From glorious fantasies of hope departed:'
> (7. 3091–92)

> 'My mind became the book through which I grew
> Wise in all human wisdom, and its cave,
> Which like a mine I rifled through and through,
> To me the keeping of its secrets gave—'
> (7. 3100–103)

Shelley makes it textually impossible here to distinguish the literal cave of Cythna's confinement from the figurative cave of mind: both are open to sources of light from a sphere beyond, and both yield the images that eventually motivate Cythna's fashioning of "'A subtler language within language'" through which she reclaims her access to earthly struggle and renewal:

> 'And thus my prison was the populous earth—
> Where I saw—even as misery dreams of morn
> Before the east has given its glory birth—
> Religion's pomp made desolate by the scorn
> Of Wisdom's faintest smile, and thrones uptorn,
> And dwellings of mild people interspersed
> With undivided fields of ripening corn,
> And love made free,—a hope which we have nursed
> Even with our blood and tears,—until its glory burst.'
> (7. 3136–44)

This is the core of Shelley's revolutionary re-vision, the key to his attempt, two years after Waterloo, to produce a poem that might restore belief in the unrealized political potential of the French Revolution. It is politically and poetically momentous that he gives this vision to a woman in the process of discovering—from the depths of tyrannical imprisonment and in the wake of seeing her maternal identity dissolve as if it were only a "'brainless fantasy'" (7. 3027)—her own imaginative, linguistic, and political power. We can recognize these dimensions of Shelley's poetic agenda without disabling ourselves from thinking seriously about the problems and limitations in Shelley's, or in any male writer's, effort to give voice to or project a woman's self-liberation.

To grasp the connection of this mythpoeic scene of autogenous linguistic empowerment to the broader political agenda of *The Revolt of Islam*, we have to take in more of its intertextual and biographical-historical make-up. Looking backward, I believe we must read Cythna's narrative as Percy Shelley's rewriting of Wollstonecraft's *The Cave of Fancy*, the fragmentary, unfinished philosophical parable printed by Godwin in

Posthumous Works of the Author of a Vindication of the Rights of Woman (1798).⁹ Wollstonecraft describes "a cavern in the very bowels of the earth, where never human foot before had trod . . . formed by the great inundation of waters" (*WMW* 1: 192). Presiding over the cavern is the reclusive sage Sagestus, "and the various spirits, which inhabit the different regions of nature, were here obedient to his potent word." I will comment later on Shelley's turning Wollstonecraft's presiding male authority into the self-authorizing female agency of Cythna's cave. Some suggestions for this transformation come from chapter 3 of Wollstonecraft's own fragment, where a female "Spirit" tells the story of her mother and of her encounter with "a girl, who stood weeping on the common" (*WMW* 1: 205).

Reading forward from Cythna's parable of the cave, we meet another version of this parable produced eight years later in the Introduction to *The Last Man. By the Author of Frankenstein* (1826). Mary Shelley here constructs a fictive authorial identity from a rewriting of Percy Shelley's rewriting of the Wollstonecraftian, by now multiply maternal, fragment. On a visit to Naples the author-narrator enters, with a "companion," the "gloomy cavern of the Cumaean Sibyl." Disappointed with the first space identified for them by their guides as the "Sibyl's Cave," she insists on going forward, through a network of "passages," into an interior cavern, where they find

> piles of leaves, fragments of bark, and a white filmy substance, resembling the inner part of the green hood which shelters the grain of the unripe Indian corn. . . . At length my friend, who had taken up some of the leaves strewed about, exclaimed, "This *is* the Sibyl's cave; these are Sibylline leaves." On examination we found that all the leaves, bark, and other substances, were traced with written characters. What appeared to us more astonishing, was that these writings were expressed in various languages . . . they seemed to contain prophecies, detailed relations of events but lately passed; names, now well known, but of modern date; and often exclamations of exultation or woe, of victory or defeat, were traced on their thin scant pages. . . . We made a hasty selection of the leaves, whose writing one at least of us could understand.¹⁰

On these "leaves" the author-narrator "labours," at first with her companion and then alone, generating a text that combines transcription ("some parts . . . I have faithfully transcribed from my materials") with "adaptation and translation." The result is *The Last Man*, Mary Shelley's troping of her mother's unfinished "tale" and of Cythna's woven inscriptions of "'A subtler language within language,'" a novel that envisions the end of human history by reimagining her own.

Between Percy Shelley's poetic imaging of a revolutionary woman's cave of prophetic self-discovery and Mary Shelley's novelistic recasting of an encounter with Sibylline leaves came an actual visit to the Grotto of the Cumaean Sibyl, on the banks of Lake Avernus just north of Naples, on 8 December 1818.[11] Some five months after this visit, Percy encouraged Mary to write a play about Beatrice Cenci, to whose tragedy as it was recorded in a manuscript history of the Cenci family that Mary had "copied or translated" in May 1818 he himself turned with great intensity. Although Mary declined the invitation to write her version of this narrative of brutal paternal incest, on 4 August 1818 she began a different kind of father-daughter incest narrative that would eventually be titled *Mathilda*.[12] Her initial title for it was *The Fields of Fancy*, an obvious allusion to Wollstonecraft's *The Cave of Fancy* and an indication of how continuously she and Percy associated their writings about women's relation to political and linguistic power with "the Author of A Vindication of the Rights of Woman," as Godwin identified Wollstonecraft on the title-page of her *Posthumous Works*.

3.

For all its psycholinguistic suggestiveness, Percy Shelley's imagining of Cythna's access to a "'subtler language within language'" is rooted historically and politically in his broader determination to reawaken the revolutionary energy of the 1790s in the face of post-Waterloo triumphalism and reaction. Fundamental to Shelley's sense of this revolutionary decade was his awareness that, in England as well as in France, women had entered public life in new ways and had made unprecedented claims to political participation and authority. Wollstonecraft was the central figure for Shelley in this regard, and in dedicating *The Revolt of Islam* to Mary Wollstonecraft Godwin he was locating his epic in relation to her mother's writing of the 1790s and its continuing relevance:

> They say that thou wert lovely from thy birth,
> Of glorious parents, thou aspiring Child.
> I wonder not—for One then left this earth
> Whose life was like a setting planet mild,
> Which clothed thee in the radiance undefiled
> Of its departing glory; still her fame
> Shines on thee, through the tempests dark and wild
> Which shake these latter days;
> (Dedication 12, 100–107)

This idealized elegiac tribute to Wollstonecraft disguises the mixed influence on *The Revolt of Islam* of her legacy—of her claims on behalf of women's liberation, and also of her reactions to the French Revolution. Reconstructing more of the Wollstonecraftian dimension of Shelley's poem will cast a politically revealing light on the theoretical issues that have caught the eye of so many recent commentators on Cythna's cave-scene of writing. In the process we will need to rethink Wollstonecraft's own identity as a writer as it evolved during the critical period of her residency in France, from December 1792 until early 1795.

Wollstonecraft's responses to the Revolution involve striking antitheses of engagement and removal, solidarity and rejection. Having fiercely defended the earliest phase of the Revolution against Burke's counterrevolutionary attack in *A Vindication of the Rights of Men* (1790), and then having challenged the male-centered restrictions of the Declaration of the Rights of Man and Citizens in *A Vindication of the Rights of Woman* (1792), Wollstonecraft went alone to live in Paris in December 1792, near the end of the period between the August overthrow of the monarchy and September Massacres, and the execution of Louis XVI in January 1793. She took lodgings in the house of French acquaintances in the Marais and was soon actively in touch with English and American expatriates such as Thomas Paine, Helen Maria Williams, Thomas Christie, Joel and Ruth Barlow—and with their Girondin friends. Yet Wollstonecraft felt more isolated from than connected to the immediacy of the Revolution. Writing to Joseph Johnson on 26 December, she describes the King's procession through the streets on his way to trial. "For the first time since I entered France I bowed to the majesty of the people, and respected the propriety of behaviour so perfectly in unison with my own feelings" (*WMW* 6: 363). But this affirmation of solidarity is quickly countered by an inexplicable sadness: "I can scarcely tell you why, but an association of ideas made the tears flow insensibly from my eyes." This leads in turn to a more general confession of haunted loneliness:

> Though my mind is calm, I cannot dismiss the lively images that have filled my imagination all the day.—Nay, do not smile, but pity me; for, once or twice, lifting my eyes from the paper, I have seen eyes glare through a glass-door opposite my chair, and bloody hands shook at me. Not the distant sound of a footstep can I hear.—My apartments are remote from those of the servants, the only persons / [indicates page-break in original printing] who sleep with me in an immense hotel, one folding door opening after another.—I wish I had even kept the cat with me!—I want to see something alive; death in so many frightful shapes has taken hold of my fancy.—I am going to bed—and, for the first time in my life, I cannot put out the candle.

This "nightmare fantasy," as Claire Tomalin characterizes it ("it cannot have been literal truth"), is moving not just because it "reads like a forecast of the Terror" but because it conveys the degree to which Wollstonecraft felt cut off from any active, practical engagement with political events.[13] As Janet Todd indicates, the situation accentuated unresolved tensions in Wollstonecraft's political thinking: "she was never a full republican though using a republican analysis to attack the injustice of all inherited privilege."[14]

The subsequent convergence—or nonconvergence—in 1793 and 1794 of Wollstonecraft's life with critical political developments in Paris is crucial to understanding her influence on *The Revolt of Islam*.[15] As the execution of the King and England's declaration of war against the French republic led to severe economic crisis and savage counterrevolutionary revolt in areas such as the Vendée, Wollstonecraft's own life was increasingly dominated by her love affair with Gilbert Imlay. "[W]hatever Mary felt on behalf of her French friends," Tomalin observes, "she had moved into a different mental world" (143). In May and June, when popular insurrection led to the Jacobins' defeat of the Girondins and the latter's expulsion from the National Convention, Wollstonecraft was in the process of moving from Paris proper to Neuilly, then still a small village separated from the city by a toll-gate or *barrière*. Throughout the summer, as events in Paris moved ominously toward the crisis of the autumn months and the Terror, Wollstonecraft gave herself to a life of erotic and domestic intimacy and seclusion that she had never known before. At the same time she was haunted by erotic anxieties with which she was all too familiar. "Yet, I shall not (let me tell you before these people enter, to force me to huddle away my letter) be content with only a kiss of DUTY," she wrote to Imlay, who was spending most of his time on business in Paris: "—you *must* be glad to see me—because you are glad—or I will make love to the *shade* of Mirabeau" (*WMW* 6: 370). Wollstonecraft was probably already pregnant when she wrote this letter to her lover in August.

"Whilst Mary remained at Neuilly," Tomalin imagines, "life inside the gates of Paris took on the inconsequence of a feverish dream" (147). But in September, with her pregnancy confirmed and Imlay away even more of the time, Wollstonecraft could no longer remain alone in Neuilly. She returned to Paris just as the Jacobin government, pushed by another insurrection from below in Paris, formally instituted the Terror as the only way to defend the Revolution. Now Wollstonecraft found herself swept up in events she could do nothing to influence: the arrest of English expatriots living in Paris on 9 October; the execution of Marie Antoinette on 16 October; the execution of the Girondin leadership on 31 October. Wollstonecraft herself avoided arrest only because Imlay registered her as his wife, giving her the protection of United States citizenship.

It was also during the autumn of 1793 that the immediate political involvment of women in the French Revolution took a decisive turn. An impressive tradition of feminist scholarship, recently supplemented for

English readers by the translation of Dominique Godineau's *Citoyennes tricoteuses: Les femmes du peuple à Paris pendant la Révolution française*, has traced the rise, suppression, and disintegration of women's active intervention in French revolutionary politics, from the fall of the Bastille and women-led march on Versailles in 1789 through the Convention's abolition of the Revolutionary Republican Women (Société des Citoyennes Républicaines Révolutionnaires) and other women's clubs on 30 October 1793.[16] Wollstonecraft's connection to this history was inevitably partial and selective, given her circumstances. Even allowing for these circumstances, however, Wollstonecraft's relation to women and politics in revolutionary Paris is difficult to understand. She admired Manon Roland, who opposed the women's clubs and political militancy—and who received no women at her twice-weekly salons in the rue de la Harpe. Wollstonecraft must have been aware of the more flamboyant women revolutionaries who associated their cause with the Girondins, Olympe de Gouges and Théroigne de Méricourt, but makes no mention of them in her writing.[17] And she was not just distant from, but disgusted by and afraid of, the Revolutionary Republican Women and the other female militants among the sansculottes who are the subjects of Godineau's book.

The threat both to foreigners and to constitutional monarchists in the autumn of 1793 has been assumed to account for Wollstonecraft's failure to engage directly with or comment on the crisis in women's participation in the Revolution. Still, given Wollstonecraft's founding status in the history of feminism, it is surprising and disturbing that Tomalin is able to conclude that "she remained entirely silent on . . . the whole feminist movement in France," that "she knew nothing of the provincial women's clubs, and . . . does not seem to have attended any of the reputable ones in Paris either" (157–58). Todd, also perplexingly, attributes Wollstonecraft's "lack of comment on the stifling of the female clubs by the Jacobins" to "her horrified reaction to the later exploits of the mob inspired by Robespierre and the Terror" (219). Whatever the balance of practical caution during the Terror, personal constraints arising from her affair with Imlay and her pregnancy, and ideological allegiance to those most suspicious of the Paris Commune and of the sansculottes, Wollstonecraft's distant, occluded relation to women's involvment in the Revolution constitutes a major difficulty in her political legacy. The difficulty decisively marks the book that she began writing in the summer of 1793 and that was published by Joseph Johnson after the fall of Robespierre and the Jacobins in late summer 1794, *An Historical and Moral View of the Origin and Progress of the French Revolution; and the Effect It Has Produced in Europe*.

Only recently has *An Historical and Moral View* received the critical attention it deserves. And even now Wollstonecraft's commentary on women's participation in the first year of the Revolution—"Volume the First," the only one written, ends with the march on Versailles to force Louis XVI to return to Paris in October 1789—has been the focus of little sustained analysis. Yet this must have been a part of the book that Wollstonecraft's contemporary readers approached with intense anticipation.

In the Preface Wollstonecraft gives slight indication of that fear of political reprisal often attributed to her, referring quite boldly to "the pressure of the calamitous horrours produced by desperate and enraged factions" while insisting that "it is the uncontaminated mass of the french [sic] nation, whose minds begin to grasp the sentiments of freedom, that has secured the equilibrium of the state" (WMW 6: 6). When she turns to the Parisian masses in Book 5, however, and particularly to the aggressive leadership of the female sansculottes in the march on Versailles, it is an overdetermined revulsion from contaminating violence and mindless "vulgarity" that drives the writing. The counterrevolutionary machinations of Marie Antoinette and the "scarcity of bread, the common grievance of the revolution," fade into the background as "on the fifth of October a multitude of women by some impulse were collected together":

> The concourse, at first, consisted mostly of market women, and the lowest refuse of the streets, women who had thrown off the virtues of one sex without having power to assume more than the vices of the other. A number of men also followed them, armed with pikes, bludgeons, and hatchets; but they were strictly speaking a mob, affixing all the odium to the appellation it can possibly import; and not to be confounded with the honest multitude, who took the Bastille. (WMW 6: 196–97)

Though Wollstonecraft goes on to claim that this mob was enflamed and paid by "assassins" in the hire of "the despicable duke of Orleans," this conviction does nothing to mitigate her condemnation of "the tumultuous concourse of women" who "arrived at Versailles" (WMW 6: 200–201). Even when flagrantly provoked to self-defensive retaliation, the aggression of these women is treated with impassioned censure:

> Some women now returning to Paris . . . were unfortunately maltreated by a detachment of body-guards, commanded by a nobleman; and the volunteers of the Bastille coming to their assistance, two men, and three horses, were killed on the spot. These same irritated women meeting, likewise, the parisian militia, on their way to Versailles, gave them an exaggerated description of the conduct of the guards. (WMW 6: 203).

Wollstonecraft's condemnatory observations culminate in her account of "the singular army of the females" who violated the Queen's private chamber:

The altar of humanity had been profaned—The dignity of freedom had been tarnished—The sanctuary of repose, the asylum of care and fatigue, the chaste temple of a woman, I consider the queen only as one, the apartment where she consigns her senses to the bosom of sleep, folded in it's [sic] arms forgetful of the world, was violated with murderous fury. (*WMW* 6: 209)

Wollstonecraft's previous description of Marie Antoinette's corruption and duplicity are forgotten in this passage, indebted as it obviously is to the very sentimentalizing of aristocratic privilege in Burke's *Reflections* that Wollstonecraft had attacked in her first *Vindication*.[18]

It is not that we expect from Wollstonecraft an endorsement, projected indirectly through her account of the events of 1789, either of Jacobin policies in 1793–1794 or of the militancy of sansculottes women during the early 1790s. Gary Kelly is right to describe her "political values" as those of "a constitutional monarchist, gradualist, supporter of capitalism and the rights of property and exponent of a merit system that would in effect ensure the social and political dominance of the professional middle class." But Kelly's specific case for *An Historical and Moral View* as a "revolutionary feminist reading of the Revolution" that successfully combines "discourses conventionally regarded as 'masculine' and 'feminine'" minimizes the contradictions and limitations of Wollstonecraft's political perspective and of her authorial positioning and agency in this text.[19] What Percy Shelley and Mary Wollstonecraft Godwin found when they read *An Historical and Moral View* in December 1814 (it was almost certainly around this time that they also read *The Cave of Fancy* in *Posthumous Works*) was not a controlled and achieved dialogic synthesis of "personal and often figurative style" with "historical detachment"—of "personal voice" and "philosophical history"—but instead a text marked throughout by the selectivity, partiality, and anxiety of Wollstonecraft's position as the ex-patriot reformer who had, in her most famous book, addressed the condition of women by "pay[ing] particular attention to those in the middle class, because they appear to be in the most natural state" (*Vindication*, 9). That the composition of Wollstonecraft's book about the French Revolution coincided with her first pregnancy and her first experience as a mother must also have left its mark on Percy's and Mary's different ways of regarding this moment in her life.

The Enlightenment tradition of "philosophical history" was, as Jane Rendall has shown, a major influence on Wollstonecraft's authorial "self-identification" in *An Historical and Moral View*. This tradition was defined by masculine voices—particularly by those of Scottish historians such as John Millar, William Robertson, Alexander Jardine, and Hugh Blair. Rendall's project of "[m]apping the masculine . . . voices she adopted" helps us grasp how Wollstonecraft went about trying to discover a distinctive historical language within language to register, as she puts it in her Preface, the "rapid changes, the violent, the base, and nefarious assassinations, which have clouded the vivid prospect that began to / spread a ray of joy and gladness over the gloomy horizon of oppression" (*WMW* 6: 6).[20] Rendall stresses "the difficulties and contradictions for a woman writer in claiming" the voice of "philosophical historian," arguing that Wollstonecraft "confronted the barriers of a gendered genre directly" but never fully overcame them.[21] This is especially evident, Rendall implies, in Wollstonecraft's account of the participation of women in the Revolution.

Ashley Tauchert has indirectly suggested some of the ways in which these matters might be pursued by taking up the "difficulties and contradictions" Rendall locates and exploring them in a speculatively psychoanalytic as well as historical direction. Although "Mary Wollstonecraft" appears on the title-page, "[t]he author/narrator of the *Historical and Moral View* does not declare her gender in the course of the narrative," as Wollstonecraft had so assertively done in the two *Vindications*. Instead, Tauchert argues, we encounter "a representative, ungendered narrator whose narrative of the Revolution could not be identified with Wollstonecraft's personal experience of that Revolution."[22] Tauchert goes on to argue, following Janet Todd and Meena Alexander, "that this performance, and the sexless discourse to which it makes a claim, are explicable in terms of Wollstonecraft's first experience of maternity."[23] Tauchert's further claim, that Wollstonecraft needed to avoid representing "the King's decapitated body" to mask a "castrating desire" of which this represented decapitation would have been the sign, may be difficult to sustain in the face of our acknowledging that Wollstonecraft's "Volume the First" stops three years short of the execution of Louis XVI. But Tauchert's analysis of the bearing Wollstonecraft's pregnancy might have had on the rhetorical strategies and political argument of *An Historical and Moral View* is worth investigating, particularly with Shelley's later construction of a revolutionary woman warrior in mind. Noting that Wollstonecraft began her account of the Revolution before she knew she was pregnant, Tauchert suggests that this knowledge would have aroused Wollstonecraft's determination to defy yet again Rousseau's assertion that the bearing of children was a woman's essential "business" in life. That Rousseau's case in *Emile* received fresh political endorsement in late 1793 when the Jacobins repudiated women's organized political intervention and exhorted them instead to bear and nurture a new generation of loyal republican citizens may well have confirmed Wollstonecraft's decision to write not as a woman but as a genderless "philosophical historian."

When Shelley returned to Wollstonecraft's own representation of the Revolution, as he must certainly have done when he began *The Revolt of Islam* in the spring and summer of 1817, he found suppression and avoidance as well as inspiration and engagement—particularly when it came to the role of women in the most important historical transformation of the era. The conflict between the personal and the political aspects of Wollstonecraft's experiences in France, her distance even from most of the middle-class women participants in the Revolution, her disgust for "les femmes du peuple" and for the Parisian men who followed them "disguised in women's clothes" (*WMW* 6: 201)—all of this would have coincided with some of Shelley's own attitudes and yet left him needing to look through and beyond as well as to Wollstonecraft for images of the heroic revolutionary woman writer. And for images of the heroic revolutionary mother. While Cythna occupies a series of overlapping female subject-positions—sister/lover/mother/daughter—it is around her enactments of mothering and self-mothering in Canto 7 that *The Revolt of Islam* weaves its overdetermined intertextual vision of the revolutionary liberation of women.

4.

One of the places Shelley looked in his need to transfigure Wollstonecraft's powerful but conflicted exemplarity was to the early poetry of Robert Southey. That Shelley was intensely interested in *Joan of Arc*, written between 1793 and 1795 during Southey's hot prorevolutionary youth—and with the substantial collaboration of Coleridge in the first edition dated 1796—should come as no surprise, given what Stuart Curran, Marilyn Butler, and others have shown about the influence on Shelley of later Southey poems, *Thalaba the Destroyer* (1801) and *The Curse of Kehama* (1811).[24] Despite his political differences with Southey, which deepened into revulsion (for reasons analyzed years ago by Kenneth Cameron) during the very months of 1817 when he was writing the poem initially titled *Laon and Cythna*, Shelley continued to take Southey seriously as a poet.[25] There are reasons for thinking that Shelley's conversations with Southey at Keswick during December 1811 and January 1812 would have come back to him as he was writing a poem that, as he says in the Preface, aimed to counter the moral ruin and "infectious gloom" that had settled over most of the early supporters of the French Revolution. On 25 July 1811, five months before his visit to Southey, Shelley ardently recommended *Joan of Arc* to Elizabeth Hitchener (*LPBS* 1: 126). It is unclear whether Shelley read Southey's epic in the first edition of 1796, the only one containing Coleridge's substantial contribution to the second book, or in the revised editions of 1798 or 1806. We do know, however, that Shelley would have read Coleridge's *The Destiny of Nations*, which contains the lines he contributed to Southey's *Joan of Arc* plus 148 additional lines on the subject that he published separately in the *Morning Post* on 26 December 1797, in *Sibylline Leaves*: he asked Ollier to send him a copy of this volume, in which *The Destiny of Nations* was first published, on 13 July 1817, two or three months after he began work on the poem he would eventually call *The Revolt of Islam*.[26] It is pertinent to what I have said about the intertextual connections between Shelley's epic and both Wollstonecraft's *The Cave of Fancy* and Mary Shelley's Introduction to *The Last Man* that Shelley encountered in Coleridge's "Collection of Poems" an explicit appropriation of the Virgilian image of the cave-scene of prophetic female writing. It may well have been the lines on Joan of Arc in *The Destiny of Nations* that sent Shelley back to Southey's *Joan of Arc*, one of the most ambitious attempts of the 1790s to address the French Revolution in verse. Southey's poem would certainly have mattered to Shelley, both at the time of his first meetings with Southey and six years later when he was writing his own revisionary revolutionary epic.

Curran puts us in touch with the force of the nineteen-year-old Southey's ambitious enterprise, begun six months after the execution of Louis XVI and seven months after England declared war on the French republic. "Everything about the poem projects an image of the *enfant terrible* . . . Southey went out of his way to ensure it," he writes: "In a climate of growing repression of Jacobin sympathizers, accompanied by a concerted attempt to muzzle the press, [Southey] audaciously celebrates a French campaign for liberation from British rule. His central figure . . . is not a man but a woman of courage, . . . vision—and also, as one might expect in the 1790s, of sensibility."[27] Looking back at Southey's epic two years after Waterloo, Shelley found an even fuller pattern than Curran indicates from which to develop his own revolutionary woman warrior: a passionately inspired militant who leads her nation to victory over its oppressors only to be sold out by her male rulers, tried as a witch and a heretic, and burned at the stake. The contradictory mythic accretions around Joan of Arc since the time of her political intervention and death, indicated by the chapter titles in Marina Warner's 1981 study, would have fascinated Shelley: "Prophet," "Harlot of the Armagnacs," "Heretic," "Ideal Androgyne," "Knight," "Amazon," "Personification of Virtue," "Child of Nature."[28] In the last of these chapters Warner places Southey's poem in the context of appropriations of Joan of Arc as peasant nationalist martyr by both Left and Right during and after the French Revolution. That by 1814 Coleridge had become disgusted with his and Southey's "transmogrification of the fanatic Virago into a modern novel-pawing

Proselyte of the age of Reason, a Tom Paine in Petticoats," indicates precisely the grounds for assuming Shelley's interest in what they had done.[29] And that Shelley saw the point of returning to Southey's early revolutionary allegory in 1817 is confirmed by his initially having tried to get *Laon and Cythna* copublished by the Olliers and by Sherwood, Neely, and Jones: the latter were responsible for the sensationally embarrassing publication of Southey's *Wat Tyler* in February of 1817.[30]

Southey—and in a different way Coleridge, both as Southey's collaborator and as a poet writing about Joan of Arc on his own—are sustainedly concerned with the source of the voices that speak to and through their "missioned Maid." Mystical voices were a traditional part of the legend, as Françoise Meltzer has recently emphasized: Joan had claimed that St. Catherine, St. Margaret, and St. Michael had told her to go to the Dauphin and lead his forces to victory, and this claim, variously recorded and interpreted, figured critically in her trial and execution. Southey and Coleridge approach the matter with a divided agenda. Southey remarks in the Preface to later editions of *Joan of Arc* that the mystery surrounding the source of Joan's authority makes her story "peculiarly fit for poetry. The aid of angels and devils is not necessary to raise her above mankind; she has no gods to lackey her, and inspire her with courage, and heal her wounds; the Maid of Orleans acts wholly from the workings of her own mind."[31] These pronouncements may seem to suggest that we have already arrived at Cythna's condition of self-generated prophetic wisdom. But in the poem itself Joan often listens to voices other than her own—never directly to the voice of God, but recurrently to voices in the phenomena of nature, as Marina Warner emphasizes. And in the section of *Joan of Arc* contributed by Coleridge to Book 2 of the first edition, she listens to a male "tutelary spirit," a "guardian Power" that may be said to represent, argues Robert Sternbach, "the will to French national self-determination—and ultimately democratic freedom—working itself through Joan."[32] The problem for Southey and Coleridge is familiar to readers of British Romantic writing: how to represent an authority higher than or beyond, yet not ultimately other than, "the workings of [Joan's] mind"—how to show her mind "Working but in alliance with the works / Which it beholds," to adapt the language of Book 2 of *The Prelude* in which *authority* is explicitly absorbed into Wordsworthian *agency*. The various textual configurations of this problem are too intricate to trace in detail here, given Southey's revisions from edition to edition and Coleridge's initial collaboration and then separate elaboration of the Joan of Arc material. What we can say for certain, though, is that this very problem about how and where to locate Joan's voice of authority would have been apparent in any version of *Joan of Arc* that Shelley might have read.

Shelley's rewriting of this earlier Romantic representation of a woman's access to discursive and political authority is in one sense an overtly feminist version of his rewriting of Wordsworth, Coleridge, and Southey in *Alastor*, *Mont Blanc*, and other earlier poems: he radically intensifies the reflexive or autogenous impulse, locates it principally in the self-realizations of a powerful female figure, and extends it through a dynamic of specular projective reciprocity. Jerrold Hogle reads this dynamic in *The Revolt of Islam* under the heading "Narcissism and the Gaze of the Other," and his doing so enables us to see both the radical brilliance of Shelley's response to the problem of authority in Southey's *Joan of Arc* and the contradictions in his revisionary alternative. The guiding principle of Hogle's analysis is Shelley's own prose fragment "On Love": "There is something within us which from the instant that we live and move thirsts after its likeness." "Primary narcissism" in the Shelleyan/Freudian/Lacanian sense elaborated by Hogle is fundamental to the formation of subjectivity—not on naively solipsistic grounds, but because the Shelleyan subject constitutes itself by finding this "thirst after its own likeness" mirrored back to it from "a specific counterpart (a person or environment or symbolic order)."[33] By extending Shelley's own reading of anthropomorphic projection in Hume's *Four Dissertations*, Hogle shows how Cythna and Laon enact this double narcissistic transference on a political as well as a personal level. Cythna's role in articulating the political implications of the dynamic Hogle emphasizes is pivotal: it is she who reveals, in her speeches to the sailors who bear her away from the sea-cave of confinement and self-realization in Canto 8, that "the most oppressive and hierarchical transfer of 'selfhood' outside the supposed 'self' [to a God or King] is . . . the same as the one in the most loving and equal of interchanges . . . the foundations of tyrannical ideology lie in what can happen to the movement of desire that also serves to promote love" (96–97).

Hogle's reading of *The Revolt of Islam* helps us articulate the difference between Shelley's and Southey's women warriors imagined as acting "wholly from the workings of [their] own mind." It also helps us understand aspects of the problem of authority I have been trying to define that are not resolved in Shelley's text. Hogle wants us to value Shelley's vision of how "the most loving and equal of interchanges" can overcome political oppression by recognizing its own deep relation to the potential for such oppression—but he sees that this idealized reflexive egalitarianism gives way to a persistent tendency toward hierarchy. At one revealing moment in his reading he indicates that the hierarchy is less a matter of gaze than of voice—the inescapable privileging of one voice over another. Cythna "can complete the process" of reciprocating self-projection "to the point of really comprehending it," he writes, "only by telling all" that she has learned through her subtler language within language "to Laon" (98). We are inevitably reminded of that moment later in Shelley's poetry when Maddalo's daughter finally tells Julian "How / All happened" (*Julian and Maddalo* 616–17), and Julian refuses to transmit what he hears the voice of the woman say.

In *The Revolt of Islam* we are told "How / All happened"—through the voice of the male protagonist. Hogle's observation repositions us to take up the question of the quotation punctuation that marks off Cythna's voice in the first printed versions of the poem. She, not Laon, is Shelley's hero of projected reflexivity. But as Nigel Leask and others have pointed out, in the rhetorical structure of *The Revolt of Islam* it is only through, or from within, Laon's voice that she speaks. The poet-narrator is guided into the presence of the two departed spirits in Canto 1 by the figure of a woman who speaks with a fierce authority ("Speak not to me, but hear!" she says in stanza 25), but this woman's words are not set off by inverted commas and thereby differentiated from the unmarked discourse that joins the poet-narrator to Laon as the poem's primary narrator.[34] I will return in a moment to this textual difference.

At this point the problem of Shelley's effort to represent the voice of the heroic woman revolutionary needs to be posed very starkly. Is Shelley not a male feminist at all but rather, in Alan Richardson's terms, just one in a line of Romantic "colonizers of the feminine"?[35] Is that what a male feminist inevitably is: a man whose identification with women's struggle against oppression is really a disguised or furtive effort to control, dominate, appropriate the power of that struggle? Leask articulates a version of this perspective in arguing that in Shelley's epic "a manifest feminism is undone by the poem's investment in a discourse of latent imperialism."[36] Reading *The Revolt of Islam* in relation to Southey's *Joan of Arc* suggests a way of taking seriously the force of Richardson's and Leask's arguments while making some further political and historical discriminations. Shelley imagines a degree of autonomy for Cythna that is quite distinct from the ambitious yet compromised depictions of Joan of Arc by Southey and Coleridge in their pantisocratic days. That Shelley's representation of Cythna's oppression and self-liberation is, in part, a wishful self-portrait—that he wants to be Cythna, not just to possess her as her fantasized masculine counterpart—makes a difference recognizable in the printed text's diacritical registering that such identification is always wishful, and always fraught with the possibility of subjection. It is a valuable ramification of Hogle's argument that the reversion to hierarchized rhetorical configurations in *The Revolt of Islam* signals an awareness on Shelley's part that the idealized mutual self-constitution he celebrates cannot be sustained. The rhetorical locating and marking off of Cythna's voice is already there in the version of the poem that makes her Laon's sister rather than his cousin, and it should be read as a sign of difference within textual processes of specular projection, as a denial of any claim of unmediated access to the feminine in a text in which the feminine is so evidently a projection of the male writer's desire. The Victorian feminist Mathilde Blind told the readers of the *Westminster Review* in 1870 that while previously "all poets creating ideals of woman . . . had depicted her invariably in her relation as either wife or mistress, mother or daughter—that is, as a supplement to man's nature," Shelley had imagined in Cythna "a new female type."[37] Some readers today will insist that Cythna remains a "supplement," yet Mathilde Blind's insight persists: in Shelley's revisionary revolutionary fiction Cythna claims her own mind as "'the *type* of all'" by becoming self-consciously the producer of historically constrained yet liberating supplements. Shelley's representation of a woman's linguistic and political agency through the figure of Cythna is not just another instance of narcissistic Romantic ventriloquism. The ventriloquist does not quote the voice of another but produces an illusion that his voice is that other's voice. This is not the structure of Shelley's rhetorical fiction in *The Revolt of Islam*.

5.

I want to conclude this chapter by bringing into sharper focus the psycholinguistic and political implications of the enfolded intertextual patterns in *The Revolt of Islam*. Some valuable help here is to be found in Kenneth Johnston's reading of Wordsworth's last effort to continue *The Recluse*, the 1826 lines "Composed when a probability existed of our being obliged to quit Rydal Mount as a Residence." For a reader unfamiliar with this poem, it comes as a shock of more than mild surprise to move from the stuffy occasional title of Wordsworth's lines to the provocative questioning title of Johnston's essay: "Narcissus and Joan: Wordsworth's Feminist Recluse?" Wordsworth's elegiac anticipation of leaving Rydal Mount and its "pellucid Spring" (called Nab Well) includes prominently paired extended references to "the fair Narcissus" (79 ff.) and "the Maid of Arc" (165 ff.). Both, Johnston shows through an attentive reading of the published lines in their manuscript variants, "are veiled versions of Wordsworth himself. . . . In the poem's obscure progression from Narcissus to Joan of Arc, we can sense Wordsworth's complicated efforts to work out, through metaphor, a formula for the sociopolitical effect of artistic creativity in the ordinary world."[38]

Johnston constructs a late Wordsworthian analogue to the politically divergent handlings of the Joan of Arc figure in Southey, Coleridge, and Shelley. If Wordsworth's "progression from Narcissus to Joan of Arc" seems more "obscure" than theirs, it may be because we are not listening closely enough to the mediations of Miltonic self-projection in the description of the waving ferns reflected in Nab Well:

> The Other, glass'd in thy unruffled breast,
> Partook of every motion, met, retired,
> And met again . . .
> (72–74)

This is Eve at the pool in Book 4 of *Paradise Lost*, as well as Wordsworth himself looking over the side of a slow-moving boat at his own reflection in Book 4 of *The Prelude*. When earlier in the poem Wordsworth asks his beloved "translucent Spring" "What witchcraft, meek Enchantress, equals thine?" (29), we know—and we know he knows—that the answer is the one given by Ovid's Narcissus: *iste ego sum: sensi, nec me mea fallit imago* ("Oh, I am he! I have felt it, I know now my own image").[39]

Wordsworth's "Maid of Arc" stands over her "Fountain of the Fairies" as a redeemed female Narcissus, as a redeemed Eve who listens not to the working of her own mind but to an echo of Milton's warning voice:

> a Voice
> Reached her with supernatural mandates charged
> More awful than the chambers of dark earth
> Have virtue to send forth.
> (174–77)

This is the Tory countertype to Shelley's Cythna, weaving within her chamber of dark earth a "'subtler language within language'" from reflections on and of her own imaginative power. Yet Wordsworth's poem reinforces an awareness that however different Cythna may be from the traditional image of a heroic woman attuned to nature and dependent on its "supernatural mandates," she remains a reflexive projection of a male writer's desire for erotic, imaginative, and political completion.

We can see more clearly now that the eventually censored and suppressed trope of sibling incest in Shelley's conception of Cythna forms part of a broader, more entangled dynamic through which the male poet's desire for self-realizing freedom is invested in the figure of a woman whose voice is "like the voice of his own soul" (*Alastor* 153). This figure incorporates at different moments in Shelley's writing the ambiguously differentiated roles of mother/sister/daughter/lover. Purged of the brutal, abusive political character it always has in Shelley's representations of father/daughter incest (Othman's rape of Cythna prefigures Cenci's rape of Beatrice) and transferred onto its erotically mystified mother/son alternative, parental incest is further displaced onto the initially open and then disguised brother/sister relationship. It is this sibling relationship, as

Richard Cronin argues, that allows Shelley to enact in interpersonal terms that condition of infinite reflexive desire said in "On Love" to be "the invisible and unattainable point to which love tends" (*SPP*, 504). Cronin connects a thematics of incest undifferentiated as to parent/child or sibling relations to Shelley's thematics of language through Lévi-Strauss's claim that "the prohibition of incest is the necessary precondition of the institution of language."[40]

But this would appear to account only for Shelley's sense of language as it is historically and socially constituted through that process in which, as he says in the *Defence*, "words ... become through time signs for portions or classes of thoughts instead of pictures of integral thoughts" (*SPP*, 512). For language in its potentially vital and continually suppressed metaphoricity—the "'subtler language'" of "'elemental shapes'" that Cythna rediscovers and writes on the sand in her cave—it is *defiance* of the prohibition of incest that is the "necessary precondition." Though the figure of Cythna carries the imprint of Shelley's incestuous and reflexively projective (narcissistic) fantasies, it is important that she does so in the process of enacting a desire for freedom and human connection that Shelley imagines as a distinctively feminine version of an innate, universal capacity for political and linguistic autonomy. Shelley's male feminist agenda makes a difference, even if it does not and cannot make a sufficient difference.

Shelley elaborates a figurative and narrative form of women's agency in terms of a reflexivity or specularity that, though already evident in the Southey-Coleridge *Joan of Arc*, is characteristically pushed to extremes in *The Revolt of Islam*. If sibling incest is initially the explicit and subsequently the elided thematic shape of this specularity, its most conspicuous formal shape is the marked enfolding of Cythna's voice within the voices of Laon and the narrator. In this diacritically marked enfolding of Cythna's voice resides an elided and censored fantasy of heterosexual sibling incest that is itself a sublimation of a prior fantasy of mother-son erotic and linguistic communion. When Cythna tells Laon that she made "'signs ... of my thought ... whose smallest change / A subtler language within language wrought,'" she articulates the circumstances of her own immediate textual status as well as a vision of women's distinctive access to discursive power within the order of human language. Cythna discovers for Shelley, in the process of making it, a "'language'" that is at once "'within language'" and "'subtler,'" *sub-tela* (from *texere*, to weave): woven fine, woven under as well as "'within'" the web or *textus* of language as it is already socially and historically constituted. In doing so she enacts, within Laon's narrative, Shelley's belief that poetry "spreads its own figured curtain" by "withdraw[ing] life's dark veil from before the scene of things" (*SPP* 533). From this perspective the marking off of

Cythna's voice as she gains access to a "'subtler language within language'" may be read as a sign not just of this self-consciously visionary poem's political and psychological limits, but also of its political and poetic fidelity to social realities.

This gesture inside Laon's narrative is significantly different from the effect produced at the beginning of *The Revolt of Islam*, where the voice of the mysterious "Woman" who meets the poet-narrator on the seashore and conducts him to the scene of Laon's narration is not marked off from the voice of the narrator. Modern printed texts have added quotation punctuation to identify this woman's powerful eloquence, but as Jack Donovan notes in the Longman edition, "The speech-marks from [line 343] until line 542 are not present in" the first printings of either *Laon and Cythna* or *The Revolt of Islam* (*PS*, 75). Although we cannot know with certainty that this difference in the textual status of women's voices is a matter of authorial agency—Donovan says that "the compositors altered S[helley]'s capitalisation and punctuation freely" (*PS*, 18)— it is possible that Shelley himself either introduced or saw reason to accept the differentiation. If Cythna is inevitably Laon's visionary reflexive projection as well as his female counterpart, she is so in a sense that gives her a significantly different status from that of the mysterious Woman in Canto 1. The latter figure is identifiably linked to the historical past in a way that Cythna is not. Gelpi follows a long line of readers in seeing that this "woman's devotion to human liberty . . . bears certain resemblances to Mary Wollstonecraft's" (*Shelley's Goddess*, 171); by implication Gelpi invites us to see her as the presiding and enabling maternal figure who makes possible this revolutionary "Vision of the Nineteenth Century." We learn that she "had looked upon / That unimaginable fight" (1. 271–72) witnessed by the poet-narrator at the beginning of Canto 1; that "She spake in language whose strange melody / Might not belong to earth" (1. 289–90); that she claimed to know "the dark tale which history doth unfold" (1. 460) as "great France sprang forth, / And seized, as if to break, the ponderous chains / Which bind in woe the nations of the earth" (1. 470–72); and finally that

> soon as the Woman came
> Into that hall, she shrieked the Spirit's name
> And fell; and vanished slowly from the sight.
> Darkness arose from her dissolving frame,
>
> (1. 616–19)

These initial dramatizations of witnessing and voicing may be read as Shelley's idealized allegorization of Wollstonecraft's truncated representations of the French Revolution—through which *he* comes to be positioned by *her*, in the space left by her dissolving form, as the one who must see and hear what is about to unfold. The last of these passages recasts into a more urgent political configuration the language at the end of the *Alastor* poet's autoerotic dream, when the "veiled maid" with her "hopes of divine liberty" "Folded his frame in her dissolving arms" (151, 159, 187).

It is consistent with the terms in which *The Revolt of Islam* articulates its relation to the historical example of Wollstonecraft that the voice of the Woman in Canto 1 was not marked off from and within the poet-narrator's unmarked discourse. This Woman's voice is not exactly ventriloquized by the poet-narrator, but it does register his bewilderment and hopelessness much more immediately than does Cythna's. From her first words ("Speak not to me, but hear!" [1. 343]) to her last ("Fear it!" [1. 542]), the Woman in Canto 1 is invested with a commanding authority that arises directly from the poet-narrator's need for interpretive guidance and prophetic access. She utters not the "supernatural mandates" of Wordsworth's Joan of Arc, but "a strange and awful tale" in which "Much must remain unthought, and more untold" (1. 334, 344). Much still remains unthought and untold even after Cythna takes up the burden of "the dark tale which history doth unfold" and gains access to a "subtler language." But in the cave of Canto 7 a hitherto unrealized potential for reaching what may be thought and told is represented through Cythna's act of political and linguistic self-discovery.

At the end of Wordworth's portrait of Joan of Arc, when "The chosen Rustic urged a warlike Steed / Tow'rd the beleaguer'd city, in the might / Of prophecy, accoutred to fulfill, // At the sword's point, visions conceived in love" (188–91), we may seem to have an aggressively armed version of Cythna's rushing in (as she often does in Shelley's poem) on her great black tartary steed. But it is Southey, not Shelley, whom Wordsworth most directly recalls here—this time the Southey who tried to placate Mary Wollstonecraft in the dedicatory lines to his *Poems* of 1797 by reminding her that in past ages women were degraded because

> No *Maid of Arc* had snatch'd from coward man
> The heaven-blest sword of Liberty . . .
> No *Corde's* angel and avenging arm
> Had sanctified again the Murderer's name.[41]

Twinned with Charlotte Corday, Southey's Joan of Arc in 1797 is already a figure for that defeated and defeatist political martyrdom mystified as the will and word of God that Cythna's "mind," as a textually differentiated projection of Laon's and of Shelley's, desires to take us beyond.

If Cythna is herself a martyr, as readers have often concluded, it is not because she "sanctified again the Murderer's name." It is because her version of Joan of Arc's death by fire bears witness to a struggle with and against arbitrary power that is larger than her own life.[42] And it is because, like the Woman who enables the poem's visionary narrative at its inception, "the dark tale which history doth unfold / I knew, but not, methinks, as others know" (1. 460–61). Cythna's "'subtler language,'" like her knowing, cannot itself exist beyond the violence of history; it can only be realized "'within language'" that is inevitably marked by the arbitrary power of political division and domination—and yet charged with an inherent potential for change. This "'subtler language'" includes but is not confined to what has already been found, given, transmitted from the past. It has to be made historically, "'wrought'" into a "'key of truths which once were dimly taught'" (7. 3113) and which still await their brighter, fuller teaching. It is Cythna's determination to enact her belief in a freer and fuller human future on the basis of knowing "the dark tale which history doth unfold" that makes her a distinctive figure within Romantic feminism. We can acknowledge the limits and contradictions of the ways in which she is produced in Shelley's writing and still value in her a daring revolutionary integrity unsurpassed in any other literary effort to confront the political "age of despair" that followed the French Revolution.[43]

6

THE LANGUAGE OF REVOLUTIONARY VIOLENCE

> [I]f the degeneracy of the higher orders of society be such, that no remedy less fraught with horrour can effect a radical cure; and if enjoying the fruits of usurpation, they domineer over the weak, and check by all the means in their power every humane effort, to draw man out of the state of degradation, into which the inequality of fortune has sunk him; the people are justified in having recourse to coercion, to repel coercion. ... The rich have for ages tyrannized over the poor, teaching them how to act when possessed of power, and now must feel the consequence.
> —Wollstonecraft, *An Historical and Moral View of the French Revolution*, 1794

> For so dear is power that the tyrants themselves neither then, nor now, nor ever, left or leave a path to freedom but through their own blood.
> —P. B. Shelley, *A Philosophical View of Reform*, 1820

1.

THE FIRST OF these justifications of insurrectionary violence was written on the eve of the Jacobin Terror; the second was begun in the year which marks "the nearest point Britain every reached to social revolution."[1] Wollstonecraft and Shelley both predicate the inevitable and necessary violence of revolution on the prior existence of an oppressive ruling-class power that is doubly arbitrary. The power that "the higher orders of society" wield over the weak and the poor is both tyrannical and capricious, absolute and irrational. As Paine puts it in his attack on Burke's celebration of hereditary monarchy, the British constitution championed by the ruling class is "a thing in imagination," "a thing as various as imagination can paint."[2] Shelley has a different understanding of the arbitrary power of imagination from Paine and from Wollstonecraft. What he derives from and shares with them, however, is the conviction that the coercive power of the ruling order ultimately leaves "the people" no alternative but to assert coercion of their own. Whether this oppositional, republican coercion can free itself from the power of the arbitrary in all its forms—

whether, for instance, it can discover forms of representation in both the linguistic and the political sense that either lie outside of or transvalue arbitrary power—is one of the organizing questions of this chapter.

Determining as the French Revolution has been to the historical formations of European and British Romanticism, the violence of the Revolution has largely remained outside of, or only tangentially or figuratively connected to, the cultural life it is taken to have produced. The violence of key events of the Revolution—the fall of the Bastille, the march on Versailles by Parisian revolutionaries in October 1789, the September Massacres, the Jacobin Terror—though frequently represented in Romantic discourse, is rarely understood as central to the production and aesthetic valuing of literary texts. Even so basic a question as the representation and reception of politically antithetical sources of violence—the Jacobin Terror and the counterrevolutionary White Terror, for example, or in Britain the Pentridge Rising of 1817 and the Tory government's ruthless suppression of it—have been slighted by kinds of historicist criticism that see power, in Foucauldian terms, as pervasive and beyond human agency, rather than as the contradictory and transformable social dynamic of class-divided society. Just how important the problem of representing revolutionary violence is to our understanding of Romantic literature, art, and culture is made dramatically evident in John Barrell's *Imagining the King's Death*. If "the struggle for ownership of the word 'imagination'" was, as Barrell argues, at the center of threats to and defenses of the British monarchical state in the 1790s, then the constitutive significance of representing revolutionary violence for the formation of what we call "Romanticism" could hardly be greater.[3] "Imagination," Barrell shows, is fundamental to the language of revolutionary violence. But in what sense exactly does the word "imagination" name a power that can be "owned" by either loyalists or reformers, by either enemies or supporters of the new French republic, by either Burke or Paine?

2.

Consider two very different revolutionary turns on the trope of the "correspondent breeze." Book 10 of the 1805 *Prelude* is organized and energized by Wordsworth's effort to come to terms retrospectively with the violence of revolutionary civil war and, eventually, of international war between republican France and his own country and its allies. The book opens with the ominous words "The King had fallen" (10. 9), and with the memory of Coalition armies descending on France "like a band / Of eastern hunters" (10. 14–15).[4] From here Wordsworth proceeds through "those September massacres" (10. 64) and circumstances that made Paris feel "Defenceless as a wood where tigers roam" (10. 82). Recalling that on his return to England, still a partisan of the revolutionary cause, he "Exulted in the triumph of my soul / When Englishmen by thousands were o'erthrown" (10. 260–61), Wordsworth characteristically converts the violence of historical conflict into internalized psychomachia as he remembers the self-alienation of his attending an Anglican worship service in commemoration of "our country's victories" even as he "Fed on the day of vengeance yet to come" (10. 270–74):

> Oh, much have they to account for, who could tear
> By violence at one decisive rent
> From the best youth in England their dear pride,
> Their joy, in England.
> (1805; 10. 275–78)

The violence done to Wordsworth by the claims of war and revolution is powerful because it penetrates and transforms his own imaginative life. Nowhere is this process more remarkably articulated than in those lines in the middle of Book 10 devoted, not ostensibly to the crisis in the poet's mind, but to what Wordsworth now sees as the "desperate" "madness of the many" in France:

> They found their joy,
> They made it, ever thirsty, as a child—
> If light desires of innocent little ones
> May with such heinous appetites be matched—
> Having a toy, a windmill, though the air
> Do of itself blow fresh and makes the vane
> Spin in his eyesight, he is not content,
> But with the plaything at arm's length he sets
> His front against the blast, and runs amain
> To make it whirl the faster.
> (1805; 10. 336–45)

Though every previous and subsequent figuration of wind and of innocent childhood impulse in *The Prelude* may be seen to converge on this passage, those that converge on it most intensely come from the earliest recollections of Wordsworth's boyhood exploits in Book 1.

> Oh, when I have hung
> Above the raven's nest, by knots of grass
> And half-inch fissures in the slippery rock
> But ill sustained, and almost, as it seemed,
> Suspended by the blast which blew amain,
> (1805; 1. 341–45)

The nine-year-old Wordsworth trapping birds on the Lake District mountain slopes prefigures the Jacobin enthusiast who sets "His front against the blast, and runs amain." The transfer of agency from nature's "blast" to human desire and effort, already an organizing perplexity in Book 1, becomes a source of political deterioration in Book 10, as what was previously individualized in the imaging of childhood recollections returns in a childhood simile for collective social experience and historical crisis. This projective transfer between natural and imaginative agency, part of *The Prelude*'s deepest thematic agenda, is already anticipated in the poem's opening image of a "breeze" that "seems half conscious" (1. 1–4), and that will quickly turn into "a tempest, a redundant energy / Vexing its own creation" (1. 46–47). The violent energy embedded in Wordsworth's personal recollections makes their poetic conversion into figures for social conflict a process that reveals but also conceals what these spheres of representation have in common. As David Bromwich observes, "what Wordsworth cannot say about the revolution he will often consent to say about his childhood, and what he cannot say of childhood he will say of the revolution."[5]

The Book 10 figuring of a breeze driven by human desire to become "A tempest, a redundant energy" is concentrated in the image of the "windmill," a childhood "toy" that spins together, as Wordsworth elaborates it, associations of play and work, the spontaneous and the purposive. The toy windmill also miniaturizes the allusions to Don Quixote in Book 5 (60, 124) while extending their function in Wordsworth's poetic historicizing of romance and the romantic. Representing the violence of the French Revolution becomes in Book 10 an historical and political realization of what was at stake in the earliest stages of Wordsworth's coming to terms with imaginative desire. "It was as if he were a part of the Terror," Bromwich writes of a later passage in this Book (*Disowned by Memory*, 141). Wordsworth's deflected recognition of what is being realized in the writing is marked by fascinated horror because it reaches so deeply into his own romance with a power whose "strength / Of usurpation" (6. 532–33) he can never appease.

It is the entanglement of this imaginative power with revolutionary violence that also brings Wordsworth, early in Book 10, to claim that he saw

> with my proper eyes
> That liberty, and life, and death, would soon
> To the remotest corners of the land
> Lie in the arbitrement of those who ruled
> The capital city;
> (1805; 10. 107–11)

Arbitrement as either "decision, determination" or "compromise" (Johnson's *Dictionary*) merges disastrously in Wordsworthian hindsight with the *arbitrary* as both "despotick; absolute; bound by no law" and "depending on no rule; capricious."[6] Little wonder that shortly after this moment Wordsworth came to counter his anxiety about revolutionary "arbitrement" in the 1850 *Prelude* with a desperate claim that "A sovereign voice subsists within the soul, / Arbiter undisturbed of right and wrong" (10. 183–84). In 1805 this "arbiter" was still too disturbed by its links with the very power it feared to make possible such a claim. The 1805 *Prelude* produces the nervous similative fantasy of running against and thus adding the child's own power to the wind's so that his romantic "toy" will "whirl the faster," turning both imaginative and revolutionary desire into forms of arbitrary power.

Though it makes no explicit reference to the French Revolution or to insurrectionary events in England inspired by those in France, Shelley's *Ode to the West Wind* is as close historically to political violence as is the 1805 *Prelude*. When Shelley drafted the poem in October 1819, he had learned only a few weeks before of the Peterloo Massacre, had drafted *The Mask of Anarchy* with "the torrent of my indignation . . . not yet done boiling in my veins" (*LPBS* 2: 117), and would soon, perhaps within a few days, begin writing *A Philosophical View of Reform*.[7] As in *The Prelude*, the *Ode* articulates a relationship among natural, imaginative, and political modes of power organized through the figure of the wind as arbitrary force. Shelley's poetic articulation of this force, though radically different from Wordsworth's, also involves the return to a "boyhood" moment when the impulse not merely to contend with and match but to "outstrip" the "speed" of the wind (power is most characteristically figured as speed in Shelley's writing) "Scarce seemed a vision" (48–51). Whether running competitively with the wind or, like the "fierce Maenad" of the second stanza and the "child" of *The Prelude*, against it, human desire and agency and language reveal themselves as urgent engagements with a power simultaneously "wild" and ineluctably directional, simultaneously determinative with respect to natural life ("Destroyer and preserver") and susceptible to the shapings of human desire, understanding, intention, and linguistic representation.[8]

Read in its mainly implicit and figurative political dimension, the *Ode* turns on Shelley's evolving, always unsettled beliefs about necessity as a philosophical construct and as a principle of historical process.[9] The wind here is the natural form and figure of determinative necessity, but its contradictory character and its dependence on human thought, language, and culture for meaningful realization open it, without making it answerable, to human need. The cycles of oppression and revolt recognized in the passage from *A Philosophical View of Reform* quoted at the beginning of this chapter play themselves out in specific historical moments through a process that not only allows for but demands human intervention. This is the prevailing perspective in Shelley's letters of late August and September 1819, as he watches events in Britain unfold from self-exile in Italy. What shifts from letter to letter is the social location of the longed-for and still uncertain intervention:

> England seems to be in a very disturbed state. . . . But the change should commence among the higher orders, or anarchy will only be the last flash before despotism. I tremble & wonder.—(to Peacock, 24 August 1819; *LPBS* 2: 115)

> The same day that your letter came, came the news of the Manchester work, & the torrent of my indignation has not yet done boiling in my veins. I wait anxiously [to] hear how the Country will express its sense of this bloody murderous oppression of its destroyers. 'Something must be done. . . . What yet I know not.' (to Ollier, 6 September 1819; *LPBS* 2: 117)

> Many thanks for your attention in sending the papers which contain the terrible and important news of Manchester. These are, as it were, the distant thunders of the terrible storm which is approaching. The tyrants here, as in the French Revolution, have first shed blood. May their execrable lessons not be learnt with equal docility! (to Peacock, 9 September 1819; *LPBS* 2: 110)

> I have received all the papers you sent me. . . . What an infernal business this is of Manchester! What is to be done? Something, assuredly. (to Peacock, 21 September 1819; *LPBS* 2: 120)

From "the higher orders" to "the Country" to the implied British counterparts of the French revolutionaries to the prophetically revolutionary question "What is to be done?"—as Shelley's anger deepens, his orientation moves from higher to lower orders, and from wondering anxiety to a decisiveness that is still open, passionately "determined" and yet, given his removal in Italy, indeterminate. The violence of historical necessity has produced a moment in which, as in Wordsworth but on profoundly different political grounds, the desire that drives the work of writing is bound in contradictory and as yet unrealized ways to the prospect of popular insurrection.

When he came to draft the *Ode* in late October, the "terrible storm which is approaching" in the 9 September letter to Peacock found its correlative in the "violent tempest of hail and rain, attended by . . . magnificent thunder and lightning" that Shelley "foresaw" in the "tempestuous wind" blowing through the woods of the Cascine just outside Florence.[10] So much of the violence in the *Ode* is located in the wind itself as a power beyond and indifferent to human agency that it is at first hard to discern a correspondent violence in either humanity's or nature's responses—though there is a kind of violence in the very urgency with which the speaker-poet apostrophizes the wind. We have to wait until the final stanza to see the wind-as-"enchanter" of stanza 1, driving the dead leaves "to their dark wintry bed," explicitly transfigured into the "incantation" of Shelley's own "verse."

In the poem's first gesture of overt political figuration, the multiracial "Pestilence-stricken multitudes" are imagined as arising from their graves like "sweet buds" in the spring through no volition of their own, violent or otherwise. It is only with the comparison of wind-scattered clouds to "the bright hair uplifted from the head / Of some fierce Maenad" in the second stanza (20–21) that we can begin to read a transfer of violent energy from extrahuman wind to human subject. That the transference is to the figure of the ecstatically aroused woman, capable of destroying a king who denies the divine power to which she has dedicated herself, connects this turn in the *Ode* to Shelley's reading and rewriting of Wollstonecraft's account of the Parisian women who marched on Versailles thirty years before, in October 1789.[11] Shelley's "fierce Maenad" is related also to his unfinished 1819 poem "On the Medusa of Leonardo Da Vinci in the Florentine Gallery," which has been read as a rendering of both revolutionary hysteria and revolutionary terror, and to Shelley's quoting lines he had recently written for Beatrice Cenci in the 6 September letter to Ollier:

> Aye, something must be done;
> What, yet I know not . . . something which shall make
> The thing that I have suffered but a shadow
> In the dread lightning which avenges it;
> *(The Cenci* 3.1.86–89)[12]

The arbitrary violence of historical necessity becomes the contrary violence of human history in the figure of the Maenad, threatened with disintegration by the very power that uplifts her (like the boy Wordsworth threatened by the wind that suspends him on a "naked crag" in *The Prelude* 1) and also threatening to the father, the king, the established male authority that would deny or contain her.

The "fierce Maenad" marks an eruption of human violence in the *Ode* that is never fully aligned with the overarching transmutation of the West Wind's violent prophetic power into the power of the speaker-poet's breath and verse.[13] In her association with the Thracian women so enflamed by Orpheus's song that they tear his body apart, the Maenad resists full incorporation into the speaker-poet's work of appropriating the wind's power by making it simultaneously humanity's and his own. He makes himself an object of violence in the staged collapse into sentimental passivity in stanza 4 — "I fall upon the thorns of life! I bleed!" — and in his momentarily seeing himself "chained and bowed," like a prisoner in the Bastille or in Newgate. But in the triumphant resurgence of prophetic will that drives the final stanza, the violence of the wind is sublimated (via two kinds of wind-instruments that may be read as sonic, musical variations on Wordsworth's toy windmill) into forms of art that circumvent — or anticipate — forms of direct political action. The "lyre" generates "The tumult of thy mighty harmonies"; the "trumpet" finally enables the poet-speaker's spirit and breath to articulate the power of the wind — but into "prophecy," not into other immediate forms of practice. The *Ode* puts itself on the verge of saying what is to come, but not of answering Shelley's question to Peacock, "What is to be done?" The speaker-poet has acquired, in summoning it, the power of revolutionary hope. The "fierce Maenad" is left to bear the burden of revolutionary action.

But "hope" in the political sense, as Chandler reminds us in the course of meditating on the *Ode*'s representation of historical cases and causality, is for Shelley a state of mind indispensably generative of historical change in purposeful alignment with human need.[14] Chandler quotes from Shelley's letter to Hunt written on May Day 1820: "The system of society as it exists at present must be overthrown from the foundations with all its superstructure of maxims & of forms. . . . If faith is a virtue in any case it is so in politics rather than religion; as having a power of producing that . . . belief in which is at once a prophesy & a cause — " (*LPBS* 2: 191). Understanding "hope" as the characteristic Shelleyan mode of "faith," we can see him here implying that hope produces not only the "prophesy" finally asserted at the end of the *Ode* but "a cause" — a power of agency, and also a "movement" in the political sense that Cythna intends in her speech to the oppressed:

> 'But soon my human words found sympathy
> In human hearts: the purest and the best,
> As friend with friend made common cause with me,'
> (*The Revolt of Islam* 9. 3543)

While the ending of the *Ode* most evidently places its hope in the causal agency of the poem's prophetic words, it does so by also implying that this agency will be realized in its contribution to a collective moment of which the poem's "dead leaves" will have become a living part, "my words among mankind" (67).[15] Underlying this agency of hope-inspired, hope-inspiring words is the "Spirit fierce" (61) of necessity, with which the speaker-poet now demands identification. Chandler's summary, with its concluding reference to Marx's *Eighteenth Brumaire*, is apt: "Shelley is led by the events of post-Revolution history to construct an account whereby he and post-Revolution history make each other. . . . human beings make their own history, but not just as they please" (554). This is the perspective from which to understand Shelley's lyric enactment of a poetic agency that insists upon intervening in and shaping a human history driven forward by the contradictory violence of necessity. What remains as a persistent and, in the *Ode*, partly evaded problem is the recognition that in making their own history, human beings are forced (as Wollstonecraft puts it) to have "recourse to coercion, to repel coercion."

3.

I will return to Shelley's engagement with the determinations of revolutionary violence after I have set the Shelleyan—and more briefly the Wordsworthian—cases against that of Blake, "the rebel *par excellence* of English poetry."[16] Alicia Ostriker's characterization in her introduction to the Penguin edition of the *Poems* confirms a view of Blake that we take for granted, even as it defamiliarizes a familiar French phrase through its casual historical pertinence. Blake has become institutionalized as "the rebel *par excellence* of English poetry" to such a degree that we rarely pause to question the integrity and efficacy of violence in his revolutionary art. There is no denying Blake's preeminence as *the* English revolutionary poet—he has a stronger claim to it than Shelley, or even than Milton. But the *excellence* of what is revolutionary about him is not beyond question. The visionary terms in which he represents revolutionary history and himself as revolutionary prophet can be coercive and objectionable as well as liberating and inspiring.

There is a current in Blake criticism that insists on softening and qualifying, rather than emphasizing, the force of the violently revolutionary Blake. John Beer wrote in 1968: "Blake's basic sympathies lay with the revolutionaries," but "the strength of his revolutionary fervour can easily be overestimated. . . . he was attracted more by the idea and promise of liberty than by the physical force which was used to achieve it. Terrors and bloodshed could give him no pleasure."[17] The assumption that real revolutionaries take pleasure in violence should itself be rejected. The claim that needs to be addressed here, though, is Beer's denying Blake's attraction to physical force. Ronald Paulson eventually comes to a version of this view at the end of his chapter on Blake in *Representations of Revolution*: "For Blake paradox seems to be the characteristic feature of revolution itself, as well as the interpretation of it. . . . The Revolution, like his art, inhabits . . . the mythic area of ambiguity and doubleness where contraries can coexist."[18]

My argument is directed against positions such as these, as it is against those who insist that Blake's later mythopoeic visions put his earlier rebellious assertions in proper perspective. In ways far more assertive and explicit than in Wordsworth and Shelley, Blake was attracted to the force unleashed in the struggle for liberty; liberty without such force would have seemed to him not just impossible but undesirable. And while I do not mean to suggest that bloodshed in itself gave him pleasure, I do think that "Terrors"—some kinds of "Terrors"—did. Blake's relation to the violence of revolution as historical event and as representable subject cannot be as conveniently accommodated within "a mythic area of ambiguity and doubleness" as Paulson—and other very good readers of Blake—claim. Blake saw and represented the terrible sacrifices and uncertainties of armed rebellion, but his art does not transcend them. It is powerfully and problematically caught up in the convulsions of his historical subject.[19]

Three problems in Blake's verbal and visual representations of revolution are especially in need of fresh critical attention. The first has to do with the limitations of representing collective, collaborative activity and struggle in an artistic mode dominated by individual symbolic figures with superhuman powers. The second has to do with the distortions of Blake's revolutionary vision by a phallocentric myth of liberating erotic potency and feminine dependency. The third has to do with Blake's idiosyncratic, personalized appropriation of Christian apocalypse and millenarian fantasy.

Each of these interconnected problems needs to be contextualized historically, beginning with Blake's involvment in the Gordon Riots of June 1780. This upheaval started when the Protestant Association led a loosely organized demonstration in London against the Catholic Relief Act; it ended, after several days of fighting, with more than eight hundred dead and with twenty-one rioters executed. Alexander Gilchrist, our only source for Blake's actual involvment, says that Blake later recalled his "involuntary participation" in the Riots:

> On the third day, Tuesday, 6th of June . . . the artist happened to be walking in a route chosen by one of the mobs at large. . . . Suddenly, he encountered the advancing wave of triumphant Blackguardism, and was forced (for from such a great surging mob there is no disentanglement) to go along in the very front rank, and witness the storming and burning of the fortress-like prison, and release of its three hundred inmates.[20]

Many Blakeans have rewritten this moment, understanding with E. P. Thompson that the Gordon Riots were not just "triumphant Blackguardism" but expressed an array of genuine if confused social grievances. David Erdman is sure "that Blake shared the sentiments of Gilchrist's 'triumphant Blackguardism' insofar as 'the mob' believed that freeing their fellows from Newgate was a step toward freeing Albion from an oppressive [American] war."[21] Jack Lindsay agrees and understands the event as preparing Blake to identify with the crowd that stormed the Bastille nine years later.[22] What motivates these Blakeans is more than a conjectural conviction that Blake's joining the Gordon rioters could not have been "involuntary"; it is their knowing that one of Blake's most famous designs, alternatively titled "Glad Day" and "Albion Rose," was sketched in 1780 and subsequently given that date when it was engraved in the 1790s, as a way of commemorating the Gordon Riots and the turning of the tide in the American colonies' fight against England.[23] Blake knew directly what it meant to participate in mass violence, and he associated that experience with the image (quoting Paulson) of "a naked male youth at the center of a sunburst, breaking the Vitruvian circle that circumscribes him, and his center of gravity is his loins."[24]

Blake was also producing other, quite different images of political violence in the early 1780s. *Poetical Sketches* of 1783 contains, in addition to the familiar pastoral lyrics, *Gwin, King of Norway*, which tells in ballad-stanzas of a time when Gwin ruled with "cruel sceptre" "Over the nations of the North" and "The Nobles of the land did feed / Upon the hungry Poor" (1–8). A giant named Gordred "rous'd himself / From sleeping in his cave" and leads the oppressed in bloody battle against the king:

> "Pull down the tyrant to the dust,
>   Let Gwin be humbled,"
> They cry; "and let ten thousand lives
>   Pay for the tyrant's head."
>   (29–32)

The poem's language seems ambiguously aroused in the scenes of carnage it appears to condemn:

> The god of war is drunk with blood,
>   The earth doth faint and fail;
> The stench of blood makes sick the heav'ns;
>   Ghosts glut the throat of hell!
>   (93–96)

Erdman stresses the importance of this poem as an anticipation of *America: A Prophecy* and says that it is "Blake's earliest and plainest account of a revolution and . . . evidence of how far he entered imaginatively into the drama of civil conflict" (19). But how are readers to enter imaginatively into the climactic moment when Gordred—"a kind of George Washington and Tom Paine in one," says Erdman (20)—meets King Gwin in single combat? "Down from the brow unto the breast / Gordred his head divides!" (107–8). Erdman's comment on the ferocity of this moment is curiously defensive: "The revolutionary act of justice ... is relatively surgical." "Relatively surgical" is, in this context, a bit like "relatively dead." At one level the political allegory may be clear, but the implications of Blake's imaginative investment in such representations of violence require greater critical candor.

Related questions arise in Blake's unfinished history play published in *Poetical Sketches*, *King Edward the Third*. The relevance of this early project to *America* and to the other revolutionary prophecies of the 1790s has been established by Erdman in careful detail. The play is filled with patriotic and bloodthirsty praise of war by the king's followers: "Grim war shall laugh and shout, decked in tears, / And blood shall flow like streams across the meadows" (scene 5, 53–54). "These are plausible imitations. They are not the real thing," Erdman hastens to remark, though he has to acknowledge that "the impulse to *expose* the sentiments of his dramatis personae interferes with the imperfect effort to give them verisimilitude.... Our problem in reading *Edward* is not simply to account for the characters' expression of delight in bloodshed but to account for the fact that much of the hidden irony which underlies that expression remains hidden" (66). Identifying a "hidden irony" only to say that it "remains hidden" is oddly evasive. Blake eventually came to question his exuberant support for the English army at the Battle of Crécy—but the terms in which he reports this questioning complicate rather than put to rest the question about "delight in bloodshed." The convolutions in Erdman's otherwise illuminating historical analysis suggest uneasiness, avertedness, and point to difficulties that do not disappear in Blake's mature revolutionary art.

The prophecies of the 1790s recurrently image revolutionary conflict as a contest among colossal individuals: historical figures in what we have of the incomplete and unpublished *French Revolution* (1791), historically informed symbolic figures in the other Lambeth prophecies. From the point of view of Blake's pictorial preferences this concentration on individual figures makes sense: crowd scenes rarely interested him. The result, nevertheless, is that very little of Blake's artistic energy goes into representing the complication, the precarious confused power, of mass action. Such images as there are of this kind are often negative, as in *The French Revolution*, where ironically the Archbishop of Paris conveys the power of mass action through the counterrevolutionary fear it provokes in him:

... a curse is heard hoarse thro' the land, from a godless race
Descending to beasts; they look downward and labour and forget my holy law; ...
For the bars of Chaos are burst; her millions prepare their fiery way
Thro' the orbed abode of the holy dead, to root up and pull down and remove;
(138–42)

In *Visions of the Daughters of Albion*, where politics and history are radically contracted to the sadomasochistic entanglement of a trio of symbolic subjects, collective social reality intrudes fleetingly as the sound of those subject to institutionalized violence:

> Bound back to back in Bromions caves terror & meekness dwell
> At entrance Theotormon sits wearing the threshold hard
> With secret tears; beneath him sound like waves on a desart shore
> The voice of slaves beneath the sun, and children bought with money.
> (2: 5–8)

Even here, though, the plural simile "like waves on a desart shore" immediately gives way in its historical tenor to a singular "voice of slaves ... and children." Oothoon later pleads eloquently on behalf of difference and the multifariousness of instincts, but Blake's own instinct in the Lambeth prophecies is to condense difference and multifariousness into the singular colossal instance. There is a related example in *America*, when Albion's Angel sends a plague to blight the rebellious colonies:

> Fury! rage! madness! in a wind swept through America
> And the red flames of Orc that folded roaring fierce around
> The angry shores, and the fierce rushing of th'inhabitants together:
> The citizens of New-York close their books & lock their chests;
> The mariners of Boston drop their anchors and unlade;
> The scribe of Pennsylvania casts his pen upon the earth;
> The builder of Virginia throws his hammer down in fear.
> (14: 10–16)

From the mass "rushing of th'inhabitants together," to the plural citizens and mariners, to the singular scribe and builder: the passage moves to a point where Franklin and Jefferson are made to represent, to "stand for" in the sense of Marx's *vertreten*, an entire population's momentary faltering under British attack. There is little representational space for internal dissension, for the diverse historical interplay of competing interests, reactions, tactics.

It has been argued that it is precisely Blake's point to show, as he says in his 1810 Notebook entry on the Last Judgment, that "Multitudes of Men in Harmony" may appear "as One Man." Erdman notes that handbills distributed during the Gordon Riots appealed to this familiar political ideal (9 n. 16). But it remains the case that representations of revolution dominated by this visionary principle often simplify the dynamics of converging mass action. There is nothing in Blake like Wollstonecraft's intensely uneasy description of the "multitude of women by some impulse ... collected together" who marched on Versailles in early October

1789, or like Wordsworth's surviving memory of early and unexpected revolutionary solidarity in Book 6 of *The Prelude*:

> it was our lot
> To land at Calais on the very eve
> Of that great federal day; and there we saw,
> In a mean city and among a few,
> How bright a face is worn when joy of one
> Is joy of tens of millions.
> (1805; 6. 355–60)

Shelley's depictions of revolutionary resistance in *The Revolt of Islam*, though at times subordinated to his own quite different fantasies of vanguardist heroism, offer unreductive responses to the questions posed about the French Revolution—plurally and singularly, with a sharp sense of irony—in the Preface: "Could they listen to the plea of reason who had groaned under the calamities of a social state according to the provisions of which one man riots in luxury while another famishes for want of bread? Can he who the day before was a trampled slave suddenly become liberal-minded, forbearing, and independent" (*SPW*, 33). The poem answers "no" more convincingly than "yes"—and does not flinch from confronting the unpredictable political consequences of mass action. In *Prometheus Unbound*, by contrast, questions related to those in Blake's prophecies do arise about how the reader is to negotiate the vast distance separating the text's mythopoeic figuring of metaphysical and political liberation from an attentive awareness of social and historical reference.

What Blake frequently does not do in the early prophetic books he powerfully does in some of the songs, where he is more engaged in representing the actual suffering and struggle of what he would call "fallen" existence. In the songs, too, he usually prefers the representative individual to the diversity of a group. But these representative individuals are socially alive and responsive, like "The Chimney Sweeper" in *Songs of Innocence*:

> Theres little Tom Dacre, who cried when his head
> That curl'd like a lambs back, was shav'd, so I said.
> Hush Tom never mind it, for when your head's bare,
> You know that the soot cannot spoil your white hair.
> (5–8)

The irony of representing socially sanctioned violence as acceptable to one of its innocent victims and recommendable to another depends upon the tension among diverse perspectives: Tom's, the speaker's, the uninnocent reader's. In the *Songs* Blake's "doctrine of contraries" produces visions of collective suffering, and of potential collective struggle, that are not so persistently subordinated to the representational demands of a gigantistic symbolism.

The politically telling effects come through viscerally concrete acts of generalizing. Though Sir Joshua Reynolds irritated Blake into protesting that "to generalize is to be an Idiot," in the *Songs* Blake practices a fiercely specifying and concretizing art of generalization. The speaker in "London" wanders through "*each* charter'd street" and "mark[s] . . . / Marks of weakness, marks of woe" "in *every* face" he meets (emphasis added). Yet as John Brenkman has argued, "The poem does not . . . articulate a single situation or a fixed relation between Blake and the city's populace; rather, the poem moves . . . through a series of such relations."[25] The motile visual force of "every" in the first stanza accumulates an even greater aural force in the five "everys" of the second—an aural force that is performed alliteratively in "The mind-forg'd manacles I hear." "Man" is caught inside the word "manacle," and yet as Brenkman says these sounding shackles start a process in which "manifestations of suffering" take on "the active power to condemn and protest" (126). The "Chimney sweepers cry" "appalls"—shocks and also blanches—the church whose hypocrisy blackens him and itself; "the hapless Soldiers sigh" runs "down Palace walls" "in blood" that may soon be his commanders' and not just his own; "the youthful Harlots curse" converts her own and her child's disease into a plague on her respectable exploiters. Each figure is every member of an oppressed class; the violence of collective suffering generates a comprehensible violence of collective retaliation.

At the end of "London" Blake sees the "youthful Harlot" tragically and also heroically, as an avenging angel. Elsewhere the subversive representation of prostitution sounds a more sinister note—in a three-line fragment from his Notebook, for example:

> In a wife I would desire
> What in whores is always found
> The lineaments of Gratified desire
> (*CPPWB*, 474)

In *Visions of the Daughters of Albion*, engraved in 1793, Oothoon is branded a harlot as soon as she is raped by Bromion. The political allegory is clear: she is at once oppressed woman, brutalized African slave, and possessed natural landscape ("thy soft American plains are mine, and mine thy north & south"). But the more immediate sexual politics of the poem are murky and pose questions about women and revolutionary violence of a kind quite different from those we have encountered in Shelley. David Bindman comments on the pictorial design at the bottom of Plate 1 [fig. 1]: "Bromion and Oothoon are stretched upon the rocks in post-coital abandon."[26] That an art historian could say this about a scene of rape testifies to the ambiguity of Blake's design, to the way it elicits a conventional eroticized response disturbingly at odds—or disturbingly in keeping?—with the violence of the text.

What is murky in Blake's representation of counterrevolutionary rape in *Visions* becomes more densely overcast in the revolutionary rape at the beginning of *America: A Prophecy* (also engraved in 1793). Most commentators acknowledge that what the youthful Orc does to the "nameless" "shadowy female" in Plate 2 of the Preludium is rape, though Paulson is not quite sure—"[Orc] . . . rapes her (or rather she allows him)"[27]—and Bloom is not at all bothered: "The silence of the shadowy female identifies her with nature, barren when not possessed by man. Orc's rape is intended to give her a voice, and succeeds."[28] Here are the relevant lines from the Preludium:

> Silent as despairing love, and strong as jealousy,
> The hairy shoulders rend the links, free are the wrists of fire;
> Round the terrific loins he siez'd the panting struggling womb;
> It joy'd: she put aside her clouds & smiled her first-born smile;
> As when a black cloud shews its light'nings to the silent deep.
> (2: 1–5)

In Orc's embrace the "shadowy female" is first reduced to a "panting struggling womb," which here, as in Oothoon's speeches in *Visions*, gets identified with the genitals, the locus of erotic arousal. As the "womb" itself is personified ("panting struggling"), the woman is depersonalized. In *America* the reduction is carried further in "It joy'd," another instance of depersonalizing personification—of personification as, paradoxically and disturbingly, reification. The "shadowy female" is deprived of subjectivity altogether, even of gender, under the pressure of Orc's revolutionary energy. That she is then made to speak and claim an identity for herself is no extenuation of the sexual, and poetic, violence. The entire scene is complicit with the worst kind of masculine fantasy, with the belief that what women need to be sexually freed is to be forced.[29]

As for Blake's political symbolism in the Preludium to *America*, grounding the unleashing of revolutionary force in such a phallocentric scenario contorts and limits his prophetic recasting of history. To image the desire, pain, and sacrifice of revolutionary struggle in these terms is historically aberrant, at least with respect to the role played by women in the early years of the French Revolution, as well as politically repellent. There is much in Blake that suggests his assent to the shift in official revolutionary iconography analyzed by Lynn Hunt, when previous feminine allegories of "Liberty marching bare-breasted and fierce of visage" were replaced, after November 1793, by depictions of the giant Hercules with his club as emblem of the Republic.[30] If Blake's range of historical reference in

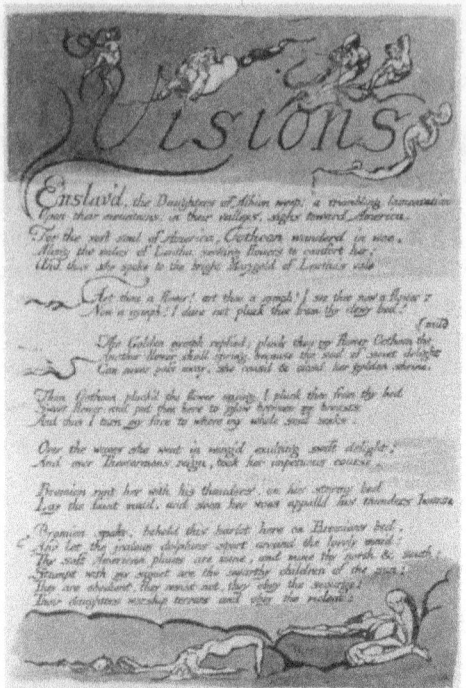

1. William Blake, *Visions of the Daughters of Albion*, plate 1. Yale Center for British Art, Paul Mellon Collection.

2. William Blake, *America: A Prophecy*, plate 5. Yale Center for British Art, Paul Mellon Collection.

America does extend, as Paulson argues, to the revolt of the slaves in Santo Domingo that began in 1791, then Orc's rape of Urthona's daughter reinforces the white myth of black male potency.[31] As in *Visions* but more triumphantly, phallic aggression is seen eventually to lead to the erotic liberation of women.

> The doors of marriage are open, and the Priests in rustling scales
> Rush into reptile coverts, hiding from the fires of Orc,
> That play around the golden roofs in wreaths of fierce desire,
> Leaving the females naked and glowing with the lusts of youth.
> (15: 19–22)

Blake's hairy youth leaves the women glowing: this is a male-dominated vision of revolutionary release, motivated by assumptions such as those that appear in Blake's annotations to Lavater's *Aphorisms of Man* of 1788: "let the men do their duty & the women will be such wonders, the female life . . . lives from the light of the male. see a mans female dependants you know the man" (*CPPWB*, 596).

Blake's vision of revolutionary energy as phallic uprising pervades his political appropriations of Christian millenarian apocalypse. In Plate 5 of *America* [fig. 2], the text represents Albion's Angel watching in fear as "the terror" Orc approaches "like a comet, or more like the planet" Mars:

> The Spectre glowd his horrid length staining the temple long
>
> With beams of blood . . .
>
> (5: 6–7)

The design surrounding the verbal text on this page is one of the most extraordinary acts of imagining the king's death in the entire 1790s; one regrets that Barrell does not offer an account of it. It depicts, in Erdman's words, "a revolutionary tribunal of three naked youths up in the heavens . . . with fiery sword and scales of justice. . . . At the top the King, bound, is tried and found wanting . . . then sent hurtling to the bottom, where his possibly decapitated body is encircled by a blood-red serpent with human face but forked tongue."[32] "Forked tongue": it is possible to see in this and in other details of both design and text indications of Blake's misgivings about such a reign of terror. Gilchrist reports that when Blake heard about the 1792 September Massacres, "he tore off his white cockade, and assuredly never wore the red cap again" (Blake had worn the pro-Revolutionary *bonnet rouge* openly in the streets of London).[33] Whatever the accuracy of Gilchrist's recollection, Blake's imaginative investment in violent apocalyptic revolution is inescapable in Plate 5 of *America*, and in the plate that follows showing a naked young man sitting with his legs spread on top of a grave-mound as he looks up in hope [fig. 3]:

The morning comes, the night decays, the watchmen leave their stations;
The grave is burst, the spices shed, the linen wrapped up;
The bones of death, the cov'ring clay, the sinews shrunk & dry'd.
Reviving shake, inspiring move, breathing! awakening!
(6: 1–4)

This amazing movement from apocalyptic violence to the dawning of a new age had been implicit in the more peaceful and reformist vision of *The French Revolution*—in the transition from the horrifying "dens" of the Bastille to the convening of the Commons: "like spirits of fire in the beautiful / Porches of the Sun, to plant beauty in the desert craving abyss, they gleam" (52–55).[34] A more overtly revolutionary anticipation of plates 5 and 6 from *America* appears in the juxtaposition of verbal images near the end of "A Song of Liberty," which Blake probably composed in the autumn of 1793 as a response to the victory of the French republican army over invading Austrian forces at Valmy:

19. Where the son of fire in his eastern cloud, while the morning plumes her golden breast,
20. Spurning the clouds written with curses, stamps the stony law to dust, loosing the eternal horses from the dens of night, crying
    Empire is no more! and now the lion & wolf shall cease.

In *America*, the terrible energy of the lion and the wolf are intrinsic to the Revolution's way toward rebirth. The innocent-looking youth who awakens to the dawning of a new age in Plate 6 is a transfiguration of the revolutionary angel flying through the night of Orc's terror in Plate 5 (upper right), his huge sword flaming between his legs. If the figure hurled into the coils of the red serpent at the bottom of the plate is "The Guardian Prince of Albion" without his head, then the flying youth holds onto—appears to be soaring aloft on—the weapon of execution. Louis XVI had been guillotined in January of the year *America: A Prophecy* was published. Blake's imagining of an apocalyptic future for Albion that will derive its impetus from what has happened in England's American colonies and in France fuses phallic mystique with the mysteries of a Christian millennium.

Blake's idiom of political apocalypse relies heavily on a vocabulary of "terror," the "terrible," and the "terrific." In *The French Revolution* such language is associated with the nobility and the old regime: the Bastille's towers are "terrible" (19); Sieyès deplores the way an enslaved populace has been "kept in awe with the whips, / To worship terrors" (214–15). But in *America* the language of "terror" acquires a different status. Orc in the Preludium is "the terrible boy" who seizes the nameless female's "terrific loins" (2: 6, 3). Albion's Prince interrupts Washington's defiant speech

3. William Blake, *America: A Prophecy*, plate 6. Yale Center for British Art, Paul Mellon Collection.

4. William Blake, *Europe: A Prophecy*, plate 15. Yale Center for British Art, Paul Mellon Collection.

with "a terrible blast" (3: 13), only to be confronted by the figure of Orc rising redundantly over the Atlantic: "his terrible limbs were fire / With myriads of cloudy terrors" (4: 9–10). I have already glanced at the textual representation of "terror" in Plate 5; many more instances from *America* might be cited. Such language is superfluously significant in Blake's version of the revolutionary—which is also for him the apocalyptic millenarian—sublime. Paulson suggests that Blake's vision of revolutionary terror is a direct response to the contradiction between Burke's enthusiastic theorizing of aestheticized terror as a primary source of the sublime in his early *Philosophical Enquiry into the Origin of our Ideas of the Sublime and Beautiful*, and his later denunciations of actual terror in *Reflections on the Revolution in France* and subsequent writings.[35] The *OED* suggests that Burke and the *Annual Register* (which he had helped to found in 1758) were instrumental in introducing the words "terrorist" and "terrorism" into English, and it is to Blake's credit that he resisted these formations: already in the 1790s the words were corrupted, as they are now, by being selectively applied only to some and not to all acts of intimidating, indiscriminate violence. What remains troubling, however, is Blake's representing revolutionary terror in the sublime terms of Christian apocalypse—in terms, that is, that subordinate individual and collective human responsibility for political violence to the worship of energy as a divinely retributive, ultimately self-validating absolute.

As a concluding example of the political and artistic problems I want to identify in Blake's apocalyptic vision, consider the final plate (15) of *Europe: A Prophecy* [fig. 4]. *Europe* represents the history of the Christian era as "the night of Enitharmon's joy," as an eighteen-hundred-year "female dream" in which woman has exerted a repressive, secretive dominion. Enitharmon calls upon Orc, her first-born son who is closely associated in this poem with Christ, to arise and take his place under her reign of sexual secrecy and institutionalized religious mystery. Instead he rises up in all his flaming energy, and at the end of the poem

> terrible Orc, when he beheld the morning in the east,
>
> Shot from the heights of Enitharmon;
> And in the vineyards of red France appear'd the light of his fury.
>
> The sun glow'd fiery red!
> The furious terrors flew around!
> On golden chariots raging, with red wheels dropping with blood;
> The Lions lash their wrathful tails!
> The Tigers couch upon the prey & suck the ruddy tide:
> And Enitharmon groans & cries in anguish and dismay.
> (14: 37–15: 8)

At this moment Los, the prophet-poet in Blake's mythic system, makes his first decisive appearance in the work of the 1790s:

> Then Los arose his head he reard in snaky thunders clad:
> And with a cry that shook all nature to the utmost pole,
> Call'd all his sons to the strife of blood.
>
> (15: 9–11)

For Erdman, Los appears here determined "to frame into prophetic symmetry the 'furious terrors' of armies of lions and preying tigers."[36] Whatever its applicability to the design of Plate 15, this is surely an idealization of what happens in the text: Los arises in language recalling Orc's own violent appearance and "Call'd all his sons to the strife of blood." In the visual design, if the frontally nude figure striding up stone steps away from the flames is Los, then Erdman might seem to be right in suggesting a benevolent pictorial alternative to the textual terror. Los, he says, is rescuing "his children (the daughters here . . .)." But in a work that has envisioned all of prerevolutionary Christian history as a delusive and corrupting dominion of the female will, this image of a powerful male removing one inert and one terrified female—both faceless—from a field of revolutionary battle to be occupied by Los and his sons, confirms the phallocentrism (this design is quite literally phallocentric) that determines so much in Blake's politics. Erdman reads the entire plate as "apocalyptic": it is visually indebted to depictions of the Last Judgment and of Christ's Harrowing of Hell. But the terms of Blake's apocalypse preserve forms of domination and mystify forms of violence. The vine that shoots out after the word "blood" at the end of the text is less a sign of hope or optimism than a gesture of prophetic self-assertion.

It is also a gesture of representational iconicity. As we noted in the first two chapters, graphic signs are frequently made to function in this hypersemiotic fashion in Blake's illuminated printing, and their doing so poses a distinctively Blakean version of the question about the relation between political and linguistic forms of the arbitrary. Hilton and Essick have both dealt with this question in revealing ways. But in textual moments such as the one I have just focused on in *Europe*, the boundary between writing and pictograph is violated on behalf of an iconicity that cannot be read as a self-validating expression of the Blakean Logos; it has to be read contextually and critically, like any other meaning-producing textual phenomenon. Elaborating the verbal representation of Los's calling "his sons to the strife of blood" into a simulacrum of organic growth and fruition confirms the appeal to phallocentric aggression in the text as a whole. If this is revolutionary violence as transgressive iconic exuberance—as an instance of the distinctively Blakean version of the "motivated sign," to use Essick's terms—we are left with aggravated rather than resolved questions about the source and consequence of such violence and of its representational status.

Is Los in the final plate of *Europe* a self-portrait of the artist as apocalyptic revolutionary? If he is, a critical reading of the plate needs to recognize in it a celebration of masculine artistic and sexual potency that makes Blake's figurings of revolutionary violence importantly different from those in Wordsworth, and also in Shelley. In *Ode to the West Wind* Shelley's imperative gesture identifying himself with the ultimate power of historical change—"Be thou me, impetuous one!" (62)—is as audacious in its way as Blake's identifying himself with Christ in *The Marriage of Heaven and Hell*. But Shelley's identification of the writing subject with historical necessity depends upon a dispersal and scattering of the subject's acts of self-representation. This process, in itself violent, is the cost for Shelley of prophetic communication. If the process is driven by an underlying erotic fantasy, it is that of dissemination, of propagation—and sometimes of projective identification with a violently inspired woman. For Blake, by contrast, representations of revolutionary violence generate a swelling concentration of productive agency. The executionary angel with the flaming phallic sword in Plate 5 of *America* is also Blake with his pen, his brush, his engraving instruments. That Blake clearly shared more pragmatic and justifiable impulses regarding revolutionary violence with radical artisans and "operatives" in the 1790s—vengeful and retaliatory fury against the ruling order, for instance—has been made clear in recent studies by David Worrall, John Mee, Saree Makdisi, and E. P. Thompson, among others.[37] But Blake's relation to the broader political context should not serve as a solvent for the fiercely phallocentric and heroically individualist qualities in his revolutionary art.

4.

Apocalypse is an operative tradition and mode in Shelley, too, but the figurative processes upon which apocalyptic writing depends are more reflexively and skeptically deployed—even when the poetic undertaking is explicitly visionary and demotic in ways that have reminded some readers of Blake.[38] Shelley sublimates the boiling rage he feels when he hears about the flagrant state violence at Peterloo into a recollected awakening from an exilic Mediterranean dream:

> As I lay asleep in Italy
> There came a voice from over the Sea,
> And with great power it forth led me
> To walk in the visions of Poesy.
> (1–4)

The four reiterated rhymes in the first stanza of *The Mask of Anarchy* contribute to the strange effect of being awakened from sleep only to be led into the realm of vision. Within this realm to which he has been summoned by the immediate political crisis in Britain, the speaker encounters the perennial forces of violent oppression and corruption masquerading as—in the momentary historical guise of—British government ministers. Frequently praised as a poem written for a popular audience, *The Mask*'s representational strategies are nonetheless characteristically subtle, even convoluted.[39] The speaker sees and discloses a hidden, disguised truth about the historical present in terms that position him and his readers in ironic, inverted relation to material reality. The Four Horsemen of the Apocalypse are disguised "like" the key figures of the current government; history provides the vehicle, not the tenor, in this version of apocalyptic discourse as waking or awakened vision.

"It is a kind of rallying hymn to nonviolent resistance": this sentence from the note in the first Norton Critical Edition aptly summarizes the main line of political interpretation of *The Mask of Anarchy*.[40] Whether the "resistance" the poem envisions is "nonviolent" or not, the forces of oppression are grotesquely brutal: Murder/Castlereagh tosses human hearts to the "Seven bloodhounds" that follow him (5–13); Fraud/Eldon knocks the brains out of the children playing around him with "mill-stones" produced by his own false tears. Anarchy himself, the only one of the four triumphant horsemen not specifically linked to a particular Tory minister (he stands for the entire government), rides "On a white horse, splashed with blood" and tramples "to a mire of blood / The adoring multitude" (31, 40–41). There is no resistance of any kind at this stage to "the triumph of Anarchy" (57): the "multitude" adore their oppressors (41) and respond to the violence used against them by obediently repeating the "mark" of arbitrary political power on Anarchy's crown, "I AM GOD, AND KING, AND LAW!" (37). The discrepancy in these early stanzas between institutionalized state violence and a mode of *non*resistance that echoes the violence of the rulers generates frustration and anger as well as a sense of hopeless desperation.

But as so often in Shelley's political writing, it is on the question of hopelessness or hope that the poem is made to turn. Just as Anarchy and his "slaves" are about to seize "the Bank and Tower" and take full possession of "his pensioned Parliament," a feminine figure and voice enter the poem. That this figure first appears as a "maniac Maid" (86) gives her an anticipatory connection to the "fierce Maenad" of *Ode to the West Wind*, as does her uncertain self-positioning between hope and despair.[41] Initially it is only her frantic act of self-naming that establishes anything like a positive identity:

> ... her name was Hope, she said:
> But she looked more like Despair,
> And she cried out in the air:
> (87–89)

Hope's behavior just after she speaks betrays her gesture of self-naming, making it seem arbitrary in an entirely degraded sense of the term. She performs a version of nonviolent resistance so abject as to problematize the subsequent status of nonviolence in the poem:

> Then she lay down in the street,
> Right before the horses' feet,
> Expecting, with a patient eye,
> Murder, Fraud and Anarchy.
> (98–101)

These lines are a partial prolepsis of the famous exhortation to passive resistance spoken by the voice of liberty near the end of the poem (299–347). They appear here to establish the preconditions for the emergence of this voice. The transitional sequence, at once inspiring and difficult in its figurative and rhetorical movement, poses a serious challenge to unqualified readings of *The Mask* as a "hymn to nonviolent resistance."

With "Hope" waiting patiently to be trampled beneath the feet of the marauding horsemen, "between her and her foes / A mist, a light, an image rose" (101–02). The agency behind or within this rising "image" is at first as textually indeterminate as the image itself; it is defined primarily by its fragility and tenuous uncertainty. Then, with astonishing speed, the image accumulates a power figured in terms of natural, and eventually of martial, violence:

> Till as clouds grow on the blast,
> Like tower-crowned giants striding fast
> And glare with lightnings as they fly,
> And speak in thunder to the sky,
>
> It grew—a Shape arrayed in mail
> Brighter than the Viper's scale,
> And upborne on wings whose grain
> Was as the light of sunny rain.
>
> On its helm seen far away,
> A planet, like the Morning's, lay;
> (106–15)

By the end of this sequence the tenuous "image" has become Lucifer, the rebellious God-defying light-bearer, whose bright armor is charged with the power of stormy "lightnings" and whose identification with the Morning Star has a long history in revolutionary discourse.[42] It is this force, which ironically makes itself felt through swift, invisible, thought-generating movement, that enables Hope to rise up from prostrate despair "ankle-deep in blood" (127) and that turns the oppressive violence of Anarchy against itself:

> And Anarchy, the ghastly birth,
> Lay dead earth upon the earth—
> The Horse of Death tameless as wind
> Fled, and with his hoofs did grind
> To dust, the murderers thronged behind.
> (130–34)

In assessing the poem's appeal to nonviolent resistance, we have to recognize and do justice to this dramatic representation of a violent undoing of state oppression. That this version of revolutionary violence springs from a liberatory energy at once armed and disarmingly mental—and that it is carried out not by the oppressed themselves but by the oppressors' own servants of war—may be both insightful and evasive. Shelley knows that the armed power of the British state somehow has to be smashed, ground to dust, before liberty can fully emerge. But he does not want to show oppressed citizens doing the grinding. The perspective in this poem is different from that of "Song to the Men of England," where workers are urged to "Forge arms, in your defense to bear" (24). The critical point is that political apocalypse in *The Mask of Anarchy* does not depend exclusively on nonviolent resistance. Shelley envisions the necessary destruction of Anarchy and his band of murderers with a very un-Blakean reluctance and with a deflection of clear political agency. The reluctance and deflection give this pivotal moment an aura of strategically evasive mystification. Yet the recognition that liberatory resistance must include the physical destruction of a genocidal oppressor is undeniably there, at the center of the poem.

The voice that emerges in the next three stanzas (135–46) to utter the great song of freedom that constitutes the second part of *The Mask* is a radically transformed elaboration of Hope's desperate two-stanza cry in lines 90–96. The voice precipitates out of images that recall the appearance of the militant Morning Star:

> A rushing light of clouds and splendour,
> A sense awakening and yet tender
> Was heard and felt—
> (135–37)

But now the "words of joy and fear" we are about to listen to come from a place defined—though only through the explicit approximation of simile—as feminine and maternal:

> As if their own indignant Earth
> Which gave the sons of England birth
> Had felt their blood upon her brow,
> And shuddering with a mother's throe
>
> Had turned every drop of blood
> By which her face had been bedewed
> To an accent unwithstood,—
> As if her heart had cried aloud:
> (139–46)

The gendered logic through which the best known part of *The Mask* is made a matter of "As if" depends, in one sense, on a conventional and traditional ideological appeal: Mother Earth cries out indignantly on behalf of the Sons of England. Shelley's quest for a revolutionary woman/mother in *The Revolt of Islam* returns here at a conjectural distance and in popular, familiar disguise, allowing the son-as-Morning Star again to revive an almost extinguished female agency: son inspires mother to inspire "Sons." There are other conventional ideological appeals woven into the song of freedom—to "some spot of English ground" (264), to "The old laws of England" (331). Countering this dimension of the rhetoric is a deeply unconventional effort to convert the tragic violence of Peterloo into a renewal of political hope rooted in popular power from below. Though the voice of maternal joy and fear and indignation will go on to counsel resolute inaction and "folded arms" (321) when the tyrants launch their next assault on a peaceful gathering of the people, this counsel is framed by a refrain that gives nonviolent resistance the power of tremendous potential militancy: "'Rise like Lions after slumber / In unvanquishable number'" (151–52, 368–69). "Lions after slumber" have not only gathered their strength, they are or will soon be hungry. By projecting an "unvanquishable number" of such lions as a figure for ordinary British people rising from a political slumber that parallels the speaker's own at the beginning of the poem, Shelley transmutes the most familiar of British royal heraldic devices into an image to make all royals and royalists tremble.[43]

But this image of popular power is entirely potential, not actual, with respect to its appeal to the necessity of "coercion, to repel coercion." In September 1819 Shelley was not simply reluctant in principle to advocate armed insurrection; he believed that circumstances in Britain were not yet favorable for a successful uprising and that an unsuccessful one would provoke more and worse brutality by the government. The view he expressed to Peacock on 24 August 1819, before he had learned of Peterloo, persisted as part of his later perspective: "anarchy will only be the last flash before despotism." Though Peterloo led him to see that *anarchy* was a term most appropriately applied to misrule by the existing *hierarchy*, his anxiety about an abortive insurrection contends with his urgent sense that "Something must be done" and that the bloody aggression of the "tyrants" must not be met with "docility." So throughout the song of freedom in *The Mask* there are repeated expressions of hope that the "Blood for blood" thirst for "revenge" may somehow be avoided, somehow sublimated into words and gestures: "'Be your strong and simple words / Keen to wound as sharpened swords'" (299–300). "Swords" takes in "words" but will not perfectly rhyme with it—a suggestion in this context of a dissonance in Shelley's hopeful thinking that has already become evident at the end of the extended definition of "Freedom": "'. . . let deeds, not words, express / Thine exceeding loveliness'" (260–61). It is not Freedom's "loveliness" alone but also its actualization in history that depends on "deeds" as well as "words"—and on "words" as "deeds."[44] Similarly, exhorting the people of Britain to meet government violence with "looks which are / Weapons of unvanquished war" (321–22), and later to trust that the "blood thus shed" in what critics have called "nonviolent resistance" will produce "hot blushes" of shame in the faces of government soldiers, are rhetorical moves that expose the uncertainty of Shelley's qualms about armed resistance. As it happened, neither the Tory government nor the Manchester militia felt any shame at all about what they had done. This is why, despite Shelley's well-founded anxiety about insurrectional violence in 1819, *The Mask* shows that Anarchy and his fellow murderers will, eventually, have to be "gr[ou]nd / To dust" (133–34). In this respect the Shelleyan apocalypse remains a self-divided vision of how ordinary British people might make a history for themselves that yields freedom rather than tyranny.

5.

It is in his most fully elaborated perspective on political reform that Shelley most fully elaborates his perspective on revolutionary violence. *A Philosophical View of Reform* was written in late 1819, with the immediate anger and anxiety provoked by Peterloo still intense and with the question "What is to be done?" posing itself more urgently than ever. Writing to Ollier on 15 December, Shelley says "I intend it to be an instructive and readable book, appealing from the passions to the reason of men" (*LPBS* 2: 164). The appeal from passion to reason drives the essay.

In his initial effort to face what most regarded as the excessive violence of the French Revolution, Shelley argues both that "The tyrants, were, as usual, the aggressors" and that when "the oppressed . . . arose and took a dreadful revenge on their oppressors" this was "in itself a mistake, a crime, a calamity" (*WPBS* 6: 13). Still he insists, inverting the irony of Mark Antony's praise of Caesar in Shakespeare's play, "the good which the Revolutionists did lives after them, their ills are interred with their bones" (*WPBS* 6: 14). Armed resistance is justified, he goes on to say, when all efforts at parliamentary and constitutional reform have been exhausted—as in most respects they had been in 1819. In these circumstances, Shelley agrees with Wollstonecraft that "The right of insurrection is derived from the employment of armed force to counteract the will of the nation"(*WPBS* 6: 53).[45]

The ruling class bears responsibility for presenting the oppressed with no alternative but "civil war." And from this grim alternative "we must not sh[rink]" (*WPBS* 6: 53). Though revolutionary civil war is always a source of "grief and horror" and "the sudden disruption of the bonds of social life," history shows that it will eventually become unavoidable: not to have "recourse to coercion to repel coercion" (Wollstonecraft) in such moments is an indefensible refusal of self-defense, of life itself. Shelley's defense of armed resistance is entwined at every turn with a repudiation of war's glory and of Fanonesque beliefs in the cleansing power of violence—and with a sense that even justifiable "confidence in brute force" is "capable of being perverted to destroy the cause [such force was] assumed to promote" (*WPBS* 6: 54). Nevertheless, the current "moral and political degradation" of Britain means that "it will be necessary to appeal to an exertion of physical strength." *A Philosophical View of Reform* ends by repudiating the calls for "Retribution" by "certain vulgar agitators" (*WPBS* 6: 55) but also by openly asserting, in a way that *The Mask of Anarchy* tries to avoid, the necessity of armed insurrection.

Some three or four months after facing the prospect of necessary self-defensive violence more directly than at any other time in his life as a writer, Shelley learned that King Ferdinand VII of Spain had been forced by liberal nationalist revolutionaries to restore the Constitution of 1812, which he had suspended when the Congress of Vienna put him back on the throne in March 1814. Shelley took the Spanish Revolution as evidence that even in the most brutally despotic of European states, determined, organized struggle from below could break through political despair and resignation.[46] About Britain itself he remained pessimistic: "I see with deep regret in today's Papers the attempt to assassinate the Ministry," he writes to Peacock from Pisa in early March 1820, having read about the Cato Street Conspiracy. "Every thing seems to conspire against Reform" (*LPBS* 2: 176). In early May he was still telling Peacock that "there is but little unanimity in the mass of the people," that "a civil war impends from the success of ministers and the exasperation of the poor" (*LPBS* 2: 193). But the revolt in Spain kept hope alive, and between March and July it gave rise to one of Shelley's most ambitious political lyrics, the *Ode to Liberty*.

The *Ode* opens with two lines from Canto 4 of *Childe Harold's Pilgrimage*, where Byron reflects defiantly on the moment when "France got drunk with blood to vomit crime": "Yet, Freedom, yet thy banner torn but flying, / Streams like a thunder-storm against the wind" (4. 874–75). Revolutionary violence for the Byron of *Childe Harold* 4, in contrast to the Byron of *Don Juan* 8. 393–408 cited in my Preface, is the memory of orgiastic and politically destructive excess, a "Saturnalia" that has since been "fatal . . . / To Freedom's cause" by providing a "pretext for the eternal fall" of oppression (4. 865–72). Instead of following the direction of his epigraph, Shelley will turn Byron's image of freedom streaming "against the wind" and bring it closer to those quite different figurations of revolutionary energy manifesting itself as counterforce to the direction of the wind in Book 10 of *The Prelude* and in *Ode to the West Wind*. There were many reasons to believe in early 1820 that the prevailing winds of history still favored the old monarchical order after all. But the Spanish Revolution disrupted the British-led restoration and consolidation of the old monarchies, signaling—Shelley dares to hope—a revived turn in the political climate.

So Shelley uses the lines from *Childe Harold* 4 to reconnect rather than to counterpose freedom and revolution, and to anticipate the rising energy of his own approaching early spring thunderstorm, the pendant to the approaching autumnal storm at the beginning of *West Wind*. Byron's "thunder-storm" is politically reconfigured, not simply echoed, in the opening lines of the *Ode to Liberty*:

> A glorious people vibrated again
>   The lightning of the nations: Liberty
> From heart to heart, from tower to tower, o'er Spain
>   Scattering contagious fire into the sky,
> Gleamed.
>
> (1–5)

"Contagious" carries forward the ambivalent aspect of Shelley's language of revolutionary apocalypse: here, as in *West Wind*, the horrifying transmission of war-engendered pestilence lurks as a threat beneath the vibrant transmission of insurrectionary "fire." The outburst of liberatory violence carries within itself a potential for degeneration in the social realm, and also in the internal realm of the speaker-poet's own revived aggression:

> My soul spurned the chains of its dismay,
> And in the rapid plumes of song
> Clothed itself, sublime and strong;
> As a young eagle soars the morning clouds among,
> Hovering in verse o'er its accustomed prey;
>   (5–9)

Insurrection in Spain has returned the poet from "dismay" to his "accustomed" aquiline instincts. The image carries a contradictory aura, given the eagle's associations with Napoleon, with Byron himself, and with the power of the nobility.[47] Revolutionary hope is taking Shelley in risky directions through such alignments of writing with dominance and predation. If the pronouns of "Ye are many, they are few" exclude the radical aristocratic poet-in-exile from active participation in *The Mask of Anarchy*'s exhorting the British people to "Rise like lions," the first stanza of the *Ode to Liberty* relocates him within a confusing vortical center of violent engagement.

Rhetorically, the *Ode to Liberty* represents itself as recording "A voice out of the deep" (15) that retraces the history of liberty as it emerges from and in opposition to both a primal "chaos" (22) and ongoing forms of tyrannical anarchy disguised as natural social hierarchy and tradition. As the poem moves from the chaotic prehistory of humanity through Greek, Roman, Renaissance, and modern attempts to establish new forms of social and cultural freedom, one of its most striking features is a sustained positive figuring of violent energy—even in passages where the emphasis initially falls on visionary tranquility:

> Athens arose: a city such as vision
>   Builds from the purple crags and silver towers
> Of battlemented clouds, as in derision
>   Of kingliest masonry: the ocean-floors
> Pave it; the evening sky pavilions it;
>   Its portals are inhabited
>   By thunder-zoned winds,
>   (61–67)

Athens derives its strength from a form of visionary parody, discovering in "battlemented clouds" shapes that derive from, but also appropriate by transforming, "kingliest" power. It is open to "thunder-zoned winds" that prefigure "The voices of its bards and sages," which "thunder / With an earth-awakening blast," "Rending the veil of space and time asunder" (80–86). This emphasis on a transformative visionary violence extends through the stanzas on Rome, imaged as a "wolf-cub" nourished by a "Cadmaean Maenad" (91–93).[48] Since the Cadmaean Maenad Agave kills her son Pentheus, Roman liberty must be understood to contain an ominous self-destructive potential.

Yet Shelley daringly associates the primal bond between "wolf-cub" and "Cadmaean Maenad" with deeds of "terrible uprightness" performed by such early Roman heroes as Camillus and Atilius. Liberty was historically unattainable without such deeds—and continues to be so when Europe finally awakens from its feudal backwardness:

> Thou huntress swifter than the Moon! thou terror
> Of the world's wolves! thou bearer of the quiver,
> Whose sunlight shafts pierce tempest-winged Error,
> (136–38)

This tenth stanza, celebrating the achievements of Luther and Milton, names Liberty as a "terror" and shows the "wolf-cub" of the seventh stanza grown from Liberty's nourished child into her targeted foe. The sequence epitomizes the *Ode*'s drive to reaffirm the inescapably painful relation between revolution and freedom, a relation that many of Shelley's politically pessimistic contemporaries, including the Byron of *Childe Harold* 4, had come to see as merely destructive.

Stanza 10, as part of a further troping of Shelley's Byronic epigraph, sets the terms for the *Ode*'s account of revolution in France and its degeneration into Napoleonic imperialist tyranny. As for the revolutionary civil war itself, stanza 12 emphasizes, it was the oppressive "slime" of feudal society clinging to power that "dyed all thy liquid light with blood and tears, / Till thy sweet stars could weep the stain away" (169–70). Echoing but shifting the political reference of Byron's calling the Jacobin Terror a "Saturnalia," Shelley defiantly holds the ruling institutions of the *ancien regime* responsible for the bloodbath:

> How like Bacchanals of blood
> Round France, the ghastly vintage, stood
> Destruction's sceptred slaves, and Folly's mitred brood!
> (171–73)

The political figuration here is daring—and again risky—since "Bacchanals" inevitably recalls liberty-as-"Cadmaean Maenad" from stanza 7, even as it sees the counterrevolutionary destroyers of freedom, not the Jacobins, as the ones guilty of drinking blood.[49] We are made to understand frenzied violence as endemic to revolutionary civil war, and as a force moving across the political spectrum. Napoleon arises from the historical vortex as a reflexive corruption of liberty's violent trajectory, as "The Anarch of thine own bewildered powers" (175). Nevertheless, the political sources of his power were different from those of the aristocratic "sceptred slaves" with whom he did battle, and Napoleon lives on in the *Ode*'s historical present as a ghost who haunts "victor kings in their ancestral towers" (180), mocking their indulgence in the "ghastly vintage" of triumphant restoration.

As the *Ode* finally turns to England, it composes a fierce harmony from the figurative keynote of thunder and what G. M. Matthews long ago called the "volcano voice" of revolution:

> England yet sleeps: was she not called of old?
>   Spain calls her now, as with its thrilling thunder
> Vesuvius wakens Aetna, and the cold
>   Snow-crags by its reply are cloven in sunder:
>   (181–84)[50]

Italy's volcanoes, with their associative links to ancient eruptions of liberatory struggle in Greece and Rome, momentarily provide the third mediating term in stanza 13 between the present breaking of Spain's "links of steel" and a future in which England's "chains," which are in reality "threads of gold," offer the fleeting possibility of a more benign kind of breaking: "she [England] need but smile / And they dissolve."

That this possibility is unlikely to be realized is the burden of the extended portrait of Arminius in stanza 14. Byron's stanzas in *Childe Harold* 4 continue to provide metaphorical points of departure: the speaker wishes that the soul of the ancient Germanic tribal hero "may stream over the tyrants' head" (198), like freedom's banner in the epigraph, liberating both Italy and Germany: "Thy victory shall be his epitaph, / Wild Bacchanal of truth's mysterious wine" (199–200).[51] The flow of Bacchic figuration appears to return at this point from its precarious status in the France stanza to its ancient Greco-Roman topos. But this place, too—and all places of Dionysian ecstasy, the *Ode* insists—contain the potential for violently destructive contradiction. So stanza 14 ends with a call for liberty's "Wild Bacchanal" of truth to turn against the false, oppressive appropriation of this libidinal energy:

> O Italy,
> Gather thy blood into thy heart; repress
> The beasts who make their dens thy sacred palaces.
>   (208–10)

Where else in Shelley's poetry is there a call for repression?[52] In the *Ode to Liberty* there has to be such a call: liberty cannot be realized in the world of this text without the violent desire and will to seize political power from the "beasts" who have possessed it.

"Repress" in the penultimate line of stanza 14 echoes back through its semantically dissonant rhyming partners ("loveliness" in line 207, "wilderness" in line 205) to "impress" in the penultimate line of the previous stanza, where England and Spain are summoned to register their crimes: "impress as from a seal / All ye have thought and done! Time cannot dare conceal" (194–95). This image of semiotic stamping comes to be obsessively elaborated in the astonishing stanza near the end of the *Ode* where the violence of representation appears as a precondition for the elimination of monarchy.

> O, that the free would stamp the impious name
>   Of KING into the dust! or write it there,
> So that this blot upon the page of fame
>   Were as a serpent's path, which the light air
> Erases, and the flat sands close behind!
>   Ye the oracle have heard:
>   Lift the victory-flashing sword,
> And cut the snaky knots of this foul gordian word,
>   Which weak itself as stubble, yet can bind
>   Into a mass, irrefragably firm,
> The axes and the rods which awe mankind;
>   The sound has poison in it, 'tis the sperm
> Of what makes life foul, cankerous, and abhorred;
>   Disdain not thou, at thine appointed term,
> To set thine armed heel on this reluctant worm.
>   (211–25)

This is Shelley's culminating rewording and reworking of the epigraphic image of freedom's banner, freedom's visible sign. The "free" are challenged to use the force necessary to constitute liberty's own historical identity and obliterate the monarchical countersign, the "name" or "word" that legitimizes social inequality and domination. One strain in this figurative skein reaches back into Shelley's radical reading and rereading of Enlightenment theories of the arbitrary sign. The word "KING" as a tangle of "snaky knots" revises Locke's assertion that "Though . . . it be the Mind that makes the Collection [of "the loose parts of . . . complex *Ideas*"], 'tis the Name which is, as it were the Knot, that ties them fast together." Locke continues: "What a vast variety of different *Ideas*, does the word *Triumphus* hold together, and deliver to us as one *Species*" (*Essay Concerning Human Understanding* 3. 5. 10, 434). Making the particular word-knot "KING" also "gordian" evokes and inverts the ancient narrative in which, as a demonstration of political power, a knot is severed by a king's sword (Alexander's) rather than painstakingly untied.

From the stanza's opening optative wish ("O, that . . .") forward, semiotic agency converts political into linguistic, graphemic violence—and vice versa.[53] "[S]tamp" in line 211 merges acts of language and acts of regicidal insurrection in an aggressive pun; this gives way to what seems an alternative act of writing that produces, however, an equivalent result, since "KING" is satanically, serpentinely written or rewritten in order that it may be erased—razed, in terms that echo the devastation of Ozymandias's "shattered visage" and "colossal" "Works." With the shift from optative to exhortative address in the middle of the stanza—"Lift the victory-flashing sword"—the *Ode* comes closest to the defiant apocalyptic vision of Plate 5 of Blake's *America*. In a pivotal iconic gesture sharply different from the related act of rhyming in *The Mask*, "sword" precedes and absorbs "word." It will take an actual sword, not just the pen as metaphorical weapon, to break "The axes and the rods which awe mankind" (221).

Here as elsewhere in Shelley, revolutionary violence is threatened and potentially contaminated by its counterrevolutionary forms and versions. The self-erasing "serpent's path" of writing coalesces again into the "snaky knots of this foul gordian word," then degenerates further in the institutionalized sign's "poison[ous]" "sound" and in its monstrous life as pestiferously generative "sperm." There are additional ties here to the degenerative dimension of the phallocentric serpent imagery in Blake's *America*, as if in rising up against the mystified oppression of "sceptred" power, insurrectional violence risks being transmuted into forms of its political antithesis. It is to resurrect the stanza's and the *Ode*'s political intention and goal that Shelley ends with a couplet paralleling the militant challenge to Italy at the end of the previous stanza: "Disdain not thou, at thine appointed term, / To set thine armed heel on this reluctant worm" (224–25). If the monarch is "reluctant" to surrender power, "the free," too, may fight back against (*reluctor*, to struggle against, resist) their historical mission by disdaining to crush tyranny when they have the power to do so. The speaker-poet asserts his own will and agency as rhetorical imperative in an effort to assure that freedom's "appointed term" is not missed in a moment of compassionate but misguided passivity and mercy.

But hope, not aggressive assurance, is the prevailing stance in Shelley's political writing. The *Ode* returns to the optative mode ("O, that . . . O, that . . .") in stanza 16, devoted to "the pale name of PRIEST," then ends three stanzas later in a series of dwindling similes recording the sudden withdrawal of "the spirit of that mighty singing / To its abyss" (271–72). The final simile—"As waves which lately paved his watery way / Hiss round a drowner's head in their tempestuous play"—evokes a stormy death by drowning that recalls the poisonous hiss of the kingly serpent in stanza 14 as well as the thunderstorm in which the spirit of liberty first appeared in stanza 1.[54]

Before reading the newspaper accounts of Peterloo, Shelley told Peacock that "change should commence among the higher orders, or anarchy will only be the last flash before despotism." The terms of Shelley's anxiety about catastrophic violence in this letter correspond to the two modes of arbitrary power traced in this book: "anarchy" and "despotism," chaotic disorder from below or within, coercive imposition from above or without. But the poem Shelley wrote in the weeks following his learning about Peterloo reveals "despotism" as the real "anarchy" and imagines popular resistance to a brutal, militarized state as a contradictory fusion of unvengeful, passive endurance and volcanic, lion-like uprising. That such an uprising could generate new and different forms of "despotism" was evident from the Napoleonic aftermath of the French Revolution. So in the extended essay on politics and political economy he drafted in the final months of 1819, Shelley grounds his revised and unfinished understanding of the right and necessity of insurrection in a fresh sense of what it would mean for "the people" to "have obtained"—and to sustain—"victory over their oppressors" (*WPBS* 6: 54). 1820 opened with news from Madrid related to but different from the news from Manchester: liberal popular forces had overthrown a corrupt dictatorial monarch. The *Ode to Liberty* dares to imagine that the history of political freedom may finally have arrived at a moment when "the impious name / Of KING" may be, like Anarchy and his throng of "murderers" in *The Mask*, ground to dust.

To imagine such a moment inevitably means for Shelley, especially given his isolation from organized collective action, to pose its historicity and its actuality, as well as its very representational status, as a question. Three powerful "what if" questions about material progress, about art, and about the "breed"-ing of "New wants, and wealth from those who toil and groan" dominate stanza 17. Then the speaker-poet responds to the beckoning of the "morning-star" in the penultimate stanza of the *Ode* by asking about

> Blind Love, and equal Justice, and the Fame
>   Of what has been, the Hope of what will be?
> O, Liberty! if such could be thy name
>   Wert thou disjoined from these, or they from thee:
> If thine or theirs were treasures to be bought
>   By blood or tears, have not the wise and free
>   Wept tears, and blood like tears?
>   (266–70)

The *Ode to Liberty* cannot answer these questions. They will have to be answered in the future ongoing process of making a history to which

Shelley's work will contribute its vision that arbitrary power—after an inevitable shedding of blood and tears—may be democratically transfigured to meet the historical evolution of human needs and desires.

All that is certain about the "Liberty" we are asked to imagine in Shelley's *Ode* is that most of humanity has desired and still desires it—and has the capacity (to use the "new verb" that Coleridge introduces in chapter 12 of *Biographia Literaria*) to "potentiate" it. The *Ode*'s concluding dialectic of hope and uncertainty emerges from a poetic return to and turning of history in which freedom's own history takes shape through recurrently violent antagonism with unfree structures and institutions of power, and through incomplete recognitions of its own difficult self-differentiation from chaos and mere contingency. To the extent that the "recourse to coercion" (Wollstonecraft) is determined by the ruling order's leaving no other "path to freedom but through their own blood" (Shelley), freedom realizes itself historically against and through arbitrary power—against and through conditions that are given and imposed, random and capricious. In the *Ode* itself, once the "spirit" momentarily awakened and animated by revolutionary struggle in Spain has "withdrawn" to "its abyss" (271–72), the poetic subject who has envisioned and recorded "Liberty's" unfolding historical self-definition dissolves in figures of arbitrary violence and disorganization—the "wild swan" shot through the "brain" without motivation (273–77), the mariner drowned instead of transported by the waves' "tempestuous play" (284–85). What survives this staging of the poem's own death is a trajectory of commitment to "Liberty's" unfinished cause.

Romanticism has conventionally been celebrated, and more recently demystified, as a cultural period especially defined by a belief in the power of the free individual subject. But from the perspective elaborated in the *Ode to Liberty* and in many of the other texts I have foregrounded in this book, human freedom has meaning only within a process of making history in which the arbitrariness of language and the arbitrariness of political domination are encountered inside as well as outside or beyond human agency. It is because these forms of the arbitrary are inside as well as outside or beyond that they can be transformed through the work of imagining and knowing, through cultural and political practice. And it is because the Romantics saw their relations to arbitrary power as diversely transformable that we most effectively read these writers as representing themselves not "at the end of history," and certainly not outside of it, but at its beginning.[55]

NOTES

PREFACE

1. James Chandler documents the "return to history" throughout *England in 1819: The Politics of Literary Culture and the Case of Romantic Historicism* (Chicago: University of Chicago Press, 1998). On the earlier "linguistic turn," see my "Romanticism and language," *The Cambridge Companion to British Romanticism*, ed. Stuart Curran (Cambridge: Cambridge University Press, 1993), 95–119. For a representative sampling of the latter development, see *Romanticism and Language*, ed. Arden Reed (Ithaca: Cornell University Press, 1984).

2. Chandler, *England in 1819*, 36, 37.

3. Fredric Jameson, *The Political Unconscious: Narrative as Symbolically Social Act* (Ithaca: Cornell University Press, 1981), 9.

4. Fredric Jameson, *The Prison-House of Language: A Critical Account of Structuralism and Russian Formalism* (Princeton: Princeton University Press, 1972), 145.

5. Richard Cronin, *The Politics of Romantic Poetry: In Search of the Pure Commonwealth* (New York: St. Martin's Press, 2000), 11–12.

6. See John Barrell, *Imagining the King's Death: Figurative Treason, Fantasies of Regicide 1793–1796* (Oxford: Oxford University Press, 2000).

7. See Marchand's note in *BLJ* 8: 78.

1. ARBITRARY POWER

1. Quoted from Mary Wollstonecraft, *A Vindication of the Rights of Woman*, ed. Carol H. Poston, 2d ed. (New York: Norton, 1988), 15.

2. *The Edinburgh Review* 32: 184.

3. See Hans Aarsleff, *From Locke to Saussure: Essays on the Study of Language and Intellectual History* (Minneapolis: University of Minnesota Press, 1982), especially "Leibniz on Locke on Language," "Locke's Reputation in Nineteenth-Century England," and "Wordsworth, Language, and Romanticism"; also Aarsleff's earlier book, *The Study of Language in England 1780–1860* (Minneapolis: University of Minnesota Press, 1983). See also the discussions of this principle in Stephen K. Land, *From Signs to Propositions: The Concept of Form in Eighteenth-Century Semantic Theory* (London: Longman, 1974), 50–74, and Murray Cohen, *Sensible Words: Linguistic Practice in England 1640–1785* (Baltimore: The Johns Hopkins University Press, 1977), 122 ff.

4. John Locke, *An Essay Concerning Human Understanding*, ed. Peter H. Nidditch (Oxford: Clarendon Press, 1975), 405. Quotations later in this chapter of the *Two Treatises of Government* are from the edition by Peter Laslett, 2d ed. with amendments (Cambridge: Cambridge University Press, 1970). All citations of Locke are from these editions and are given parenthetically within the text. Throughout the text, emphasis is in the original source unless otherwise stated.

5. Shelley ordered a new edition of Locke's *Essay* from his bookseller in Sep-

tember 1815 (*LPBS* 1: 431). According to Mary Shelley's *Journals*, he read Locke regularly from November 1816 to January 1817 and returned to him again in March and April 1820 (*The Journals of Mary Shelley*, ed. Paula R. Feldman and Diana Scott-Kilvert [Baltimore: The Johns Hopkins University Press, 1995], 144–58, 314).

6. During a conference at Northwestern University several years ago, John Brenkman dissented from this line of argument by saying that I wanted to make "arbitrary power" the "founding contradiction" of Romantic writing. My response was, and is, that "arbitrary power" is not *the* but *a* founding contradiction of Romantic writing.

7. Hugh Roberts, *Shelley and the Chaos of History: A New Politics of Poetry* (University Park: Pennsylvania State University Press, 1997), 252, 253.

8. For discussions characteristically emphasizing Locke's "conventional" theory of language, see Neal Wood, *The Politics of Locke's Philosophy: A Social Study of "An Essay Concerning Human Understanding"* (Berkeley: University California Press, 1983), 168, and Michael Ayers, *Locke Vol. I: Epistemology* (London and New York: Routledge, 1991), 289–99. The latter considers Locke's philosophy of language in relation to Chomskyan theory.

9. For an argument that Shelley's poetry "attempts to work beneath, and in defiance of, the words of which it is composed" by turning conventional political language against itself, see Richard Cronin, "Shelley's Language of Dissent," *Essays in Criticism* 27 (1977): 203–15.

10. Jacques Derrida, *Of Grammatology*, trans. Gayatri Chakravorty Spivak (Baltimore: The Johns Hopkins University Press, 1974), 44. See also Derrida's "Scribble (writing-power)," *Yale French Studies* 58 (1979): 117–47, esp. 141: "Arbitrariness is a ruse to conceal motivation and power by creating the illusion of an *internal* system of language or writing in general."

11. Paul de Man, "Shelley Disfigured," *Deconstruction and Criticism* (New York: Seabury Press, 1979), 62–63.

12. Umberto Eco, *A Theory of Semiotics* (Bloomington: Indiana University Press, 1979), 190–99. The "arbitrary"/"motivated" distinction structures Robert N. Essick's detailed survey of linguistic theory in *William Blake and the Language of Adam* (Oxford: Clarendon Press, 1989; see especially Ch. 2, "In Pursuit of the Motivated Sign"). But Essick never acknowledges that the term "motivated" was not part of eighteenth- or early nineteenth-century semiotic discourse, and he says nothing about the concept of the "arbitrary" and its complex relationship to ideas of motivation.

13. Symptomatic in this respect is John Carlos Rowe's essay on "Structure" in *Critical Terms for Literary Study*, ed. Frank Lentricchia and Thomas McLaughlin, 2d ed. (Chicago: University of Chicago Press, 1995); see especially 26–27: "By the mid-1970s, Saussure's theories would be common assumptions of most literary critics . . . , especially the theory of the arbitrariness of the sign."

14. The only entry under "arbitrary" in *The Encyclopedia of Language and Linguistics*, ed. R. E. Asher and J.M.Y. Simpson (Oxford: Pergamon Press, 1994) is an article by W.P.M. Meyer Viol (1: 205–6) devoted to "Arbitrary Objects," a term used in mathematics and logic with reference to the principle of "generic attribution." See K. Fine, *Reasoning with Arbitrary Objects* (Oxford: Basil Black-

well, 1985). In his article on "Sign" in the *Encyclopedia*, P.A.M. Seuren provides a general explanation for this state of affairs: "Although there is a general if only implicit agreement in modern linguistics that natural languages are a specific kind of sign system, there is hardly any mention of the notion of 'sign' in contemporary theoretical and philosophical linguistic literature" (7: 3885). In *A Dictionary of Linguistics and Phonetics*, 3d ed. (Oxford: Basil Blackwell, 1991), David Crystal defines only "arbitrary reference," "a term used in *Generative Grammar*, especially in *Government-Binding Theory*, in connection with the understood *Subject* of certain *Infinitives*" (emphasis in original to indicate q.v.).

15. Roy Harris, *Reading Saussure* (London: Open Court, 1987), 55 ff. Subsequent page-references are given parenthetically in the text.

16. Emile Benveniste, "The Nature of the Linguistic Sign" [1966], *Problems in General Linguistics*, trans. Mary Elizabeth Meek (Coral Gables: University of Miami Press, 1971), 43–45.

17. Noam Chomsky, *Cartesian Linguistics: A Chapter in the History of Rationalist Thought* (Lanham, MD: University Press of America, 1966). See Hans Aarsleff's critique, "The History of Linguistics and Professor Chomsky," *Language* 46 (1970): 570–85, reprinted in his *From Locke to Saussure*, 101–19.

18. Oswald Ducrot and Tzvetan Todorov, *Encyclopedic Dictionary of the Sciences of Language*, trans. Catherine Porter (Baltimore: The Johns Hopkins University Press, 1983), 134.

19. Steven Pinker, *The Language Instinct: How the Mind Creates Language* (New York: Harper Collins, 1994), 237. For an indication of current debates over the status within the tradition of generative grammar of words as arbitrary pairings of sounds and meanings, as distinct from rules as universally set cognitive operations that assemble words into meaningful combinations, see John Searle's review of Pinker's *Words and Rules: The Ingredients of Language* (New York: HarperPerennial, 2001) in the *New York Review of Books* (14 March 2002) and the subsequent exchange between Pinker and Searle (27 June 2002). See also Searle's review of Chomsky's *New Horizons in the Study of Language and Mind* in the *New York Review of Books* (28 February 2002), Sylvain Bromberger's response to this review (25 April 2002), and the exchange between Chomsky and Searle (18 July 2002).

20. See James C. McKusick, *Coleridge's Philosophy of Language* (New Haven: Yale University Press, 1986), 4–32, 119–48.

21. Raymond Williams, *Marxism and Literature* (Oxford and New York: Oxford University Press, 1977), 38. Subsequent page-references are given parenthetically in the text.

22. Tony Bennett, *Formalism and Marxism* (London and New York: Methuen, 1979), 60.

23. John B. Thompson, ed., "Editor's Introduction" to *Language and Symbolic Power* (Cambridge, MA: Harvard University Press, 1991), 30. This volume includes all but two essays originally published in Bourdieu's *Ce que parler veut dire: l'économie des échanges linguistiques* (1982), plus five pieces published elsewhere. Subsequent page-references to this edition are given parenthetically in the text.

24. Bourdieu refers briefly to Williams in *The Rules of Art: Genesis and Struc-

ture of the Literary Field, trans. Susan Emanuel (Stanford: Stanford University Press, 1996), 55. This book appeared in French in 1992 as *Les Règles de l'art*.

25. Olivia Smith, *The Politics of Language 1791–1819* (Oxford: Clarendon Press, 1984), 224.

26. Smith, *The Politics of Language*, 214, 215.

27. Tom Furniss, *Edmund Burke's Aesthetic Ideology: Language, gender, and political economy in revolution* (Cambridge: Cambridge University Press, 1993), 90. Furniss is quoting James T. Boulton's edition of *A Philosophical Enquiry into the Origin of Our Ideas of the Sublime and Beautiful* (London: Routledge and Kegan Paul, 1958), 123.

28. Alan Richardson places this passage from Coleridge's letter to Godwin in a fascinating new context in *British Romanticism and the Science of the Mind* (Cambridge: Cambridge University Press, 2001), 3–5.

29. See McKusick's discussion of Coleridge and natural language, *Coleridge's Philosophy of Language*, 4–19, 101–3, 108–10, 117–18, 149–50; also the relevant pages in Timothy Corrigan, *Coleridge, Language and Criticism* (Athens: University of Georgia Press, 1981), Raimonda Modiano, *Coleridge and the Concept of Nature* (Tallahassee: Florida State University Press, 1985, and A. C. Goodson, *Verbal Imagination: Coleridge and the Language of Modern Criticism* (New York: Oxford University Press, 1988).

30. There is little indication that Coleridge was interested in Tooke's emphasis on speed and efficiency as factors in the development of language; see McKusick's fine chapter on "Coleridge and Horne Tooke," *Coleridge's Philosophy of Language*, 33–52.

31. Jerome Christensen, *Lord Byron's Strength: Romantic Writing and Commercial Society* (Baltimore: The Johns Hopkins University Press, 1993), 313.

32. The entirety of Chandler's third chapter, "Representing Culture, Romanticizing Contradiction: The Politics of Literary Exemplarity," is relevant here and forms the main enabling critical context for the concluding section of my own chapter.

33. I offer an English translation that follows the German text more closely than the one in the International Publishers edition (1977) quoted by Chandler and many others. The passage runs as follows in the second, revised edition of *The Eighteenth Brumaire* (Hamburg, 1869): "Die Menschen machen ihre eigene Geschichte, aber sie machen sie nicht aus freien Stücken, nicht unter selbstgewählten, sondern unter unmittelbar vorgefundenen, gegebenen und überlieferten Umständen."

34. For an impressive attempt to extend Althusser's account of "overdetermination"—in *For Marx* (1965)—that is particularly relevant to the concerns of this chapter, see Michel Pêcheux, *Language, Semantics and Ideology*, trans. Ben Brewster (New York: St. Martin's Press, 1982). Pêcheux's book was published in French in 1975.

2. WORDS ARE THINGS

1. Although the formal discourse of the aesthetic explicitly privileges poetry from Baumgarten's *Reflections* forward, there is no sustained treatment of the

status of poetic language within this discourse as it emerges and develops through Kant and Hegel. Terry Eagleton's chapters on eighteenth- and early nineteenth-century developments in *The Ideology of the Aesthetic* (Oxford: Basil Blackwell, 1990) say little about language, which, however, emerges as a key issue in the chapter on Marx (197–99) and in his discussion of Freud, Heidegger, Adorno, Benjamin, and Habermas. "Language" does not appear in the index to Luc Ferry's *Homo Aestheticus: The Invention of Taste in the Democratic Age* (Chicago: University of Chicago Press, 1990)

2. See Alexander Baumgarten, *Reflections on Poetry*, trans. Karl Aschenbrenner and William B. Holther (Berkeley: University of California Press, 1954), 38–39: "By *sensate representations* we mean representations received through the lower part of the cognitive faculty.... By *sensate discourse* we mean discourse involving sensate representations.... By *perfect sensate discourse* we mean discourse whose various parts are directed towards the apprehension of sensate representations.... By *poem* we mean a perfect sensate discourse." These preliminary deductions are foundational to Baumgarten's culminating movement at the end of the *Reflections* from "poetry" as "measure" and "verse" to "philosophical poetics" and "the science of perception, or *aesthetic*" (73–78).

3. In addition to the Romanticist work on the materiality of language taken up directly in the following pages, Marjorie Levinson's account of "the dynamically materializing agent in our acts of knowing" ("Romantic Poetry: The State of the Art," *Modern Language Quarterly* 54 [1993]: 183–235) has been an abiding speculative challenge, though I take quite different positions from hers on "the difference between ideology and reality" (212) and on "the power of negative thinking" (213).

4. Much of the recent work on literary texts as commodities was anticipated and has been enabled by Kurt Heinzelman's *The Economics of the Imagination* (Amherst: University of Massachusetts Press, 1980). Also influential on current debates about literature and the market is John Guillory, *Cultural Capital: The Problem of Literary Canon Formation* (Chicago: University of Chicago Press, 1993) and the work of Mary Poovey; see especially her "Aesthetics and Political Economy in the Eighteenth Century: The Place of Gender in the Social Constitution of Knowledge," *Aesthetics and Ideology*, ed. George Levine (New Brunswick: Rutgers University Press, 1994), 79–105.

5. See James McKusick's helpful comment on "this rather obscure passage" in *Coleridge's Philosophy of Language* (New Haven: Yale University Press, 1986), 41–52.

6. What I say about Byron in this chapter is indebted to L. E. Marshall's "*Words* are *things*: Byron and the Prophetic Efficacy of Language," *SEL* 25 (1985): 801–22.

7. Kurt Heinzelman, "Byron's Poetry of Politics: The Economic Basis of the 'Poetical Character'," *TSLL* 23 (1981): 361–88. For excellent analysis of Keats's connection to some of the questions raised in this chapter, see Heinzelman's "Self-Interest and the Politics of Composition in Keats's *Isabella*," *ELH* 55 (1988): 159–93, and (on both Byron and Keats) Sonia Hofkosh, "The Writer's Ravishment: Women and the Romantic Author—The Example of Byron," *Romanticism and Feminism*, ed. Anne K. Mellor (Bloomington: Indiana University Press, 1988), 93–114.

8. Sheila Emerson, "Byron's 'one word': The Language of Self-Expression in *Childe Harold* III," *SIR* 20 (1981): 363–82. I am also indebted to Emerson's article in my later discussion of *Childe Harold* 3. 97.

9. Michel Foucault, *The Order of Things: An Archaeology of the Human Sciences* (New York: Random House, 1970), 238–42.

10. Foucault, *The Order of Things*, 61.

11. Michel Foucault, *The Archaeology of Knowledge*, trans. A. M. Sheridan Smith (London: Tavistock, 1972), 49.

12. Fredric Jameson, *The Political Unconscious: Narrative as a Socially Symbolic Act* (Ithaca: Cornell University Press, 1981), 45. Lacan's psychoanalytic concept of "the Thing" is recurrently taken up in the special issue of *Critical Inquiry* devoted to "Things," ed. Bill Brown (vol. 28, Autumn 2001); see Brown's introductory essay, "Thing Theory," 5–6, and Peter Schwenger's "Words and the Murder of the Thing," 106–13.

13. Derek Attridge, *Peculiar Language: Literature as Difference from the Renaissance to James Joyce* (Ithaca: Cornell University Press, 1988), 154 n. 34. Attridge's entire chapter on "Literature as Imitation: Jakobson, Joyce, and the Art of Onomatopoeia" is pertinent to the semiotic dimension of my argument.

14. Thomas Sprat, *History of the Royal Society*, ed. Jackson I. Cope and Harold Whitmore Jones (St. Louis: Washington University Press, 1959), 27.

15. Jonathan Swift, *Gulliver's Travels (1726)*, ed. Herbert Davis (Oxford: Basil Blackwell, 1959), 185.

16. All quotations of Locke's *Essay Concerning Human Understanding* are from Peter H. Nidditch's edition (Oxford: Clarendon Press, 1975); subsequent citations are, like this one, given parenthetically in the text.

17. John Locke, *Two Treatises of Government*, ed. Peter Laslett (Cambridge: Cambridge University Press, 1970), 292–93; see also 299–301.

18. *PWWW* 2: 513. Wordsworth's extended note on "The Thorn" first appeared in the second edition of *Lyrical Ballads* (1800).

19. Frances Ferguson, *Wordsworth: Language as Counter-Spirit* (New Haven: Yale University Press, 1977), 14.

20. For a different view of Foucault's bearing on "this new, heightened perception of thingness" in Romantic writing, see W.J.T. Mitchell's "Romanticism and the Life of Things" in the special issue of *Critical Inquiry* (vol. 28, Autumn 2001): 173, 176.

21. Mitchell writes insightfully about passages such as this in "Romanticism and the Life of Things," 171–73.

22. From a notebook entry in MS. Egerton 2801, f. 145; see *Inquiring Spirit: A Coleridge Reader*, ed. Kathleen Coburn (London: Routledge & Kegan Paul, 1951), 101.

23. Kurt Heinzelman, *The Economics of the Imagination* (Amherst: University of Massachusetts Press, 1980), 200. Subsequent page-references are given parenthetically in the text.

24. McKusick, *Coleridge's Philosophy of Language*, 48.

25. John Horne Tooke, *The Diversions of Purley* (London, 1786–1805; rpt. Menston, England: Scolar Press, 1968), 2: 405–6.

26. McKusick, *Coleridge's Philosophy of Language*, 48.

27. See my "Romanticism and Language," *The Cambridge Companion to British Romanticism*, ed. Stuart Curran (Cambridge: Cambridge University Press, 1993), 113–14.

28. Ralph Waldo Emerson, *Essays & Lectures*, ed. Joel Porte (New York: The Library of America, 1983), 20–21.

29. Kenneth Burke, *Language as Symbolic Action: Essays on Life, Literature, and Method* (Berkeley: University of California Press, 1966), 360–61.

30. *Table Talk* in CC 2: 353; quoted in Heinzelman, *Economics of the Imagination*, 300, n. 40.

31. See Robert Essick's reference to this passage in the context of his chapter called "In Pursuit of the Motivated Sign" in *William Blake and the Language of Adam* (Oxford: Clarendon Press, 1989), 48.

32. Nelson Hilton, *Literal Imagination: Blake's Vision of Words* (Berkeley: University of California Press, 1983), 9. Subsequent references are given parenthetically in the text.

33. Essick, *William Blake and the Language of Adam*, 128, 107, 167, 191, 192.

34. Clifford Siskin, *The Historicity of Romantic Discourse* (New York: Oxford University Press, 1988), 153.

35. For an argument challenging some aspects of this judgment, see Joseph Viscomi, "The Myth of Commissioned Illuminated Books: George Romney, Isaac D'Israeli, and 'ONE HUNDRED AND SIXTY designs . . . of Blake's,'" *Blake / An Illustrated Quarterly* 23 (1989): 48–74. For brief overviews of recent debates concerning Blake's relation to London book publishing and the literary market, part of ongoing debates about his actual and intended audience, see John Mee, *Dangerous Enthusiasm: William Blake and the Culture of Radicalism in the 1790s* (Oxford: Clarendon Press, 1992), 214–27, and *Historicizing Blake*, ed. Steve Clark and David Worrall (New York: St. Martin's Press, 1994), 2–4.

36. Paul Fry, "Made men: a review article on recent Shelley and Keats studies," *Texas Studies in Language and Literature* 21 (1979): 451.

37. Margaret Homans, *Bearing the Word: Language and Female Experience in Nineteenth-Century Women's Writing* (Chicago: University of Chicago Press, 1986), 5. Subsequent page-references are given parenthetically in the text.

38. Quotations of Mary Shelley's *Frankenstein* are from the Penguin Classics edition, ed. Maurice Hindle (1992). Subsequent page-references are given, like this one, parenthetically in the text.

39. *A New Translation of Volney's Ruins; or Meditations on the Revolution of Empires. Made Under The Inspection of The Author*, 2 vols. (Paris: Levrault, 1803), 1: ix. This translation, begun by Thomas Jefferson and completed by Joel Barlow, has been reprinted by Garland Publishing (New York and London, 1979), with an introduction by Robert D. Richardson, Jr.

40. Peter Brooks, "'Godlike Science/Unhallowed Arts': Language, Nature, and Monstrosity," *The Endurance of Frankenstein: Essays on Mary Shelley's Novel*, ed. George Levine and U. C. Knoepflmacher (Berkeley: University of California Press, 1979), 207–8. Subsequent page-references are given parenthetically in the text.

41. Marchand notes that "Byron used this phrase of Mirabeau in *Don Juan*,

Canto III, stanza 88" (*BLJ* 4: 74 n.). I have been unable to trace the source in Mirabeau's writings or speeches.

42. For Byron's initial refusal and eventual willingness to accept payment for his writing, see Leslie A. Marchand, *Byron: A Biography*, 3 vols. (New York: Alfred A. Knopf, 1957), 2. 556, 2. 654, 2. 696, 2. 713, 3. 1039 ff., 3. 1052.

43. Jerome Christensen, "Theorizing Byron's Practice: The Performance of Lordship and the Poet's Career," *SIR* 27 (1988): 487.

44. Eagleton, *The Ideology of the Aesthetic*, 196, 208.

3. THE POLITICS OF RHYME

1. John O. Hayden, *The Romantic Reviewers, 1802–1824* (London: Routledge & Kegan Paul, 1969), 188–96; Theodore Redpath, *The Young Romantics and Critical Opinion 1807–1824* (London: Harrap, 1973), 418–21; Jerome J. McGann, "Keats and the Historical Method in Literary Criticism," *MLN* 94 (1979): 996–99; Marjorie Levinson, *Keats's Life of Allegory: The Origins of a Style* (Oxford: Basil Blackwell, 1988), 1–45; Nicholas Roe, *Keats and the Culture of Dissent* (Oxford: Clarendon Press, 1997), 1–50; Susan Wolfson, *Formal Charges: The Shaping of Poetry in British Romanticism* (Stanford: Stanford University Press, 1997), 136; Jeffrey N. Cox, *Poetry and Politics in the Cockney School: Keats, Shelley, Hunt and their Circle* (Cambridge: Cambridge University Press, 1998), 27–28, 104, 161–63; Richard Cronin, *The Politics of Romantic Poetry: In Search of the Pure Commonwealth* (New York: St. Martin's Press, 2000), 181–99.

2. McGann, "Keats and the Historical Method," 996.

3. Walter Jackson Bate, *John Keats* (Cambridge, MA: Harvard University Press, 1963), 366–67.

4. *The Keats Circle: Letters and Papers 1816–1878*, ed. Hyder Edward Rollins (Cambridge, MA: Harvard University Press, 1948), 1: 34.

5. "Cockney School of Poetry. No. IV," *Blackwood's Edinburgh Magazine* 3 (August 1818): 522.

6. All quotations are from *The Poems of John Keats*, ed. Jack Stillinger (Cambridge, MA: Harvard University Press, 1978).

7. "Cockney School of Poetry. No. IV," 524.

8. "Art. VII.—*Endymion: A Poetic Romance*. By John Keats," *The Quarterly Review* 19, no. 37 (April 1818): 205–06.

9. *The Spectator*, ed. Donald F. Bond (Oxford: Clarendon Press, 1965), 1: 256.

10. See Wolfson, *Formal Charges*, 282–83, note.

11. (London: J. Murray; W. Blackwood; Cumming, 1816), p. xv. Subsequent quotations are from this edition. In "The Return of the Enjambed Couplet" (*ELH* 7, 1940: 239–52), Earl Wasserman argued that Hunt's and Keats's originality in opening up the closed Augustan couplet had been exaggerated, that "the versification of Keats and Hunt is . . . the fulfillment of a movement that had its beginnings in the last quarter of the eighteenth century" (251).

12. We need to remember that a majority of the reviewers of both Keats's early volumes were encouraging. See Hayden, *The Romantic Reviewers*, 188, 190.

13. Leigh Hunt, "An Answer to the Question What is Poetry? Including Remarks on Versification," *Imagination and Fancy* (New York: Wiley and Putnam, 1845), 2.

14. Leigh Hunt, *The Feast of the Poets*, 2d ed. (London: Gale and Fenner, 1815), 32.

15. See P.M.S. Dawson, "Byron, Shelley, and the 'new school,'" *Shelley Revalued: Essays from the Gregynog Conference*, ed. Kelvin Everest (Totowa, NJ: Barnes and Noble, 1983), 89–108, esp. 91–101.

16. "Cockney School of Poetry. No. IV," 520.

17. *Mary Shelley's Journal*, ed. Frederick L. Jones (Norman: University of Oklahoma Press, 1947), 15.

18. Bate, *John Keats*, 349–50.

19. Douglas Bush notes that the source of Keats's image here is Hazlitt's "On Milton's Versification" (1815): "Dr. Johnson and Pope would have converted his [Milton's] vaulting Pegasus into a rocking-horse" (John Keats, *Selected Poems and Letters* [Boston: Houghton Mifflin 1959] 312).

20. "Some Observations upon an Article in *Blackwood's Edinburgh Magazine*," *Lord Byron: The Complete Miscellaneous Prose*, ed. Andrew Nicholson (Oxford: Clarendon Press, 1991), 117. For valuable commentary on Pope and British Romanticism relevant to my argument here, see Robert J. Griffin, *Wordsworth's Pope: A Study in Literary Historiography* (Cambridge: Cambridge University Press, 1995), esp. chapter 1, "The eighteenth-century construction of Romanticism," and chapter 2, "Refinement, Romanticism, Francis Jeffrey."

21. See Nicholson's note in *Miscellaneous Prose*, 358–59, and Leslie A. Marchand, *Byron: A Biography* (New York: Knopf, 1957), 2: 845 and note.

22. See Nicholson, *Miscellaneous Prose*, 358–59. Marchand, *BLJ* 6: 257 (note) says: "It is still a question as to whether John Wilson wrote the review."

23. *The Quarterly Review* Vol. 23, no. 46 (July 1820): 400–34.

24. *BLJ* 7: 217 (4 November 1820). Bowles's own preference for the open, enjambed couplet is an aspect of the "Pope controversy" that doubtless exacerbated Byron's antipathy to Bowles as it did his antipathy to Keats. See Wasserman, "The Return of the Enjambed Couplet," 248–49.

25. *Miscellaneous Prose*, 156–57.

26. Peter Manning, "Tales and Politics: *The Corsair, Lara,* and *The White Doe of Rylstone*," *Salzbürger Studien zur Anglistik und Amerikanistik* 13 (1980): 204–30; and "The Hone-ing of Byron's Corsair," *Textual Criticism and Literary Interpretation*, ed. Jerome J. McGann, ch. 6 (Chicago: University of Chicago Press, 1985), 107–26.

27. Quotations of *The Corsair* are from the third volume of *The Complete Poetical Works*, ed. Jerome J. McGann (Oxford: Clarendon Press, 1981). The references to Byron's Preface are on 3: 148–49.

28. See Manning, "Tales and Politics," 209.

29. Wolfson, *Formal Charges*, 137–38.

30. "Cockney School of Poetry. No. IV," 522.

31. M. R. Ridley, *Keats' Craftsmanship: A Study in Poetic Development* (London: Methuen, 1963), 241–49, 305, Note J, and Walter Jackson Bate, *The Stylistic Development of John Keats* (New York: Humanities Press, 1945), 19–28, 147–55.

32. 6 and 13 July 1817, reprinted in Redpath, *The Young Romantics and Critical Opinion*, 455–56.

33. Ibid., 451–52.

34. *The London Magazine* Vol. 1, no. 4 (April, 1820): 383. In *The London Magazine* review of Keats's 1820 volume, John Scott observed of the attacks on Keats's earlier volumes: "Mr. Keats, though not a political writer, plunged at once, with what we shall take the liberty of calling a boyish petulance, and with an air of rather insulting bravado, into some very delicate subjects" (Vol. 2, no. 9 [September 1820]: 315).

35. *The Poetical Works of Leigh Hunt* (London: Edward Moxon, 1832), xxxvi–xxxvii.

36. Jerome McGann, "Romanticism and its Ideologies," *SIR* 21 (1982): 576.

37. *The Edinburgh Review* Vol. 34, no. 67 (August 1820): 204–5.

38. Cronin, *The Politics of Romantic Poetry*, 185.

39. P. N. Medvedev / M. M. Bakhtin, *The Formal Method in Literary Scholarship: A Critical Introduction to Sociological Poetics*, trans. Albert J. Wehrle (Baltimore: The Johns Hopkins University Press, 1978), 122 (quoted by McGann in "Keats and the Historical Method," 990); David Simpson, "Criticism, Politics, and Style in Wordsworth's Poetry," *Critical Inquiry* 11 (1984): 67.

40. McGann, "Keats and the Historical Method," 996–97.

41. See Kingsley Amis, "The Curious Elf: A Note on Rhyme in Keats," *EIC* 1 (1951): 189–92. The quoted comment on the sources of Cockney rhyming slang is from Peter Wright, *Cockney Dialect and Slang* (B.T. Batsford: London, 1981), 94–95. For an interesting comment on Keats's relation to other aspects of Cockney pronunciation and rhyme, see Lynda Mugglestone, *'Talking Proper': The Rise of Accent as Social Symbol* (Oxford: Clarendon Press, 1997), 100–102.

42. *The Letters of John Keats*, ed. Hyder Edward Rollins (Cambridge, MA: Harvard University Press, 1958), 2: 139. On the biographical context see James Chandler, "The Week When Keats Wrote 'To Autumn,'" *England in 1819*, 425–32.

43. Helen Vendler emphasizes the influence of the Mutability Cantos on "To Autumn" in *The Odes of John Keats* (Cambridge, MA: Harvard University Press, 1983), 242–43. She mentions the September stanza in passing but says nothing about its appearance in *The Examiner*.

44. *The Examiner* 610 (5 September 1819): 574. For a fuller assessment of this text in relation to "To Autumn," see Roe, *John Keats and the Culture of Dissent*, 257–63.

45. *The Examiner* 527 (1 February 1818): 76.

46. See P.M.S. Dawson, *The Unacknowledged Legislator: Shelley and Politics* (Oxford: Clarendon Press, 1980), 50–51.

47. References are to *Aeneid* 1. 430–36 in the Loeb Classical Library edition (Cambridge, MA: Harvard University Press, 1934).

48. See especially Manning, "The Hone-ing of Byron's *Corsair*," 107–26.

49. See McGann's commentary, *CPWB* 5: 692–93 and 735–37.

50. For Frere's life and career, see the *Dictionary of National Biography* and the prefatory memoir by W. E. and Sir Bartle Frere in the first volume of *The Works of John Hookham Frere in Verse and Prose* (London: Basil Montagu Pick-

ering, 1872). There is a good introductory account of Byron's relation to Frere and to Rose in Elizabeth French Boyd, *Byron's Don Juan: A Critical Study* (New York: The Humanities Press, 1958), 4–16, 49–54.

51. See *CPWB* 2: 42 and McGann's commentary, 2: 281–82.

52. See *BLJ* 6: 78 and 7: 46.

53. See Jerome J. McGann, *"Don Juan" in Context* (Chicago: University of Chicago Press, 1976), 51. In "'Mixed Company': Byron's *Beppo* and the Italian Medley," *Shelley and His Circle*, ed. Donald H. Reiman (Cambridge, MA: Harvard University Press, 1986), 7: 238, McGann follows Marchand's view that Frere's poem was brought to Byron by "either Rose or the Kinnairds" (*Byron: A Biography* [New York: Knopf, 1957], 2: 709). My account of Rose's life and career is based primarily on the article in the *Dictionary of National Biography*.

54. The first volume of Rose's translation of Ariosto appeared in 1823; this was preceded by a translation, mainly in prose but with exemplary passages in English *ottava rima*, of Berni's *rifacimento* of Boiardo's *Orlando Innamorato*.

55. See Byron's letter to Pryce Gordon, June 1816: "I cannot tell you what a treat your gift of Casti has been to me; I have almost got him by heart. I had read his 'Animali Parlanti,' but I think these 'Novelle' much better. I long to go to Venice to see the manners so admirably described" (*BLJ* 5: 80 and note 1).

56. Peter Vassallo, *Byron: The Italian Literary Influence* (New York: St. Martin's Press, 1984), 43–63.

57. Byron uses this phrase about *Don Juan* in his letter to Douglas Kinnaird of 26 October 1819 (*BLJ* 6: 232).

58. *CPWB* 1: 45.

59. On Merivale, see the *Dictionary of National Biography* article, and the text of and commentary on Byron's letter to Merivale commending him on the *Orlando in Roncesvalles* in *Shelley and His Circle* 6: 1134–36 (SC 566).

60. *Blackwood's Edinburgh Magazine* 6 (December 1819): 290.

61. "Translation from the 'Morgante Maggiore' of Luigi Pulci," *Poems Original and Translated*, 2 vols. (London: William Pickering, 1844), 2: 2. Merivale explains in this introduction that "the following translated specimens formed part of a series of papers, under the title 'Remarks on the Morgante Maggiore of Luigi Pulci,' which made their appearance in several successive numbers of the Monthly Magazine, during the years 1806 and 1807; those contained in the last number of the series, viz, for June, 1807, being afterwards incorporated in the poem called 'Orlando in Roncesvalles.'" The *Orlando* follows the Pulci translations in this edition of Merivale's collected poems.

62. *CPWB* 3: 90–91, #214, "[On Southey's Laureateship]"; see McGann's commentary, 3: 427, and *"Don Juan" in Context*, 53.

63. Vassallo, *The Italian Literary Influence*, 44–45.

64. Letter to Landor, 20 February 1820; quoted in Redpath, *The Young Romantics and Critical Opinion*, 259.

65. *Works of John Hookham Frere* 1: clviii.

66. *The Quarterly Review* 21 (1819): 503. Frere himself describes Whistlecraft as "a thoroughly common, but not necessarily low-minded man" (*Works of John Hookham Frere* 1: clix).

67. Quoted from *The Monks and the Giants*, ed. R. D. Waller (Manchester: Manchester University Press, 1926).

68. *The Monks and the Giants*, 42. Waller's comment that "Frere's Tristram is compared with Lord Wellington" seems, at best, only partly correct. See Rose's *Thoughts and Reflections* (London: John Murray, 1825), 214–15; he quotes the two stanzas on Sir Tristram (18–19) and asks: "Who can read this description, without recognizing in it, the portraits (flattering portraits perhaps) of two military characters well known in society?"

69. *CPWB* 5: 737. Cf. Foscolo, *The Quarterly Review* 21 (1819): 487: "[Casti] does not ridicule the religion, or the politics, or the ethics of any peculiar sect or nation; he laughs at all faith, and all patriotism . . . his satire has not been always understood; and politicians and party-men have been so simple as to quote the verses of Casti, imagining that the laughter would be on their side."

70. Vassallo, *The Italian Literary Influence*, 123–24.

71. "Giambattista Casti's 'Novelle Galanti' and Lord Byron's 'Beppo,'" *Italica* 28 (1951): 263.

72. *Works of John Hookham Frere* 1: clvii; the quotation is from Rose's *Rhymes* (Brighton, 1837).

73. In the opening line of this sequence Byron's narrator, seeming to quote himself, is in fact quoting Cowper, *The Task*, 2. 206 (*Poetical Works*, ed. H. S. Milford [Oxford: Oxford University Press, 1967]). Cowper's passage continues: "Though thy clime / Be fickle, and thy year most part deform'd / With dripping rains, or wither'd by a frost, / I would not yet exchange thy sullen skies, / And fields without a flow'r, for warmer France / With all her vines . . ." (2. 209–14). The political implications of Byron's quoting Cowper's patriotic lines from the other side of the channel may be extended in relation to later passages from this book of *The Task*: "True, we have lost an empire—let it pass. / True; we may thank the perfidy of France, / That pick'd the jewel out of England's crown, / With all the cunning of an envious shrew" (2. 263–66). Byron's references to Cowper in his letters are consistently parodic and denigrating: "Cowper was not a poet" (*BLJ* 3: 179); "that maniacal calvinist & coddled poet" (*BLJ* 7: 101).

74. Boyd, *Byron's Don Juan*, 12.

75. In a letter to Scott of 17 March 1818; see Samuel Smiles, *A Publisher and His Friends: Memoirs and Correspondence of the Late John Murray* (London: John Murray, 1891), 2: 8.

76. See Marchand, *Byron* 2: 763–66. Hobhouse says in his diary: "I called on Hookham Frere . . . he was decisively against publication . . . I felt I was talking in some sort to a rival of *Don Juan's* style" (quoted in Redpath, *The Young Romantics and Critical Opinion*, 248).

77. Willis W. Pratt, *Byron's "Don Juan": Notes on the Variorum Edition* (Austin: University of Texas Press, 1957), 190, quotes Beranger's "Complainte d'une de ces Demoiselles à l'Occasion des Affaires du Temps" (*Chansons* [1821] 2: 17: "Faut qu'lord Villain-ton ait tout pris; / N'y a plus d'argent dans c'gueux de Paris"). In *The Works of Lord Byron. Poetry*, 7 vols. (London: John Murray, 1905), Ernest Hartley Coleridge quotes an epigram from a contemporary newspaper written in retaliation against De Beranger: "These French *petit-maitres*

who the spectacle throng, / Say of Wellington's dress *qu'il fait vilain ton!* / But, at Waterloo, Wellington made the French stare / When their army he dressed *à la mode Angleterre!*"

78. Pratt, *Notes on the Variorum Edition*, 190, says that lines 9–10 of Byron's "Ode (From the French)," first published in the *Morning Chronicle* of 15 March 1816 and beginning "We do not curse thee, Waterloo!," refer to Ney: "With that of him whose honoured grave / Contains the 'bravest of the brave.'"

79. Boyd, *Byron's Don Juan*, 5.

80. *CPWB* 4: 509: Byron's translation of Pulci's *Morgante Maggiore* "stands at the centre of his whole revisionist project in poetry."

81. Quoted in Redpath, *The Young Romantics and Critical Opinion*, 259.

4. VULGAR IDIOMS

1. Harold Bloom, ed., *The Selected Poetry and Prose of Shelley* (New York: The New American Library, 1966), xvii; Donald Davie, *Purity of Diction in English Verse*, rev. ed. (London: Routledge & Kegan Paul, 1967), 143: "the lunatic's raving . . . tiresome and unpoetic as it is, impairs but does not ruin the whole" because Shelley "presents it (plausibly enough) as a verbatim report."

2. Kelvin Everest, "Shelley's doubles: an approach to *Julian and Maddalo*," *Shelley Revalued: Essays from the Gregynog Conference*, ed. Kelvin Everest (Totowa, NJ: Barnes & Noble, 1983), 79–80.

3. An exception is Tony Crowley's *Language in History: Theories and Texts* (London and New York: Routledge, 1996), esp. ch. 3, "Wars of words: The roles of language in eighteenth-century Britain," on which I have drawn throughout this discussion. Peter Trudgill's work, particularly *The Social Differentiation of English in Norwich* (Cambridge: Cambridge University Press, 1974), is helpful, even though his subject is twentieth-century usage in a circumscribed geographical area. Literary scholarship informed by sociolinguistic method, such as Susie I. Tucker's *Protean Shape: A Study in Eighteenth-Century Vocabulary and Usage* (London: Athlone Press, 1967) and Carey McIntosh, *Common and Courtly Language: The Stylistics of Social Class in 18th-Century English Literature* (Philadelphia: University of Pennsylvania Press, 1986), has yet to be done on the period from the French Revolution to the first Reform Bill. Though there is some valuable commentary on this period in Lynda Mugglestone's *'Talking Proper': The Rise of Accent as Social Symbol* (see Chapter 3, note 41 above), her main focus is on the middle and later nineteenth century.

4. Don Bialostosky's *Wordsworth, dialogics, and the practice of criticism* (Cambridge: Cambridge University Press, 1992) offers an instructive dialogic reading of Wordsworth based on Bakhtinian principles, but his attempt to address the question of poetic language by saying that "in certain times and places verse composition can itself become 'novelized' and incorporate the dialogic interplay of the novel" (66) leaves important formal differences relatively unexplored. This is also the case in Part I of Michael Macovski's insightful *Dialogue and Literature: Apostrophe, Auditors, and the Collapse of Romantic Discourse* (New York and Oxford: Oxford University Press, 1994), 1–101. Yury Lotman comments usefully on the exclusion of the "vulgar lexicon" from the "classical"

poetic tradition in *Analysis of the Poetic Text*, trans. D. Barton Johnson (Ann Arbor: Ardis, 1976), 83–85.

5. David Simpson, *Wordsworth's Historical Imagination: The Poetry of Displacement* (London and New York: Methuen, 1987); Peter J. Manning, "The Hone-ing of Byron's *Corsair*" and other essays in *Reading Romantics: Texts and Contexts* (New York and London: Oxford University Press, 1990); Marjorie Levinson, *Keats's Life of Allegory: The Origins of Style* (New York: Basil Blackwell, 1988); John Barrell, *The Idea of Landscape and the Sense of Place, 1730–1840: An Approach to the Poetry of John Clare* (Cambridge: Cambridge University Press, 1972) and "Being is Perceiving: James Thompson and John Clare" in his *Poetry, Language and Politics* (Manchester: Manchester University Press, 1988).

6. *Das Kapital*, "Nachwort zur zweiten Auflage," in Karl Marx, Friedrich Engels, *Werke* (Berlin: Dietz Verlag, 1962) 23: 20–21: "Es war die Periode wie der Vulgärisierung und Ausbreitung der Ricardosichen Theorie"; "Auch diesen letzten Stachel zog die Freihändelsgesetzgebung seit Sir Robert Peel der Vulgärökonomie aus"; ". . . des flachsten und daher gelungensten Vertreters vulgärökonomischer Apologetik."

7. David Simpson, "Literary Critics and 'History,'" *Criticial Inquiry* 14 (1988): 737; Fredric Jameson, *The Political Unconscious* (Ithaca: Cornell University Press, 1981), 82.

8. Jacques Derrida, *Of Grammatology*, trans. Gayatri Chakravorty Spivak (Baltimore: The Johns Hopkins University Press, 1974), 86; the French text of the clause I call attention to here reads "ce concept vulgaire et mondain de la temporalité" (Paris: Les Editions de Minuit, 1967, 128). See also Derrida's reference to "a vulgar concept of writing" in the Spivak translation (55).

9. Pierre Boudieu, *Distinction: A Social Critique of the Judgement of Taste*, trans. Richard Nice (Cambridge, MA: Harvard University Press, 1984), 4. Subsequent page-references are given parenthetically in the text.

10. Quoted from James Creed Meredith's translation of *The Critique of Judgment* (Oxford: Clarendon Press, 1928; reprinted 1952), 151; this is the English translation used by Nice in his translation of *Distinction*.

11. Quotations here and elsewhere in this chapter are from the Loeb Classical Library Edition of the *Satires, Epistles and Ars Poetica*, trans. Rushton Fairclough (Cambridge, MA: Harvard University Press, 1961).

12. Jerome Christensen, *Romanticism at the End of History* (Baltimore: The Johns Hopkins University Press, 2000); see especially Introduction and chapter 1, "The Romantic Movement at the End of History." For his notion of "demotic speech," see esp. 24–34.

13. On Hone, see Manning, "The Hone-ing of Byron's *Corsair.*" On the piracies of Shelley's *Queen Mab*, see Richard Holmes, *Shelley: the Pursuit* (New York: E. P. Dutton, 1975), 660–62; Iain McCalman, *Radical Underworld: Prophets, Revolutionaries, and Pornographers in London, 1795–1840* (Oxford: Clarendon Press, 1993), 155, 160, 189, 193, 211–21; Neil Fraistat, "Illegitimate Shelley: Radical Piracy and the Textual Edition as Cultural Performance," *PMLA* 110 (1994): 409–23.

14. Jon Klancher, *The Making of English Reading Audiences, 1790–1832* (Madison: University of Wisconsin Press, 1987), 15, 23 and passim.
15. *Blackwood's Edinburgh Magazine* 3 (May 1818): 197.
16. Ibid., 453.
17. Ibid., 520, 521.
18. Ibid., 4 (January 1819): 475–82.
19. *The Quarterly Review* 21 (April 1819): 469–70.
20. *Blackwood's Edinburgh Magazine* 7 (September 1820): 686.
21. *The Edinburgh Review* 29 (February 1818): 303–4; quoted in Theodore Redpath, *The Young Romantics and Critical Opinion* (London: Harrap, 1973), 225–26.
22. Leigh Hunt, *Lord Byron and Some of His Contemporaries* (Philadelphia: Carey, Lea & Carey, 1828), 48.
23. *The Letters of John Keats, 1814–1821*, ed. Hyder Edward Rollins (Cambridge, MA: Harvard University Press, 1958), 17–27 (September 1819). See Sonia Hofkosh, "The Writer's Ravishment: Women and the Romantic Author—The Example of Byron," *Romanticism and Feminism*, ed. Anne K. Mellor (Bloomington: Indiana University Press, 1988), 107.
24. On Byron's reference to the "pleasure" of an "Italian fiddler" as involving *le coup de corde* and "a distinctly lower-class character in a perversion associated with aristocratic refinement," see Marjorie Levinson, *Keats's Life of Allegory*, 22–23.
25. Tucker, *Protean Shape*, 251–52. The 1805 *Prelude* is full of instances of this hesitation, this wavering between the neutral and the derogatory; see 1. 493, 1. 609, 1. 625, 5. 595, 8. 455, 8. 651, 8. 695, 12. 188, 12. 362, 13. 140.
26. *CWTP* 51, 58–59.
27. Mary Wollstonecraft, *A Vindication of the Rights of Woman*, ed. Carol H. Poston, 2d ed. (New York: Norton, 1988), 179. Cf. *A Vindication of the Rights of Men*: "The vulgar, and by this epithet I mean not only to describe a class of people, who, working to support the body, have not had time to cultivate their minds; but likewise those who, born in the lap of affluence, have never had their invention sharpened by necessity are, nine out of ten, the creatures of habit and impulse" (*"A Vindication of the Rights of Men" and "A Vindication of the Rights of Woman,"* ed. D. L. Macdonald and Kathleen Scherf [Peterborough, Ontario: Broadview Press, 1997], 45–46).
28. Mary Poovey, *The Proper Lady and the Woman Writer* (Chicago: University of Chicago Press, 1984), 61.
29. See Tara Ghoshal Wallace's introduction to her edition of *A Busy Day* (New Brunswick: Rutgers University Press, 1984), 15: "Whenever she shows vulgarity and rudeness, she also implies moral coarseness, and in the depiction of this there are no class boundaries." Burney took the manuscript of *A Busy Day* with her when she joined her husband in Paris in 1802; she returned to England in 1812. The loss of direct contact with London theatres meant that the play was never staged in her lifetime. There have been several successful productions in recent years, most recently a production mounted by the Bristol Old Vic in 2000.
30. *Indicator* 1 (13 October 1819): 1.

31. Percy Bysshe Shelley, *The Masque of Anarchy* (London: Edward Moxon, 1832), xv. Subsequent page-references to Hunt's preface to this edition are given parenthetically in the text.

32. *The Complete Works of William Hazlitt*, ed. P. P. Howe (London and Toronto: J. M. Dent, 1931), 8: 156. Subsequent page-references to this edition are given parenthetically in the text.

33. See Klancher, *The Making of English Reading Audiences*, 126: "As he extends the eighteenth century's demonology of the urban crowd, Cobbett reverses what the crowd signifies. No longer the emblem of an amoral, anarchic, potentially violent lower class, the crowd is now an amoral, congealed form of the aristocracy."

34. *Leigh Hunt as Poet and Essayist*, ed. Charles Kent (London: Frederick Warne, 1889), xxv.

35. *Blackwood's Edinburgh Magazine* 3 (August 1818): 522.

36. Everest, "Shelley's Doubles," 63.

37. *The Edinburgh Review* 11 (July 1824): 499–500, reprinted in *Shelley: The Critical Heritage*, ed. James E. Barcus (London: Routledge and Kegan Paul, 1975), 340–41.

38. Shelley's point here may be indebted to, though it differs from, the distinction Wordsworth makes near the end of the *Essay, Supplementary to the Preface* of 1815 between "emotions of the pathetic that are simple and direct, and others—that are complex and revolutionary" (*PWWW* 3: 82). Owen and Smyser connect this passage to John Dennis's discussion of "vulgar passion" and "Enthusiasm" (*PWWW* 3: 104–5).

39. On the political import of the debate between Julian and Maddalo, see Michael Henry Scrivener, *Radical Shelley: The Philosophical Anarchism and Utopian Thought of Percy Bysshe Shelley* (Princeton: Princeton University Press, 1982), 184–87.

40. This aspect of the maniac's represented speech is related to Shelley's explicit address in the Preface to *Prometheus Unbound* and elsewhere in his later poetry to "the more select classes of poetical readers"; see Stephen C. Behrendt, *Shelley and His Audiences* (Lincoln: University of Nebraska Press, 1989).

41. Pope's lines address God as one who "Yet gave me, in this dark Estate, / To see the Good from Ill; / And binding Nature fast in Fate, / Left free the Human Will" (9–12); quoted from *The Poems of Alexander Pope*, ed. John Butt (London: Methuen, 1965).

42. See David Crystal, *A Dictionary of Linguistics and Phonetics*, 3d ed. (Oxford: Basil Blackwell, 1991), 170 ("*idiolect* A term used in *Linguistics* to refer to the linguistic *System* of an individual speaker—one's personal *Dialect*. . . . Some linguists give the term a more restricted definition, referring to the speech habits of a person as displayed in a particular *Variety* at a given time"), and 319 (*sociolect* A term used by some sociolinguists to refer to a linguistic *Variety* [or *Lect*] defined on social [as opposed to regional] grounds, e.g., correlating with a particular social class or occupational group"). Both entries refer to Peter Trudgill's *Sociolinguistics: An Introduction*, 2d ed. (Harmondsworth: Penguin, 1984). Michael Riffaterre makes a sustained attempt to appropriate these terms and cat-

egories for a formalist semiotics in *Semiotics of Poetry* (Bloomington: Indiana University Press, 1978).

43. Anna Jameson, *Characteristics of Women, Moral, Poetical, and Historical*, 3d ed (London: Saunders and Otley, 1835), 1: 33–35.

44. See David Simpson, ed., *The Origins of Modern Critical Thought* (Cambridge: Cambridge University Press, 1988), 264; Simpson's note refers to the Penguin edition of the *Preface to Shakespeare*, ed. W. K. Wimsatt (Harmondsworth, 1969), 62 ff. According to the *Dictionary of National Biography* Jameson went to Germany in 1833 for a considerable stay and met Schlegel, along with other German writers.

45. Barrell, *Poetry, Language and Politics*, 73–74, 141–47, 165–66. See *The Friend* 1: 450–51 in *CC*.

46. Later in the Introduction to *Characteristics of Women* Medon launches an extended denunciation of "political women." When he says to Alda "but you never talk politics," she replies: "Indeed I do, when I can get any one to listen to me; but I prefer listening." She continues: "Women, however well read in history, never generalize in politics: never argue on any broad or general principle; never reason from a consideration of past events, their causes and consequences. But they are always political through their affections, their prejudices, their personal *liaisons*, their hopes, their fears" (1: 46–48).

5. "'A SUBTLER LANGUAGE WITHIN LANGUAGE'"

1. Accounts of men dressed as women during the early years of the Revolution appear in a number of recent studies examining gender and the role of women. Those on which I have most consistently drawn are Lynn Hunt, *Politics, Culture, and Class in the French Revolution* (Berkeley: University of California Press, 1984) and *The Family Romance of the French Revolution* (Berkeley: University of California Press, 1992); Joan B. Landes, *Women and the Public Sphere in the Age of the French Revolution* (Ithaca: Cornell University Press, 1988); Dominique Godineau, *The Women of Paris and their French Revolution* (Berkeley: University of California Press, 1998), English translation by Katherine Streip of *Citoyennes tricoteuses: Les femmes du people à Paris pendant la Révolution française* (Paris: Alinea, 1989); Dorinda Outram, *The Body and the French Revolution* (New Haven: Yale University Press); and Madelyn Gutwirth, *Twilight of the Goddesses: Women and Representation in the French Revolutionary Era* (New Brunswick: Rutgers University Press, 1992).

2. For textual evidence pertinent to Shelley's marking of voice in *The Revolt of Islam*, see my review of *The Bodleian Shelley Manuscripts. Volume XVII. Drafts for Laon and Cythna. Cantos V–XII*, ed. Steven E. Jones (New York: Garland Publishing, 1994), in *Keats-Shelley's Journal* 45 (1996): 199–200. In "The Composition and Publication of 'The Revolt of Islam,'" Donald Reiman says that "Shelley devoted considerable pains to preparing his poem for the press, giving attention even to details of punctuation and orthography" (*Shelley and his Circle* [Cambridge, MA: Harvard University Press, 1973], 5. 153). Reiman notes that, in contrast to early printed texts, "the intermediate fair copy . . . contains only

minimal punctuation." In his introduction to *Laon and Cythna* in the second volume of the new Longman edition, by contrast, Jack Donovan says that "while S. saw *L&C* through the press and later supervised the alterations that turned it into *RofI*, it is unclear whether he read all the proofs himself" (*PS*, 17). Donovan also concludes, on the basis of the slight surviving fair-copy manuscripts, "that the compositors altered S.'s capitalisation and punctuation freely" and that "the punctuation of *L&C* [is] generally more elaborate and more rhetorical than the sparser practice of syntactical pointing in the MSS" (*PS*, 18). All quotations of *The Revolt of Islam* are from *PS*.

3. Paul Fry, "Made men: a review article on recent Shelley and Keats studies," *Texas Studies in Language and Literature* 21 (1979): 451.

4. Jerrold Hogle, *Shelley's Process: Radical Transference and the Development of His Major Works* (New York and Oxford: Oxford University Press, 1988); William Ulmer, *Shelleyan Eros: The Rhetoric of Romantic Love* (Princeton: Princeton University Press, 1990); Laura Claridge, *Romantic Potency: The Paradox of Desire* (Ithaca: Cornell University Press, 1992); Barbara Gelpi, *Shelley's Goddess: Maternity, Language, Subjectivity* (New York and Oxford: Oxford University Press, 1992); Margaret Homans, *Bearing the Word: Language and Female Experience in Nineteenth-Century Women's Writing* (Chicago: University of Chicago Press, 1986). See also Laura Claridge, "The Bifurcated Space of Desire: Shelley's Confrontation with Language and Silence," *Out of Bounds: Male Writers and Gender(ed) Criticism*, ed. Laura Claridge and Elizabeth Langland (Amherst: University of Massachusetts Press, 1990), 92–109.

5. Sandra M. Gilbert and Susan Gubar, *The Madwoman in the Attic: The Woman Writer and the Nineteenth-Century Literary Imagination* (New Haven: Yale University Press, 1979), 95.

6. Daniel Stern, *The Interpersonal World of the Infant* (New York: Basic Books, 1985), 42–69; subsequent page-references are given parenthetically in the text. See also Stern's earlier book, *The First Relationship* (Cambridge, MA: Harvard University Press, 1977) and "Affect Attunement" in *Frontiers Of Infant Psychiatry*, ed. J. D. Call, E. Galenson, and R. L. Tyson, 2 vols. (New York: Basic Books).

7. L. S. Vygotsky, *Thought and Language*, trans. and ed. Alex Kozulin (Cambridge, MA: MIT Press, 1986), 232–36; subsequent page-references are given parenthetically in the text.

8. Bénédicte de Boysson-Bardies, *How Language Comes to Children: From Birth to Two Years*, trans. M. B. DeBevoise (Cambridge and London: MIT Press, 1999), 8. Shelley critics have often debated the enigmatic parentage of Cythna's child; see especially E. B. Murray, "'Elective Affinity' in *The Revolt of Islam*," *JEGP* 67 (1968): 570–85.

9. Although she does not specifically comment on Wollstonecraft's influence on *The Revolt of Islam*, Claudia Johnson's analysis in *Equivocal Beings: Politics, Gender, and Sentimentality in the 1790s* (Chicago: University of Chicago Press, 1995), introduction and chapters 1–2, has been particularly important for the argument of this chapter. In addition to Gelpi, other critics who have commented on Wollstonecraft's significance for Shelley's epic include A.M.D. Hughes, *The Nascent Mind of Shelley* (Oxford: Clarendon Press, 1947), 206–13; Carlos

Baker, *Shelley's Major Poetry: The Fabric of a Vision* (London: Oxford University Press, 1948), 271–83; Kenneth Neil Cameron, *Shelley: The Golden Years* (Cambridge, MA: Harvard University Press, 1974), 319–22; Nathaniel Brown, *Sexuality and Feminism in Shelley* (Cambridge, MA: Harvard University Press, 1979), 187–88; Alan Richardson, "The Dangers of Sympathy: Sibling Incest in English Romantic Poetry," *Studies in English Literature* 25 (1985): 737–54.

10. *The Novels and Selected Works of Mary Shelley*, ed. Jane Blumberg, with Nora Crook (London: William Pickering, 1996), 4: 7.

11. See *The Journals of Mary Shelley 1814–1844*, ed. Paula R. Feldman and Diana Scott-Kilvert (Baltimore: The Johns Hopkins University Press, 1987), 242: "Teusday [sic] 8th Go on the sea with S.–Visit Cape Micenae–The Elysian fields–Avernus Solfatara–The Bay of Baiae is beautiful but we are disappointed by the various places we visit." Writing to Peacock on 17 or 18 December 1818, Percy says: "After passing the Bay of Baiae & observing the ruins of its antique grandeur standing like rocks in the transparent sea under our boat, we landed to visit Lake Avernus. We passed thro the cavern of the Sybil [sic] (not Virgils Sybil [sic]) which pierces one of the hills which circumscribe the lake" (*LPBS* 2: 61). It is unclear what Shelley means by "not Virgils Sybil [sic]," unless he is referring to the fact that the temple of the Cumaean Sibyl is some miles away from the Grotto above Lake Avernus. See Richard Holmes, *Shelley: the Pursuit* (New York: E. P. Dutton, 1975), 462–63.

12. For a summary of these developments see my "The Shelleys and Dante's Matilda," *Dante's Modern Afterlife: Reception and Response from Blake to Heaney*, ed. Nick Havely (New York: St. Martin's Press, 1998), 60–61.

13. Claire Tomalin, *The Life and Death of Mary Wollstonecraft* (New York: New American Library, 1974), 122; subsequent page-references are given parenthetically in the text.

14. Janet Todd, *Mary Wollstonecraft: A Revolutionary Life* (New York: Columbia University Press, 2000), 206; subsequent page-references are given parenthetically in the text.

15. The best general accounts of these years are still Albert Soboul, *A Short History of the French Revolution, 1789–1799* (Berkeley: University of California Press, 1977) and George Rudé, *The French Revolution* (New York: Grove Press, 1988). See also Soboul's *The Parisian Sans-culottes and the French Revolution, 1793–4* (London: Oxford University Press, 1964).

16. See especially Godineau, *The Women of Paris and Their French Revolution*, 97–196. See also George Rudé, *The Crowd in the French Revolution* (New York and London: Oxford University Press, 1959), 33–64; Lynn Hunt, *Politics, Culture, and Class in the French Revolution*, 52–86, 93–97, 109–10; and Darlene G. Levy and Harriet B. Applewhite, "Women, Radicalization and the Fall of the Monarchy," *Women and Politics in the Age of Democratic Revolution*, ed. Darlene G. Levy and Harriet B. Applewhite (Ann Arbor: University of Michigan Press, 1990), 81–108.

17. See Tomalin, *Life and Death of Mary Wollstonecraft*, 147–58. For broader assessments of Wollstonecraft's relation to women in the Revolution, see Vivien Jones, "Women Writing History: Narratives of History and Sexuality in Wollstonecraft and Williams," *Beyond Romanticism: New Approaches to Texts and*

Contexts, 1780–1832, ed. Stephen Copley and John Whale (London: Routledge, 1992), and Harriet Devine Jump, "'The cool Eye of observation': Mary Wollstonecraft and the French Revolution," *Revolution in Writing: British Literary Responses to the French Revolution*, ed. Kelvin Everest (Milton Keynes: Open University Press, 1991).

18. See Claudia Johnson, *Equivocal Beings*, 26–46; also Elissa S. Guralnick, "Radical Politics in Mary Wollstonecraft's *A Vindication of the Rights of Woman*," *Studies in Burke and His Time* 18 (1977): 155–66; Mitzi Meyers, "Politics from the Outside: Mary Wollstonecraft's First *Vindication*," *Studies in Eighteenth-Century Culture* 6 (1977): 114–26; Marilyn Butler and Janet Todd, "General Introduction," *WMW* 1: 9–20; Virginia Shapiro, *A Vindication of Political Virtue: The Political Theory of Mary Wollstonecraft* (Chicago: University of Chicago Press, 1992), 186–222.

19. Gary Kelly, *Revolutionary Feminism: The Mind and Career of Mary Wollstonecraft* (New York: St. Martin's Press, 1992), 156–59.

20. Jane Rendall, "'The grand causes which combine to carry mankind forward': Wollstonecraft, history and revolution," *Women's Writing* 4 (1997): 155–56. It is important to acknowledge that Millar held quite progressive views on the education and social role of women; see James Chandler, *England in 1819: The Politics of Literary Culture and the Case of Romantic Historicism* (Chicago: University of Chicago Press, 1998), 128–30.

21. Rendall, "Wollstonecraft, history and revolution," 167.

22. Ashley Tauchert, "Maternity, Castration and Mary Wollstonecraft's *Historical and Moral View of the French Revolution*," *Women's Writing* 4 (1997): 174–75.

23. Tauchert, "Maternity, Castration," 176. See Meena Alexander, *Women in Romanticism: Mary Wollstonecraft, Dorothy Wordsworth and Mary Shelley* (London: Macmillan, 1989), 67–8 and Janet Todd, ed., *Mary Wollstonecraft: Political Writings* (Oxford: Oxford University Press, 1994), xxvi–xxvii.

24. See Stuart Curran, *Poetic Form and British Romanticism* (New York and Oxford: Oxford University Press, 1986), 133–35; Marilyn Butler, "Revising the Canon," *TLS* (December 4–10, 1987), 1349, 1350–51, and "Repossessing the Past: the Case for an Open Literary History," *Rethinking Historicism*, introduction by Marjorie Levinson (Oxford: Blackwell, 1989), 64–84. Neither Southey, Coleridge, nor Shelley is mentioned in Françoise Meltzer's *For Fear of the Fire: Joan of Arc and the Limits of Subjectivity* (Chicago: University of Chicago Press, 2001). For Meltzer (13), "After having been nearly forgotten during several centuries . . . Joan was revived as an icon" by Schiller in *Die Jungfrau von Orleans* (1801). Southey's and Coleridge's *Joan of Arc* antedates Schiller's play by five years. Shelley speaks of having read *Die Jungfrau von Orleans* in a letter to John Gisborne of 22 October 1821: "a fine play, if the 5th Act did not fall off" (*LPBS* 2: 364).

25. Kenneth Cameron, "Shelley vs. Southey: New Light on an Old Quarrel," *PMLA* 57 (1942): 489–512.

26. For the relation of Coleridge's contribution to *Joan of Arc* to his own "The Destiny of Nations," see *Coleridge: The Complete Poems*, ed. William Keach

(Harmondsworth: Penguin, 1997), 468. For Shelley's letter to Ollier ordering *Sibylline Leaves*, see *LPBS* 1: 548.

27. Curran, *Poetic Form and British Romanticism*, 167.

28. Marina Warner, *Joan of Arc: The Image of Female Heroism* (London: Vintage, 1981).

29. Letter to J. J. Morgan, 16 June 1814, *CLSTC* 3. 510.

30. See Donald H. Reiman, "The Composition and Publication of *The Revolt of Islam*," *Shelley and His Circle 5*, ed. Donald H. Reiman (Cambridge, MA: Harvard University Press, 1973), 156.

31. *The Poetical Works of Robert Southey, Collected by Himself*, 10 vols. (London: Longman, Orme, Brown, Green, and Longmans, 1837–1838), 1: xxii. On the issue of voice in Joan of Arc narratives, see Meltzer, "*Responsio Mortifera*: The Voice of the Maid," *For Fear of the Fire*, 165–211.

32. Robert Sternbach, "Coleridge, Joan of Arc, and the Idea of Progress," *ELH* 46 (1979): 252–53.

33. Hogle, *Shelley's Process*, 97, 98; subsequent page-references are given parenthetically in the text.

34. Ulmer writes informatively about the "hierarchical structure of power" in the poem; see his *Shelleyan Eros*, 66–73.

35. Alan Richardson, "Romanticism and the Colonization of the Feminine," *Romanticism and Feminism*, ed. Anne K. Mellor (Bloomington: Indiana University Press, 1988), 13–25.

36. Nigel Leask, *British Romantic Writers and the East: Anxieties of Empire* (Cambridge: Cambridge University Press, 1992), 131.

37. *Westminster Review* 38 n.s. (July–October 1870), 88–89, quoted in Brown, *Sexuality and Feminism in Shelley*, 181.

38. Kenneth Johnston, "Narcissus and Joan: Wordsworth's Feminist Recluse?" *SIR* 29 (1990): 197–223; the quoted passage is on 203.

39. Ovid, *Metamorphoses* 3. 436, English translation by Frank Justus Miller (Cambridge, MA: Loeb Library, 1916).

40. Richard Cronin, "Shelleyan Incest and the Romantic Legacy," *Keats-Shelley Journal* 45 (1996): 66.

41. Robert Southey, *Poems* (London: Joseph Cottle and G. G. & J. Robinson, 1797).

42. The word *martyr* derives from Greek μάρτῠρ, "witness," which has an Aryan root meaning "to remember" (*OED*). Cf. Byron, *Don Juan* 1. 1687–88: "they tell me . . . that the Edinburgh Review and Quarterly / Treat a dissenting author very martyrly."

43. Preface, *The Revolt of Islam* (*PS*, 2: 35).

6. THE LANGUAGE OF REVOLUTIONARY VIOLENCE

1. Asa Briggs, *The Age of Improvement 1783–1867* (London and New York: Longman, 1979), 208.

2. *The Rights of Man*, *CWTP* 1: 323, 373.

3. John Barrell, *Imagining the King's Death: Figurative Treason, Fantasies of Regicide 1793–1796* (Oxford: Oxford University Press, 2000), 38.

4. See Alan Liu's commentary on this passage in which "Wordsworth perceives the Revolution's foreign enemies through a Miltonic lens," *Wordsworth: The Sense of History* (Stanford: Stanford University Press, 1989), 378–79.

5. David Bromwich, *Disowned by Memory: Wordsworth's Poetry of the 1790s* (Chicago: University of Chicago Press, 1998), 2. Subsequent page-references are given parenthetically in the text.

6. The Wordsworth concordance gives *Prelude* 10. 127 as the only instance of "arbitrement." The word does not appear in Shelley's poetry, but compare "arbiter" in *The Revolt of Islam* 4. 1616, *The Mask of Anarchy* 330, and the Prologue to *Hellas* 28 (*SPW*, 449).

7. The notebook in which Shelley drafted *A Philosophical View* (Pforzheimer Library) also contains a draft of his note on the composition of the *Ode*; see Donald Reiman, *Shelley and His Circle* (Cambridge, MA: Harvard University Press, 1973), 6: 1066–69.

8. Reiman and Fraistat quote Shelley's commentary on four Maenad figures he had seen in a relief sculpture in Florence (see *WPBS* 6: 323). On Shelley's efforts to record effects of motion and speed in his descriptions of sculpture he saw in Rome and Florence, see my *Shelley's Style* (London: Methuen, 1984), 172.

9. For the background and context of Shelley's thinking about "necessity," see Stuart Sperry, "Necessity and the Role of the Hero in Shelley's *Prometheus Unbound*," *PMLA* 96 (1981): 242–54, and *Shelley's Major Verse: The Narrative and Dramatic Poetry* (Cambridge, MA: Harvard University Press, 1988), 1, 4, 92–99, 118.

10. Reiman concludes that the note was "certainly written after October 25 and almost certainly before the end of 1819," *Shelley and His Circle*, VI: 1067–68 (SC 547).

11. On the maenad as figure for women's uncontrollable violence during the Revolution, see Madelyn Gutwirth, "The Maenad Factor; or Sex, Politics, and Murderousness," *The Twilight of the Goddesses: Women and Representation in the French Revolutionary Era* (New Brunswick: Rutgers University Press, 1992), 307–40. See also Barbara Gelpi, *Shelley's Goddess: Maternity, Language, Subjectivity* (New York and Oxford: Oxford University Press, 1992), 250–58 on maenads as nursing mothers in the Dionysian *thiasos*.

12. Of the important textual and critical work on this poem, see especially Neville Rogers, "Shelley and the Visual Arts," *Keats-Shelley Memorial Bulletin* 12 (1961): 9–10; Daniel Hughes, "Shelley, Leonardo, and the Monsters of Thoughts," *Criticism* 12 (1970): 195–212; and Carol Jacobs, "On Looking at Shelley's Medusa," *Yale French Studies* 69 (1985): 163–79. On the figure of Medusa in relating to French revolutionary culture, see also Neil Hertz, "Medusa's Head: Male Hysteria Under Political Pressure," *Representations* 4 (1983): 27–54, and Catherine Gallagher, "More on Medusa's Head," *Representations* 4 (1983): 55–72. There is a fine discussion of the political meanings attributed to Medusa in Ashley Cross, "Fashionable Discourse and Impressionable Minds: Language and Feminine Subjectivity from Locke to Mary Shelley" (Ph.D. dissertation, Brown University, 1994).

13. Jonathan Culler's "Apostrophe," *Diacritics* 7 (1977): 59–69, is pertinent to the rhetoric of address in Shelley's *Ode*.

14. James Chandler, *England in 1819: The Politics of Literary Culture and the Case of Romantic Historicism* (Chicago: University of Chicago Press, 1998), 553–54: "In the period he saw as critical for English society, his hopes for improvement seemed to rest on an act of political faith that he hoped would be self-fulfilling. . . . The Wind makes Shelley make the Wind make Shelley make the Wind. But perhaps better: Shelley is led by the events of post-Revolution history to construct an account whereby he and post-Revolution history make each other."

15. The *OED* notes that "cause" in the sense of "that side of a question or controversy which is espoused, advocated, and upheld by a person or party; a movement which calls forth the efforts of its supporters" was specifically used during the English Revolution and Commonwealth by Puritan antimonarchical forces. Cythna's words in *The Revolt of Islam* 9. 3543 predate the earliest example of "made common cause with" given in the *OED* (1844).

16. *William Blake: The Complete Poems*, ed. Alicia Ostriker (Harmondsworth: Penguin, 1977), 7.

17. John Beer, *Blake's Humanism* (Manchester: Manchester University Press, 1968), 95.

18. Ronald Paulson, *Representations of Revolution* (New Haven: Yale University Press, 1983), 110.

19. Jerome McGann's recent reflections on "our heritage of violence" as it relates to Blake ("The Third World of Criticism," *Rethinking Historicism: Critical Readings in Romantic History* [Oxford: Basil Blackwell, 1989], 85–107) are pertinent to, though quite different in emphasis from, my argument here.

20. G. E. Bentley, Jr., *Blake Records* (Oxford: Clarendon Press, 1969), 18.

21. David Erdman, *Blake: Prophet Against Empire. A Poet's Interpretation of the History of His Own Times* (Princeton: Princeton University Press, 1954), 8. Subsequent page-references to this work will be given parenthetically in the text. For E. P. Thompson on the Gordon Riots, see *The Making of the English Working Class* (New York: Vintage, 1966), 62, 71–72, 78, 85.

22. Jack Lindsay, *William Blake: His Life and Work* (New York: George Braziller, 1978), 14–15.

23. See Paulson, *Representations of Revolution*, 89, and Erdman, *Prophet Against Empire*, 9.

24. Paulson, *Representations of Revolution*, 89. For a reading of Blake's representations of political violence that differs significantly from the one I offer here, see Saree Samir Makdisi's "Blake's Metropolitan Radicalism," *The Urban Scene in British Romanticism, 1780–1840*, ed. James Chandler and Kevin Gilmartin (Cambridge: Cambridge University Press, in press).

25. John Brenkman, *Culture and Domination* (Ithaca: Cornell University Press, 1987), 125.

26. David Bindman, *Blake as an Artist* (Oxford: Phaidon, 1977), 74. For readings that call attention to the representational confusions I refer to here, see Susan Fox, "The Female as Metaphor in William Blake's Poetry," *Critical Inquiry* 3 (1977): 507–19; Anne K. Mellor, "Blake's Portrayal of Women," *Blake: An Il-*

lustrated Quarterly 63 (1982–83): 148–55; and Brenda S. Webster, *Blake's Prophetic Psychology* (Athens: University of Georgia Press, 1981), 91–109.

27. Paulson, *Representations of Revolution*, 88.

28. *CPPWB*, 902.

29. The mysterious four-line passage erased from all but three copies of *America* ("The stern Bard ceas'd, asham'd of his own song . . .") might be read as a self-critical retraction of the rape scene in the Preludium. But the rest of the poem will not, in my view, support such a reading.

30. Lynn Hunt, *Politics, Culture, and Class in the French Revolution* (Berkeley: University of California Press, 1984), 93–94.

31. Paulson, *Representations of Revolution*, 93.

32. David Erdman, *The Illuminated Blake: All of William Blake's Illuminated Works with a Plate-by-Plate Commentary* (Garden City, NY: Doubleday/Anchor, 1974), 143.

33. Bentley, *Blake Records*, 40–41. Gilchrist's remark about the white cockade is puzzling; Erdman, *Prophet Against Empire*, 141, points out that "the white cockade happens to have been a royalist symbol, not a republican."

34. See Jean Starobinski, *1789: The Emblems of Reason*, trans. Barbara Bray (Cambridge, MA: MIT Press, 1988; originally published 1973), 43–46.

35. Paulson, *Representations of Revolution*, 59–73.

36. Erdman, *Illuminated Blake*, 173.

37. David Worrall, *Radical Culture: Discourse, Resistance, and Surveillance 1790–1820* (Detroit: Wayne State University Press, 1992); John Mee, *Dangerous Enthusiasm: William Blake and the Culture of Radicalism in the 1790s* (Oxford: Oxford University Press, 1992); E. P. Thompson, *Witness Against the Beast: William Blake and the Moral Law* (New York: The New Press, 1993). For a more recent view that questions previous efforts to position Blake within the radical political culture of the 1790s, see Saree Makdisi, *William Blake and the Impossible History of the 1790s* (Chicago: University of Chicago Press, 2002).

38. See F. R. Leavis, "Shelley," *Revaluation* (Harmondsworth: Penguin, 1964), 189, who cites and agrees with Oliver Elton, *Survey of English Literature, 1780–1830*, 2: 202. But see Richard Cronin, *Shelley's Poetic Thoughts* (New York: St. Martin's Press, 1981), 42: "Shelley, unlike Blake . . . , patronises the popular style in which he writes."

39. For suggestive interrogations of Shelley's poetic tactics in *The Mask* as they relate to political issues in the poem, see Jerrold Hogle, *Shelley's Process: Radical Transference and the Development of His Major Works* (New York and Oxford: Oxford University Press, 1988), 134–38; and Susan Wolfson, *Formal Charges: The Shaping of Poetry in British Romanticism* (Stanford: Stanford University Press, 1997), 202–6.

40. In Reiman's and Fraistat's revised second edition of *Shelley's Poetry and Prose* the headnote says that "the Reform Bill [of 1832] had won the battle for which Shelley had intended his poem as a kind of rallying hymn" (315).

41. The most insightful commentary on the figuring of women in *The Mask* is Janowitz's in *Lyric and Labour in the Romantic Tradition* (Cambridge: Cambridge University Press, 1998), 98–105.

42. See Paul Foot, *Red Shelley* (London: Bookmarks, 1984), 175–77.

43. See, for example, the drawings by Philippe de Loutherbourg for a publication celebrating British naval victories included in David Bindman, *The Shadow of the Guillotine: Britain and the French Revolution* (London: British Museum Publication, 1989). Number 188, "Allegorical design of the Battle of the Nile," shows a ferocious "British lion crushing the inflated pretentions of a French cock"; no. 214, "Britannia before a bust of George III," shows the king as conquering lion "in a symbolic role as source of the prosperity and naval power of Britain at the end of the eighteenth century, identifying the monarchy completely with patriotism." See also Linda Colley, "The apotheosis of George III: loyalty, royalty and the British nation 1760–1820," *Past and Present* 102 (1984): 126 ff.

44. On "words" and "deeds" in Shelley's *Julian and Maddalo*, see my *Shelley's Style*, pp. 201–2.

45. See Gerald McNeice, *Shelley and the Revolutionary Idea* (Cambridge, MA: Harvard University Press, 1969), 91–92.

46. Shelley begins an extended paragraph early in *A Philosophical View of Reform* with the observation that "in Spain and in the dependencies of Spain good and evil in the forms of Despair and Tyranny are struggling foot to foot. That great people have been delivered bound hand and foot to be trampled upon and insulted by a traitorous and sanguinary tyrant" (*WPBS* 6: 16). Reiman comments: "We know that the passage on the political situation in Spain . . . was drafted before news of the Spanish insurrection of January 1820 had reached Shelley" (*Shelley and His Circle* 6: 954).

47. On the figure of the eagle in Shelley's writing, see Charles E. Robinson, *Shelley and Byron: The Snake and Eagle Wreathed in Fight* (Baltimore: The Johns Hopkins University Press, 1976), 4–5, 68–69, 164–65.

48. Cf. the Moon's speech in *Prometheus Unbound* 4. 473–75: "I . . . Maniac-like around thee move, / Gazing, an insatiate bride, / On thy form from every side / Like a Maenad round the cup / Which Agave lifted up / In the weird Cadmaean forest." Reiman and Fraistat provide the pertinent mythological details for reading this passage and the reference to "a Cadmaean Maenad" in the *Ode to Liberty*: "Agave, daughter of Cadmus, became a maenad (one of the female devotees of Dionysus); in a fit of blind intoxication, she killed her own son Pentheus. See Euripides, *The Bacchae*" (*SPP*, 282 n).

49. Fantasies of the Jacobins and the sansculottes as drinkers of blood and eaters of human flesh proliferated in England during the later 1790s, especially in antirevolutionary satire and cartoons: see, for example, James Gillray's "Petit souper a la Parisienne;—or—A Family of Sans-Culottes refreshing, after the fatigues of the day" (1792) in Richard Godfrey, *James Gillray: The Art of Caricature* (London: Tate Gallery Publishing, 2001), 95.

50. G. M. Matthews, "A Volcano's Voice in Shelley," *ELH* 24 (1957): 191–228.

51. "Germanic tribal leader (18 B.C.–A.D. 19) who annihilated a Roman army (A.D. 9) and freed the German tribes from foreign oppression" (*SPP*, 313 n). Known in Germany as Hermann der Cherusker, Arminius is the hero of Klopstock's *Hermanns Schlact* (1769) and *Hermanns Tod* (1787), of Kleist's *Hermannsschlact* (1809), and of F. de la Motte Fouqué's *Hermann* (1818).

52. Ellis's *Concordance* in fact shows this as the only such instance. But compare *The Revolt of Islam* 4. 1609–10 ("Her voice, whose awful sweetness doth repress / All evil") and *Prometheus Unbound* 1. 326–30 ("And who are those with hydra tresses / And iron wings that climb the wind, / Whom the frowning God represses / Like vapours streaming up behind, / Clanging loud, an endless crowd—").

53. See Stuart Curran's reference to "optative wishes that kings and priests had never existed" in *Shelley's Annus Mirabilis: The Maturing of an Epic Vision* (San Marino: Huntington Library, 1975), 177.

54. The simile also recalls the extended image of political and imaginative despair as drowning at the beginning of *Lines written among the Euganean Hills* (16–26).

55. See Jerome Christensen, *Romanticism at the End of History* (Baltimore: The Johns Hopkins University Press, 2000), 11–16, and Marx, Preface to *A Contribution to the Critique of Political Economy*: "The bourgeois relations of production are the last antagonistic form of the social process of production—antagonistic not in the sense of individual antagonism, but of one arising from the social conditions of the life of the individuals; at the same time the productive forces developing in the womb of bourgeois society create the material conditions for the solution of that antagonism. This social formation brings, therefore, the prehistory of human society to a close" (*The Marx-Engels Reader*, ed. Robert C. Tucker, 2d ed. [New York: W.W. Norton, 1978], 5).

INDEX

Aarsleff, Hans, 2
Addison, Joseph, 48
aesthetic, discourse of: hegemony of, 44–45; invention of, 23; the vulgar and, 70–71
agency: the arbitrary and, 4, 158; authority and, 113; historical necessity and for Shelley, 126–30; historical situation and, ix; natural and imaginative for Wordsworth, 125; natural *vs.* arbitrary, 9; power and, 123; in Romantic discourse, 17; women's, Shelley's representation of, 118–19. *See also* determination/indeterminacy
Alexander, Meena, 110
Althusser, Louis, 22, 164n34
Amis, Kingsley, 55
Anti-Jacobin Review and Magazine, The, 15, 62, 65
apocalypse: Blake's idiom of political, 139–44; Shelley's self-divided vision of, 144–49
arbitrary, the: agency and, 4, 158 (*see also* agency); determination and the problem of, 20–22 (*see also* determination/indeterminacy); doubleness of (*see* doubleness of "arbitrary"); language and the discourse of, 1–3; meanings of, 1–6; in political discourse (*see* arbitrary power); power (*see* arbitrary power); the problem of, approaches to, 6–13; rhyme as dramatizing, 46 (*see also* rhyme); Romantic writing, range of regarding, 13–20
arbitrary power: Bourdieu on, 11–13; contemporary politics and, xii; democracy and, 157–58 (*see also* democracy); of historical necessity in Shelley, 126–29; in Locke and Shelley, 4–6; as the name of a problem in Romanticism, 2; in political discourse, 1, 4–6; republican coercion and, 122–23; semiotic and poststructuralist theory on, 6–7; Wordsworth on, 125–26
Attridge, Derek, 25

Bailey, Benjamin, 47
Bakhtin, Mikhail, 69

Barlow, Joel, 105
Barlow, Ruth, 105
Barrell, John, 69, 93, 123, 139
Bate, W. J., 52
Baumgarten, Alexander, 23, 163n2
Beer, John, 130
Benaglia-Sangiorgi, Roberto, 64
Benbow, William, 73
Benjamin, Walter, 44
Bennett, Tony, 10–11
Benveniste, Emile, 7
Beranger, Pierre Jean, 170n77
Berkeley, George, 9
Bialostosky, Don, 171n4
Bindman, David, 136
Blackwood, William, 47
Blackwood's Edinburgh Magazine, 47, 49–57, 62, 74–75, 85
Blake, William: *America: A Prophecy*, 36, 132, 134, 137–42, 144, 156; "Annotations to Lavater's *Aphorisms on Man*", 34, 139; "Annotations to Reynolds's *Discourses*", 34, 136; "A Song of Liberty," 140; *Edward the Third*, 133; *Europe: A Prophecy*, 141–44; *The French Revolution*, 133–34, 140; *Gwin, King of Norway*, 141–44; "London," 136; *The Marriage of Heaven and Hell*, 35–36, 144; revolutionary violence, representation of, 130–44; *Songs of Innocence and Experience*, 34, 36, 135; "The Chimney Sweeper," 135–36; *Visions of the Daughters of Albion*, 36, 134–38; the vulgar and, 72; on words-as-things, 34–36, 39
Blind, Mathilde, 116
Bloom, Harold, 69, 137
Boehme, Jakob, 34
Bourdieu, Pierre: Marxism and, 11; on the problem of the arbitrary, 11–13, 16; on the vulgar, 70–72, 94
Bowles, William Lisle, 50
Boyd, Elizabeth, 67
Boysson-Bardies, Bénédicte de, 100
Brandreth, Jeremiah, 51
Brenkman, John, 136, 160n6
Bromwich, David, 125

Brooks, Peter, 38–39
Brougham, Henry, 49
Burke, Edmund: *An Enquiry Concerning the Origin of Our Ideas of the Sublime and the Beautiful,* 15–17, 142; Locke's philosophy of words and, 15–16; Paine's critique of, 79, 122; *Reflections on the Revolution in France,* 16; terror, contradictory response to, 142; Wollstonecraft's critique of, 105, 109
Burke, Kenneth, 33
Burney, Fanny, 80
Bush, Douglas, 167n19
Butler, Marilyn, 111
Byron, George Gordon, Lord: the arbitrary in, 18–20; *Beppo* (Byron), 61, 64–66, 76–77; *Childe Harold's Pilgrimage,* 40–41, 60, 151, 153–54; *The Corsair,* 51–52, 73; *Don Juan,* x–xii, 18–20, 24, 41–44, 48, 50, 59–61, 66, 151; *English Bards and Scotch Reviewers,* 50, 67; Hunt and, 85; Jeffrey on, 82; on Keats, 50–51, 78; *Letter to [John Murray], on the Rev. W. L. Bowles' Strictures on the Life and Writings of Pope,* 51; revolution, representations of, x–xii, 151, 153–54; rhyme in, 19–20, 25–26, 48, 51–52, 59–67; Shelley, influence on, 76–77; "Some Observations upon an Article in *Blackwood's Edinburgh Magazine*", 50; the vulgar, class awareness and, 73; on words-as-things, 24–26, 40–44

Cameron, Kenneth, 111
Canning, George, 60, 65
Carlile, Richard, 73
Casti, Giambattista, 61, 64
Cenci, Beatrice, 104, 128
Chandler, James, ix, 20–22, 58, 129–30, 181n14
Chomsky, Noam, 8–9, 11, 17
Christensen, Jerome, 18, 44, 73
Christie, Thomas, 105
Claridge, Laura, 97
Clarke, William, 73
class: gender and, 93–94; literary style and, 68–69. *See also* vulgar, the
Clootz, Jean Baptiste, xii
"Cockney School of Poetry," 46–59, 71, 74–75, 78, 80–82

Coleridge, Ernest Hartley, 170n77
Coleridge, John Taylor, 75
Coleridge, Samuel Taylor: arbitrariness of words, resistance to, 2; on the arbitrary sign, problem of, 9; *Biographia Literaria,* 158; class and gender, confounding of, 93; *The Destiny of Nations,* 112; *Frost at Midnight,* 32; Joan of Arc, interest in, 112–13; on language and the discourse of the arbitrary, 17–18; *Notebooks,* 30–32; "poentiate" introduced by, 158; *Sibyllina Leaves* (1817), 112; Southey's *Joan of Arc,* contribution to, 111–12; *The Statesman's Manual,* 27–28; *Table-Talk,* 33; on words-as-things, 23–28, 30–34
commodification: of Blake's art, 35–36; of Byron, 44; of words, 24, 26 (*see also* words-as-things); of writing, 44–45. *See also* materiality
contingency: the arbitrary and, 4; Chomsky on language and, 8
Coward, Rosalind, 25
Cowper, William, 170n73
Cox, Jeffrey, 47
Crabbe, George, 87
Croker, John Wilson, 47–49
Cronin, Richard: incest, on the thematics of in Shelley, 118; on poetry as political, x; political implications of Keats's style, recognition of, 47, 54; popular style, Shelley compared to Blake regarding, 182n38; the vulgar in critical analysis of, 71
Crystal, David, 161n14, 174n42
Culler, Jonathan, 10
cultural materialism, 9–10, 12
Curran, Stuart, 111–12, 184n53

Davie, Donald, 68–69, 82, 171n1
Declaration of Independence of the United States, 1
De Man, Paul, 6, 21–22
democracy: arbitrary power and, 157–58 (*see also* arbitrary power); Byron on, 64; language and, 15; republican coercion and, 122–23 (*see also* revolution); vulgar, judgment of and, 81
Dennis, John, 174n38
Derrida, Jacques: on the arbitrary, 6; Coleridge and, 17; "vulgar," use of, 69–71, 79

determination/indeterminacy: doubleness of arbitrary and, 4; historical situation and, ix; problem of the arbitrary and, 22. *See also* agency
D'Israeli, Isaac, 50
Donovan, Jack, 119, 176n2
doubleness of "arbitrary": anarchy and despotism, correspondence to, 157; Bourdieu's sense of, 12–13; political *vs.* linguistic usages, 1–2, 4–6; problems of representation/determination and, 20–22
Ducrot, Oswald, 8

Eagleton, Terry, 44–45, 163n1
Eco, Umberto, 6–7
Edinburgh Review, The, 1, 53, 60
Ellis, John, 25
Emerson, Ralph Waldo, 33
Emerson, Sheila, 24
Erdman, David, 131–34, 139, 143, 182n33
Essick, Robert N., 34–35, 143, 160n12
Everest, Kelvin, 69, 85, 91

feminism: male (*see* women, representations of); Shelley's representations of women and current theories of language, 96. *See also* gender
Ferguson, Frances, 27
Ferry, Luc, 163n1
Foot, Paul, 182n42
form, rhyme. *See* rhyme
Foscolo, Ugo, 63
Foucault, Michel, 24–26, 28, 32
French Revolution: the mythic Joan of Arc and, 111–13; Shelley's re-vision of, 102; violence, Shelley on the responsibility for, 150; Wollstonecraft and, 105–11, 119; women, role of in, 95, 97, 105–9; Wordsworth's representation of, 122–26. *See also* revolution
Frere, John Hookham, 59–67, 169n66
Fry, Paul, 37, 97
Furniss, Tom, 15–17

Gellius, Aulus, 3
Gelpi, Barbara, 97–100, 119
gender: language and subject-formation in childhood and, 97–100; representations of women by men (*see* women, representations of); the vulgar and, 91–94. *See also* feminism
Gifford, William, 60, 65
Gilbert, Sandra, 98
Gilchrist, Alexander, 131, 139
Glieg, Bishop George, 47
Godineau, Dominique, 107
Godwin, William, 39
Gordon Riots, 131–32, 134
Gouges, Olympe de, 107
Gubar, Susan, 98

Hallam, Henry, 61
Harris, James, 9
Harris, Roy, 7–8, 10, 19
Hayden, John, 47
Hazlitt, William, 73, 80–87; "On Familiar Style," 82–83; "On the Prose-Style of Poets," 84–85; "On Vulgarity and Affectation," 80–82
Heinzelman, Kurt, 24, 27, 30, 33, 35–36
Hilton, Nelson, 34–35, 143
Hitchener, Elizabeth, 111
Hobhouse, John Cam, 170n76
Hofkosh, Sonia, 78
Hogle, Jerrold, 97, 114–15
Holland, Henry Fox, 3rd Baron, 61
Homans, Margaret, 37–39, 97
Hone, William, 51, 73
Horace, 72, 81
Horne Tooke, John, 17–18, 31
Hume, David, 114
Hunt, Henry, 56, 85
Hunt, John, 59, 85
Hunt, Leigh: *The Feast of the Poets,* 49; *Hero and Leander,* 75; on Keats, 57; Keats, influence on, 46, 52–53; *Lord Byron and Some of His Contemporaries,* 78, 80; on Shelley, 80; *The Story of Rimini,* 48, 77, 84; style of, 48–49, 83–85; the vulgar and class awareness, 68, 73–78, 87–88; "vulgar" applied across classes, 79–80; "What is Poetry?", 48–49
Hunt, Lynn, 137

Imlay, Gilbert, 106–7

Jameson, Anna, *Characteristics of Women: Moral, Poetical, and Historical,* 68, 92–94

Jameson, Fredric, ix, 25, 69
Janowitz, Anne, 182n41
Jeffrey, Francis, 53–54, 76–77, 82
Joan of Arc, 96–97, 111–17, 120–21
Johnson, Joseph, 107
Johnson, Samuel: "arbitrary," definition of, 2–4, 35, 67; "vulgar," definition of, 70, 79; vulgarity and sublimity, proximity of, 93
Johnston, Kenneth, 116

Kant, Immanuel, 23, 70–71
Keats, John: *To Autumn*, 55–59; *Endymion*, 46–47, 50–51, 53, 55–56; *Hyperion*, 49, 76; *I Stood Tip-toe*, 53–54; *Lamia*, 53; *Ode to a Nightingale*, 55; *Poems* (1817), 46; the Pope controversy and, 48–51; rhyme and Cockney style of, 46–48, 52–59; "Robin Hood," 56; Shelley on, 76; *Sleep and Poetry*, 47, 49, 51; the vulgar and class awareness, 74–75, 78; "Written in Disgust of Vulgar Superstitions," 58
Kelly, Gary, 109
Klancher, Jon, 73, 174n33
Kristeva, Julia, 98

Lacan, Jacques, 25, 37, 97–100, 164n12
language: acquisition of and psycholinguistic theory, 97–100; as an arbitrary production, 1–3, 8–9 (*see also* arbitrary); arbitrary power of, range of Romantic writing regarding, 13–20; arbitrary signs, approaches to the problem of, 6–13; class and (*see* class; vulgar, the); democracy and, 15; and the doubleness of "arbitrary" (*see* doubleness of "arbitrary"); materiality of in *Frankenstein*, 39; Nature and, 33; origins of, 17, 97–101; power and, x, 5–6, 46 (*see also* arbitrary power); problems of representation/determination and, 20–22; property and, 26–27; Saussure on, 8; words-as-things (*see* words-as-things)
Leask, Nigel, 115
Levinson, Marjorie, 47, 55, 69, 163n3
Lévi-Strauss, Claude, 118
Lewis, Monk, 41, 72
Lindsay, Jack, 132
literary form. *See* rhyme
literary style. *See* style

Liu, Alan, 180n4
Locke, John: *An Essay Concerning Human Understanding*, 2, 5, 26, 155; "arbitrary," implications of use of, 10; on the arbitrary in language, 2, 6, 8; on the arbitrary in politics, 4–6; Blake and, 34; Burke and, 15–16; Coleridge and, 17; on property, 26–27; Shelley and, 36, 159–60n5; *Two Treatises of Government*, 4, 26–27; on words, 26, 31, 155; Wordsworth's response to, 14
Lockhart, John Gibson, 47, 75
Logos: Blake, 33–36, 143–44; Coleridge, 30–33
London Magazine, The, 52
Lotman, Yury, 171n4
Loutherbourg, Philippe de, 183n43
Lowther, William, 49
Lucretius, 3

Makdisi, Saree, 144
male feminism. *See* women, representations of
Manning, Peter, 51–52, 69
Marchand, Leslie A., 165–66n41
Marx, Karl: on the bourgeois relations of production, 184n55; Coleridge, anticipation by, 33; on human beings making history, 22; reference to by Chandler, 129; *vertreten* in, 134; *Vertretung* and *Darstellung*, distinction between, 20; "vulgar," use of, 69–70, 79
Marxism: Bourdieu and, 11–12; language and, 25; problem of the arbitrary in, 9–11
materiality: the aesthetic and, 44–45; Byron and, 42–44; of language for Coleridge, 30–31; of language for Wordsworth, 28–30; of language in *Frankenstein*, 39; linguistic and nonlinguistic, distinction between in Blake, 34–35. *See also* commodification; words-as-things
Matthews, G. M., 154
Mauss, Marcel, 44
McGann, Jerome, 47, 53–55, 61–62, 64, 67
McKusick, James, 31, 163n5
Medvedev, P. N., 54
Mee, John, 144
Meltzer, Françoise, 113, 178n24

Méricourt, Théroigne de, 107
Merivale, John Herman, 61–62, 169n61
Milton, John, 46, 117, 130
Moore, Thomas, 40, 51, 77
Morton, Thomas, 81
Murray, John, xi, 40, 50, 59–66

"natural," the, the arbitrary vs., 9
Natural Law, 27

OED. See *Oxford English Dictionary*
Ollier, Charles, 68, 75
origins, of language, 17, 97–101
Ostriker, Alicia, 130
Ovid, 117
Oxford English Dictionary (OED), 2–3, 74, 142, 181n15

Paine, Thomas, 79, 105, 122
Patmore, P. G., 52
Paulson, Ronald, 130–32, 137, 139, 142
Peacock, Thomas Love, 73, 76
Pêcheux, Michel, 25
Peterloo Massacre, 56, 144–49
Piaget, Jean, 99
Pinker, Steven, 8, 18
politics: class and literary style, 68–69 (*see also* vulgar, the); literary form and (*see* rhyme); oratory, 41; return to history in literary studies and, ix–xii; revolutionary (*see* revolution). *See also* arbitrary power; democracy
Poovey, Mary, 79
Pope, Alexander, 48–50, 90, 174n41
poststructuralist theory: the arbitrary in, 7; Bourdieu and, 11; words-as-things and, 25
power: arbitrary (*see* arbitrary power); language and, x, 5–6, 46
property, language and, 26–27
psycholinguistic theory, 97–100
Pulci, Luigi, 60, 62

Quarterly Review, The, 47–57, 60, 62–63, 74–75

Redpath, Theodore, 47
reification: Coleridge's anticipation of Marx on, 33; the creature in *Frankenstein* as, 39; of words, Byron's awareness of, 44

Reiman, Donald, 175–76n2, 180n10, 183n46
Rendall, Jane, 109–10
representation: power and, x; problem of the arbitrary and, 20 (*see also* determination/indeterminacy); of revolutionary violence (*see* revolution); of women (*see* women, representations of)
revolution: Blake's idiom of political apocalypse and, 139–44; Blake's representation of, 130–39; Byron's representation of, x–xii, 151, 153–54; French (*see* French Revolution); Gordon Riots, 131–32, 134; problem of representing, 122–23; representations of women and, 107–16; Shelley's perspective on reform and, 149–58; Shelley's representation of, 102, 126–30, 135, 144; Shelley's self-divided vision of apocalypse and, 144–49; Wordsworth's representation of, 122–26, 135
Reynolds, John Hamilton, 52
Reynolds, Sir Joshua, 34, 136
rhyme: the arbitrary and, 21, 46; Byron and, xi, 19–20, 25–26, 51–52; Byron's *ottava rima* style, politics and, 59–67; Keats's Cockney style, politics and, 46–48, 52–59; the Pope controversy and politics, 48–51
Ricardo, David, 70
Richardson, Alan, 115
Ridley, M. R., 52
Roberts, Hugh, 3–4
Roe, Nicholas, 47
Roland, Manon, 107
Rose, George, 61
Rose, William Stewart, 59, 61–67, 170n68
Rousseau, Jean-Jacques, 110
Rowe, John Carlos, 160n13

Saussure, Ferdinand de, 2, 7–12, 19
Schlegel, A. W., 93
Scott, John, 168n34
Scott, Sir Walter, 41, 61
semiotic theory: actual social and material life, ignoring of, 14; the arbitrary in, 6–7, 19
Serres, Michel, 3
Seuren, P. A. M., 161n14
Shakespeare, William, 92–94

Shelley, Mary: *Frankenstein*, 37–40; *The Last Man*, 103, 112; *Mathilda*, 104
Shelley, Percy Bysshe: *Alastor*, 114, 117; on apocalypse and revolution, 144–49; the arbitrary in language, 1–2, 8; the arbitrary in political writings of, 4–6; *The Cenci*, 128; Chandler on, 21–22; Coleridge and, 17; *A Defence of Poetry*, 1–2, 5–6, 36–37, 118; De Man on, 21–22; "England in 1819," 21–22; *Essay on Christianity*, 4; familiar style and class awareness of, 87–91; implications of use of "arbitrary" in, 10; *Julian and Maddalo*, 68–69, 74–76, 82, 84–95; Locke, reading of, 159–60n5; *The Mask of Anarchy*, 80, 94, 144–50, 152, 157; *Mont Blanc*, 39–40, 114; *Ode to Liberty*, 151–58; *Ode to the West Wind*, 126–30, 144–45, 151; "On Life," 36; "On Love," 118; *A Philosophical View of Reform*, 5, 122, 126, 149–50, 183n46; politics of style in the couplets of, 83–87, 89; *Prometheus Unbound*, 39–40, 75, 96–98, 100, 135, 183n48, 184n52; *Queen Mab*, 73; on reform and revolution, 149–58; *The Revolt of Islam/Laon and Cythna*, 57, 75, 95–98, 100–104, 111–21, 129, 135, 148, 184n52; revolution, representations of, 102, 122, 126–30, 135, 144; rhyme in, 57–58; self-criticism and the feminine in, 91–94; skeptical and idealist impulses in, efforts to reconcile, 3–4; Southey, influence of, 111–15; *The Triumph of Life*, 6; the vulgar and class awareness, 68–69, 73–80, 80, 82–83, 94; Wollstonecraft, influence of on, 96, 102–5, 111, 119–20; women, representation of and the formation of human subjectivity, 97–104; women, representations of, 95–97, 117–21; women, representations of as heroic, 111–16; on words-as-things, 34, 36–37, 39–40; on Wordsworth, 49
Sheridan, Richard Brinsley, 41
sign, linguistic: agency and, 118–19, 155–56; apocalyptic writing and, 144–45; the arbitrary and, 1–2, 15–19; the doubleness of "arbitrary" and, 4–13; language acquisition and, 98–100; words-as-things and, 23–27, 30–33, 36–39

Simpson, David, 54, 69
Siskin, Clifford, 36
Smith, Olivia, 15, 73
Southey, Robert: Byron and, 24, 67; *The Curse of Kehama*, 111; on Frere, 63; *Joan of Arc*, 96, 111–16, 118, 120; *Thalaba the Destroyer*, 111; *Wat Tyler*, 113
Spenser, Edmund, 57–58
Spivak, Gayatri, 20
Sprat, Thomas, 26
Staël, Anne-Louise-Germaine de (Madame), 41, 93–94
Stern, Daniel, 98–101
Sternbach, Robert, 113
style: Keats's Cockney, 46–51; making history through, Shelley and, 21–22; politics and language, convergence of and, x–xii; politics of class and, 68 (*see also* vulgar, the)
Swedenborg, Emmanuel, 33, 34
Swift, Jonathan, 26

Tauchert, Ashley, 110
Taylor, John, 47
"terrorist"/"terrorism," 142
Thompson, E. P., 131, 144
Todd, Janet, 106–7, 110
Tomalin, Claire, 105–6
Tucker, Susie, 79

Ulmer, William, 97–98

Vassallo, Peter, 61–62, 64
Vendler, Helen, 168n43
violence, revolutionary. *See* revolution
Volney, C. F., 38
Vološinov, Valentin Nikolaevich, 9
vulgar, the: the common and, 82–83; concept of, 69–72; gender and, 91–94; Hazlitt on, 80–83; as judgment extended across classes, 78–80; Shelley, familiar style in, 87–91; Shelley and class awareness, 68–69, 73–78; Shelley's couplets and, 83–87
Vygotsky, L. S., 99–100

Wallace, Tara Ghoshal, 173n29
Waller, R. D., 63, 170n68
Warner, Marina, 112–13
Wasserman, Earl, 96, 166n11
Wellesley, Arthur, x–xi, 63, 66–67

Wellington, Duke of. *See* Wellesley, Arthur
Whiter, Walter, 32
Williams, Helen Maria, 105
Williams, Raymond, 9–10, 12, 14
Wilson, John, 47, 50, 62
Wolfson, Susan, 47, 51
Wollstonecraft, Mary: *The Cave of Fancy,* 102–3, 112; the French Revolution and, 105–11, 119; *An Historical and Moral View of the Origin and Progress of the French Revolution,* 96, 109–11, 122, 128; insurrection, on the right of, 150, 158; Parisian women, account of, 128, 134; *Revolt of Islam,* impact on the creation of, 96, 102–5, 111; on revolutionary violence, 122; on Rousseau, 1, 4; *A Vindication of the Rights of Men,* 105; *A Vindication of the Rights of Woman,* 1, 105, 107, 109; on the vulgar, 79–80, 93, 173n27
women, representations of, 95–97; formation of human subjectivity and, 97–104; by Shelley, 97–104, 111–21; by Wollstonecraft, 107–11; by Wordsworth, 116–17, 120
words-as-things, 23; Blake and Shelley on, 34–40; Byron and, 40–44; Coleridge and Wordsworth on, 27–33; implications of, 23–26; materiality and, 44–45
Wordsworth, William: arbitrariness of words, resistance to, 2; blank verse, association with, 49; Coleridge and, 17; "Composed when a probability existed of our being obliged to quit Rydal Mount," 116–17; emotions, distinction between simple and complex, 174n38; *The Excursion,* 49; Keats on, 49; on "language really used by men," 13–15; *Lyrical Ballads,* 13–15, 17, 27, 30; *Ode: Intimations of Immortality,* note on, 29; *The Prelude,* 28–30, 113, 123–26, 135, 151; *The Recluse,* 116; *Resolution and Independence,* 28; revolution, representation of, 122–26, 135; "A Slumber Did My Spirit Seal," 28; "The Thorn," note on, 27, 29; *Tintern Abbey,* 28; the vulgar and, 72; women, representations of, 116–17, 120; on words-as-things, 27–30
Worrall, David, 144

GPSR Authorized Representative: Easy Access System Europe - Mustamäe tee 50, 10621 Tallinn, Estonia, gpsr.requests@easproject.com

www.ingramcontent.com/pod-product-compliance
Lightning Source LLC
Chambersburg PA
CBHW031437160426
43195CB00010BB/764